Contemporary South Korean Society

The growing importance of the Korean economy in the global arena and the spread of the so-called 'Korean wave' in Asia means there is an increasing desire to understand contemporary Korean society. To this end, this book provides a critical and progressive analysis of the diverse issues that impact on and shape contemporary Korean society at both local and national levels.

The contributors address issues and movements which include:

- the state and regime
- human rights
- gender
- civil society and social movements
- culture
- religion
- domestic and migrant labour
- welfare.

The chapters in this volume provide a critical perspective on Korean society, and draw upon interdisciplinary research from across the social sciences. With contributions from leading Korean scholars and academics from around the world, this is a welcome addition to the growing field of Korean studies, and will be of great interest to students and scholars interested in Korean studies, Korean and Asian culture and society, and Asian studies more generally.

Hee-Yeon Cho is Professor at the School of Social Science and NGO Graduate School, Sungkonghoe University, Seoul, South Korea.

Lawrence Surendra currently holds a Chair in Economics at the University of Mysore, South India.

Hyo-Je Cho is Professor of sociology at Sungkonghoe University, Seoul, South Korea.

Routledge advances in Korean studies

1 **The Politics of Economic Reform in South Korea**
A fragile miracle
Tat Yan Kong

2 **Market and Society in Korea**
Interest, institution and the textile industry
Dennis McNamara

3 **Social and Economic Policies in Korea**
Ideas, networks and linkages
Dong-Myeon Shin

4 **North Korea in the World Economy**
Edited by E. Kwan Choi, Yesook Merrill and E. Han Kim

5 **Legal Reform in Korea**
Edited by Tom Ginsburg

6 **Women, Television and Everyday Life**
Journeys of hope
Youna Kim

7 **Transformations in Twentieth Century Korea**
Edited by Chang Yun-Shik and Steven Hugh Lee

8 **The Development of Modern South Korea**
State formation, capitalist development and national identity
Kyong Ju Kim

9 **Industrial Relations in Korea**
Diversity and dynamism of Korean enterprise unions from a comparative perspective
Jooyeon Jeong

10 The Global Korean Motor Industry
The Hyundai Motor Company's global strategy
Russell D. Lansbury, Chung-Sok Suh and Seung-Ho Kwon

11 Korean Workers and Neoliberal Globalisation
Kevin Gray

12 Korea in the New Asia
East Asian integration and the China factor
Francoise Nicolas

13 Foreign Direct Investment in Post-Crisis Korea
European investors and 'mismatched globalization'
Judith Cherry

14 Korea Confronts Globalization
Edited by Chang Yun-Shik, Hyun-ho Seok and Donald L. Baker

15 Korea's Developmental Alliance
State, capital and the politics of rapid development
David Hundt

16 Capitalist Development in Korea
Labour, capital and the myth of the developmental state
Dae-oup Chang

17 Political Protest and Labour Movements in Korea
Solidarity among Korean white-collar workers
Doowon Suh

18 Retirement, Work and Pensions in Ageing Korea
Edited by Jae-jin Yang and Thomas R. Klassen

19 South Korea under Compressed Modernity
Familial political economy in transition
Kyung-Sup Chang

20 New Millennium South Korea
Neoliberal capitalism and transnational movements
Edited by Jesook Song

21 Human Rights Discourse in North Korea
Post-colonial, Marxist and Confucian perspectives
Jiyoung Song

Contemporary South Korean Society

A critical perspective

Edited by Hee-Yeon Cho, Lawrence Surendra and Hyo-Je Cho

Routledge
Taylor & Francis Group
LONDON AND NEW YORK

First published 2013
by Routledge
2 Park Square, Milton Park, Abingdon, Oxon OX14 4RN

Simultaneously published in the USA and Canada
by Routledge
711 Third Avenue, New York, NY 10017

Routledge is an imprint of the Taylor & Francis Group, an informa business

British Library Cataloguing in Publication Data
A catalogue record for this book is available from the British Library

Library of Congress Cataloging in Publication Data
Contemporary South Korean society: a critical perspective/edited by Hee-Yeon Cho, Lawrence Surendra and Hyo-Je Cho.
p. cm. – (Routledge advances in Korean studies)
Includes bibliographical references and index.
1. Korea (South)–Social conditions–1988– 2. Korea (South)–Economic conditions–1988– 3. Korea (South)–Politics and government–2002–
I. Cho, Hui-yon, 1956– II. Surendra, Lawrence. III. Cho, Hyo-Je.
HN730.5.A8C67 2012
306.095195–dc23

2012017493

ISBN: 978-0-415-69139-0 (hbk)
ISBN: 978-0-203-08437-3 (ebk)

Typeset in Times New Roman
by Wearset Ltd, Boldon, Tyne and Wear

Contents

Contributors

Dr. Hee-Yeon Cho is the Professor of School of Social Science and NGO Graduate School at Sungkonghoe University in Seoul. He established the Democracy and Social Movements Institute there, and has worked as its director. Outside campus, he works as Co-representative of National Association of Professors for Democratic Society, and of Korea Council of Progressive Academic Associations. He stayed for teaching at USC in the USA, National Chiao Tung University in Taiwan, and the Keisen University in Japan. His research area includes social movements, civil society, relation between movements and party politics, and radicalism. He has written many books including *Class and Poverty, Social Movement and Organizations in South Korea*; *The State, Democracy and the Political Change in South Korea*; *Park Chung-Hee and Developmental Dictatorship*; *Mobilized Modernization* (all in Korean), and *Breaking the Barrier: Inter-Asia Reader on Democratization and Social Movements* and *States of Democracy: Oligarchic Democracies and Asian Democratization* (both in English). He belongs to the editorial board of the journal, *Inter-Asia Cultural Studies* (Routledge) and *Globalizations* (Routledge).

Professor Lawrence Surendra is an environmental economist with over two decades of working experience in East and Southeast Asia, and recognized for his contributions relating particularly to Environment and Democracy in Asia. He has been a member of the Asian Perspectives Project of the United Nations University, has worked with UN-ESCAP, Bangkok and was more recently Deputy-Director of UNECO-APCEIU, in Seoul, South Korea. He is an internationally recognized scholar and specialist on Asia, has taught and teaches at several universities, and presently holds a chair in Economics at the University of Mysore, South India. He is the founder-director of the Asian Regional Exchange for New Alternatives (ARENA), an Asian community of scholars and activists, which is currently based in Seoul, South Korea. He is on the editorial board of several journals and has co-edited as well as contributed to several volumes on Asia.

Hyo-Je Cho is Professor of sociology at SungKongHoe University, Seoul. He has written extensively on human rights and civil society. Among his works are *Human Rights and Civic Activism in Korea* (2005), *A Grammar of Human Rights* (2007) and *In Search of Human Rights* (2011). He was closely involved with the creation of the National Human Rights Institution in South Korea and sat on a special policy advisory panel for the Ministry of Justice with special reference to the revision of Penal Code. Dr. Cho studied at Oxford and the London School of Economics, and was human rights fellow of Harvard Law School and Visiting Professor of Free University Berlin.

Uhn Cho is Professor of Sociology at Dongguk University, South Korea.

Dong-Choon Kim is Professor of School of Social Science and the Director of the Democracy and Social Movement Institute (DsSM) at SungKongHoe University, South Korea.

Kyounghee Kim is Associate Professor of Sociology and the head of the Institute of Sociology at Chung-Ang University, Seoul, South Korea.

Wang-Bae Kim is Professor of Sociology at Yonsei University, Seoul, South Korea.

Mee-Hae Kong is a Professor and a chairperson of the Department of Social Welfare for Families and Elders at Silla University, South Korea.

Byoung-Hoon Lee is a Professor in the Department of Sociology, Chung-Ang University, South Korea.

Jinsun Lee is Assistant Professor at the Department of Communication and Theater Arts and Joint Professor at Department of English at Old Dominion University, USA.

Yoonkyung Lee is Assistant Professor in Sociology and Asian and Asian-American Studies at the State University of New York at Binghamton, USA.

John Minns is Associate Professor in Politics and International Relations at the Australian National University.

Rajiv Narayan holds a doctorate from the University of London. He is currently Researcher (East Asia) for Amnesty International based in London, UK.

Dong-Hoon Seol is Professor of Sociology, Chonbuk National University, South Korea.

Kwang-Yeong Shin is Professor of Sociology at Chung-Ang University, Seoul, South Korea.

Sungbok Yun is Lecturer in Sociology and senior research fellow at the Institute of Social Science, Sogang University, South Korea.

Preface

The current compilation of chapters included in this edited volume aims to achieve three objectives. First, the editors attempted to put together in a single volume a wide array of "critical" social research in English language on contemporary Korean society. Just as there has been an explosion of interest, at the academic as well as the public level, in all things Korean during the last decade so does a proliferation of social scientific investigation into socio-political dimension of Korea with English language as a medium of communication. The latter's category represents width and depth both in terms of research interests and of writers with different disciplinary backgrounds. Thus the editors duly felt the need to collate those rapidly increasing body of works in one place in a systematic manner so that English-speaking readers can appreciate the range and scholarship of social scientific research in contemporary Korean society. So far as the editors are aware there is a dearth of collected works in this direction, among them the ones with "critical" approaches are even fewer. Therefore the simple fact that this kind of collection has finally come into being may be of significance to the concerned public, reflective practitioners, as well as to the academics and scholars in this field. It is our hope that the readers will now be able to get a grasp of contemporary Korean society through a critical lens, written by a pool of keen observers and commentators in this area.

Second, related to the first point, the volume was intended to give outside observers of Korean society a "balanced" perspective, a taste of richness and variety, and, above all, an objective picture of Korean society in a scientific manner. This point cannot be over-emphasized because most existing studies into the subject have tended to possess a sort of "systematic bias" in their philosophical and ideological perspectives and assumptions, and their political starting point. So much so in fact that there seemed to be an unspoken consensus among the majority of vernacular commentators writing in English on Korean society which favored weaving a rather conservative narrative of contemporary Korean society. This volume intends to challenge this kind of established tendency and to offer a countervailing frame of reference. The basic premise of this endeavor is that a modern society needs to be approached and analyzed in a multi-layered way that reflects and accommodates the structural, institutional, ideational, and psychological dimensions of society, including the result of committed actions as well as of omitted ones. Only in this way, the editors believe, are we able to get closer to the "heart of the matter" in understanding Korean society, or any other society for that matter. This kind of approach has another, more practical dimension to consider as well, i.e., an asymmetry of represented works in English language along the conservative-progressive continuum of ideological spectrum. This skewed representation means that those new entrants to this field with a limited historical and linguistic background in Korean affairs may have a difficulty in acquiring the whole variety of competing interpretations and analyses which are indeed vigorously played out in the public debate in Korea. This volume therefore is expected to provide English-speaking readers with a new way of critical thinking toward Korean society.

Last but not least the book is expected to play a role in developing a new path of research for a future multi-level epistemological approach and in triggering a cross-fertilization between scholars inside and outside Korea. It is well known that there is a wide variety, in terms of level of understanding, of the focus of attention, and of the meaning drawn from investigation, among researchers on a same topic with very different backgrounds. For example, a detailed analysis of a particular social problem written by a Korean scholar may be hard to understand or at least not immediately relevant for those who are new to the subject. Nevertheless these kinds of hands-on studies written by vernacular scholars may become more pertinent and interesting when a reader becomes more and more versed to the situation on the ground level. Likewise, a piece of analysis on certain aspects of Korean society written by an external observer may apparently look either too sweeping a generalization or too idiosyncratic a focus to the eyes of conventional Korean readers. Nevertheless domestic readers could learn from these studies how to see themselves from a new bird's eye view, and how to shed new light on to those aspects of society which "insiders" tend to take for granted but which still are important in their own right. In other words, by doing this a new way of seeing can be instilled into domestic readers who will realize that the social reality that they have long assumed to be "theirs" is not their monopolized reality after all. Of course these processes can be produced and reproduced in numerous ways. In the event, all of us, regardless of their nationality, familiarity with the reality, or the medium of communication, could benefit from inter-subjectivity and reflexivity resulting from a "spiral" sort of knowledge circulation.

It was very fortunate for us editors to have been able to enlist the enthusiastic participation of some of the finest social scientists in contemporary Korea for this book project. Not only did they allow their papers to be included in the edition but also some of them gave us valuable advice on editorial policy. The editors are also grateful to various academic journals and the presses for their kind permission for us to use works which had been originally published in their media. Thanks are also due to postgraduate students at SungKongHoe University in Seoul who have helped locate the material and process the cumbersome database works. A collaborative endeavor of this kind necessarily involves many sources of support, obvious as well as less obvious, so our deep gratitude to all of them for making this project possible. It is our sincere hope that the final result would be of some value in seeing contemporary Korean society from fresh and critical perspectives.

Hee-Yeon Cho, Lawrence Surendra, and Hyo-Je Cho
March 2012

1 The structure of the South Korean developmental regime and its transformation

An analysis of the developmental regime of statist mobilization and authoritarian integration in the anticommunist regimentation

Hee-Yeon Cho

Preface

Before the economic crisis, the South Korean development model was a 'successful' model to be emulated by others. Such a conception of a successful model means that the contradictions and problems inherent in this model have not been illuminated at all. However, the crisis of the South Korean economy provided the momentum for an epistemological turning moment, which has allowed us to recognize the 'unsuccessful' aspects, and approach the South Korean development model as a model of crisis and contradiction.

This chapter aims to analyze the structure of the Korean development model as simultaneously a basis for rapid successful growth and its sudden crisis around the mid-1990s in the wake of the East Asian financial crisis. The chapter looks at the model's characteristics of operation and its transformations. In this study, I explore: the structure that enabled this growth, especially political-social structure; how the same structure came to be a factor in the crisis; and in what direction the South Korean development model is currently transforming.

Characteristics of the South Korean developmental regime

Growth as a socio-political process and 'the South Korean developmental regime'

The 'developmental state theory' (Johnson 1987, 1999; Amsden 1989; Evans 1995; Wade 1990; Gereffi and Wyman 1990) focused on an interventionist role for the achievement of economic growth. The developmental state theory explaining the East Asian economic miracle focuses only on the relation between the state intervention and the resulting phenomenon, that is, growth (Cho and Kim 1998: 128–132). My preference is to use the term 'the developmental regime' (rather than 'the developmental state'), in order to bring to the fore the systemic and multi-faceted characteristics of the South Korean growth-oriented regime, not the phenomenal aspects of the 'autonomous' state intervention. I think we should not focus only on the state's role but also see the whole structure in which more factors than the state interact.

In addition, the concept 'regime' is also preferred because it allows me to talk about socio-political reorganization as well as economic. Even when 'the developmental state theory' scholars discuss this growth, they approach it only as an economic process. In my view the growth is as much a socio-political process as it is an economic one. This is because economic growth is growth of not only the secondary industry, industrial production growth or the material production, but also socio-political reorganization of a society towards growth (Bonefeld 1987).

Conceiving of the growth as a socio-political reorganization includes the following two aspects. The first is the raising and distributing of material and human resources towards growth, especially in 'resources-poor countries' (Perkins 1994). The second is the societal integration of the members of one society towards the target of growth, that is, a kind of pro-growth integration of the working class, the popular sector and other classes. The way of raising and distributing resources is diverse from maximal intervention of the state to minimal one, while the way of the integration from very much authoritarian to very much democratic one.

Raising and distributing such resources is performed basically through the market. However, the state intervenes in this process. It is not correct to regard the state theory and market theory in East Asian development analysis as directly opposite. Rather, we can say that raising and distributing resources is performed in the interaction between the market and the state. Such interaction varies from the maximal intervention of the state to minimal one, all of which are combined with the market. Maximal intervention of the state and minimal one can be posited as poles in the same continuum, rather than the state and the market. The point is that the state's intervention in economy is not seen as contrary to the market so the question is really whether the state's intervention is market friendly or anti-market. For example, the state's intervention in South Korea was market friendly: it just aimed to make business and market flourish and develop rapidly, overcoming diverse obstacles to market and business development.

In addition, we should see the difference in the way of political integration in the process of economic growth. One regime achieving a high economic growth can be democratic, however other one achieving the same growth can be authoritarian. We can characterize diverse regimes from democratic to authoritarian ones according to their political features of the developmentally oriented system.

In this sense the South Korean developmental regime, especially Park Chung-Hee's regime, can be defined as that of maximal state intervention and authoritarian integration. This can be shown Figure 1.1. In the view of mobilization and distribution of resources, it can be defined as the regime of maximal intervention of the state, while the regime of authoritarian integration in the view of integration. I would define the maximal intervention of the state in South Korea as statist mobilization.

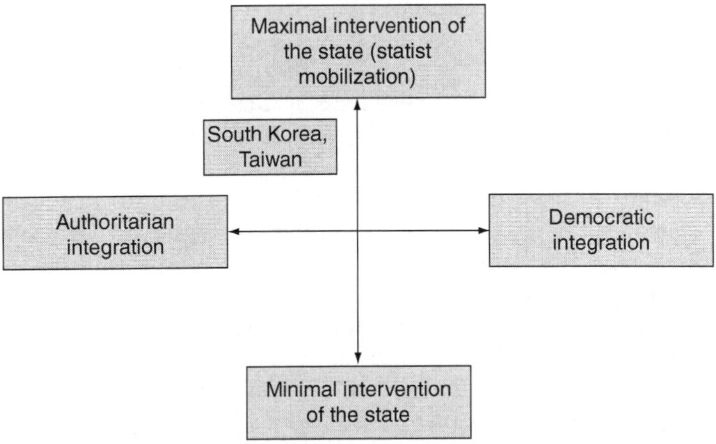

Figure 1.1 The mode of developmental state in South Korea and Taiwan.

The precondition of the developmental regime – the anticommunist regimented society

There has been a precondition for the developmental regime to emerge and function smoothly. I want to conceptualize such a precondition as 'the anticommunist regimented society'. The mobilization for growth in the maximal statist form and integration in the authoritarian form has been helped by the anticommunist regimented social situation and has been made possible by utilizing and amplifying such a situation.

If social regimentation means that a certain society is regimented in a way to promote disciplinarization of social and political behavior to be accommodated to the dominant rule, factors which contribute to this social regimentation can come from many origins (e.g. Confucian culture, militaristic confrontation with foreign country, a specific historical experience, a certain ideological situation). By the concept of 'the anticommunist regimented society', I want to imply that such regimentation in South Korea comes mainly from societal confrontation with communism, although many other factors were involved.

The formation and reproduction of the developmental regime in South Korea can not be fully analyzed without considering interactional influences of the Cold War and the civil war. In South Korea, the intense conflict after Independence in 1945, in which social forces were polarized into left-wing and right-wing groupings, developed into the civil war. This civil war ended up dividing the Korean peninsular into a capitalist-oriented 'right-wing' 'region' and a socialist-oriented 'left-wing' 'region' (South and North Korea).

What is important in the formation of 'the anticommunist regimented society' is that, in the process of the violent conflicts accompanying the civil war, oppositional figures and groups were widely removed from the public arena. Actually as a result of oppression by the American Occupation Forces and the South Korea government (together with impact of the civil war), the working class movement and popular opposition movement were nearly crushed. Only pro-governmental right-wing organizations could exist without the threat of death or imprisonment. Such a civil war, and the hot confrontation between them, transformed the external logic of the Cold War into an internalized consensual one, which continued to regulate social and class relations.

The internalization of the Cold War logic was helped by the popular conception that the commitment of the US had been decisive for the survival of South Korea during the Korean War. If we say that the rise of the East Asian developmental state was born out of the 'politics of survival' (Castells 1992), the strongest evidence can be found in South Korea. In this situation, the confrontation between South Korea and North Korea was mechanically reproduced on its own without any regard to the origins of such a confrontation. What is unique to this situation is that such self-reproduction of confrontation was internalized to become a self-censoring mechanism. This anticommunist regimented society has been reproduced easily by the fact that the Civil War was not over, but stayed in truce. That is, this characteristic of 'society in truce' made possible the continual domestic reproduction of Cold War-like confrontation. In contemporary histories in South Korea, this situation has been systematically fortified by the purposeful efforts of the dominant group to preserve the logic of confrontation.

In this respect, 'the anticommunist regimented society' in postwar South Korea can be defined as one in which the Cold War logic was, through the historical experience of the civil war, transformed into an internally consensual one and it regulated social relations and behaviors of the populace, resulting in labor discipline and popular acquiescence.

The phenomenon, which emerged in the formation of the anticommunist regimented society, is that the old landlord class was weakened so as not to block the socio-political reorganization by the developmental regime. Ironically, the confrontation between the socialist North Korea and capitalist South Korea pushed South Korea to carry out relatively progressive land reform, thus weakening the landlord class.

Although the discontent and the demands for land reform by peasants functioned as a driving force for the passing and enforcement of the land reform law in the parliament, in which assemblypersons with landlord class background occupied a majority, the land reform was forwarded by the radical North Korea land reform and an experience of revolutionary land distribution during the civil war. Land reform 'law was passed, but not one hectare was redistributed before the North Koreans occupied the South Korea in the summer of 1950: whence came a revolutionary dispossession in all but the "Pusan perimeter" holding area' (Cumings 1989: 12).

The 'quite progressive' land reform, the erosion of the material base of the landlord class and the breakdown of the former landlord class as a dominant class with effective oppositional potential against pro-bourgeoisie modernization (Lie 1991: 71) were factors that made East Asian societies go on different routes from the most Latin American societies. Because the landed oligarchies can function as potent brakes on economic growth, removal of the landlord class is an important social condition for capitalist industrialization. It is the peculiarity of the East Asian Cold War (unlike Latin America) that it contributed to land reforms, weakening the landlord class as a result. Here we can see the dual impact of the Cold War confrontation: on the one hand it contributed to opposition movements being wiped out, and, on the other hand, it led to yhe demise of the landlord class. Only under these social conditions, could the developmental regime from the 1960s become possible. And only under these conditions could statist mobilization and authoritarian integration proceed without serious threat because, in the anticommunist regimented social condition, the socio-political barrier to statist mobilization and authoritarian integration has lowered.

The formation of the anticommunist regimented society brought with it the reversion of the power in capital–labor relation in favor of the former, and the reversion of the power in state–civil society relation in favor of the former. In such an anticommunist regimented society we can see a great imbalance between both the state and civil society and between capital and labor, facilitating both statist mobilization and authoritarian integration.

In a sense, capitalism depends on the regimentation and disciplinarization of labor to fit into capitalistic order: an organization of labor in an industrial army analogous to a military army. The developmental regime from the 1960s could integrate the working class to the new capitalistic order as well as stabilize capital's domination over the labor process by extending the existing social regimentation and disciplinarization in anticommunist regimented society to the labor process.

What is emphasized here is that the anticommunism in this period has been very hostile to North Korea. This anticommunist regimentation was like regimentation based on the 'pseudo-wartime' control, in particular via creating a social atmosphere of threat in the name of national security.

The statist mobilization and authoritarian integration by Park's regime

Under the condition of the anticommunist regimented society, the Korean developmental regime went on to perform the statist mobilization and authoritarian integration from the early 1960s. The statist mobilization and authoritarian integration for growth happened in the following way. First, concerning the statist mobilization of the whole society towards growth, the state intervened to support export-oriented companies and give massive support to birth of new capitals. State intervention activities, directed to constructing capital itself and valorizing constructed capital, was economic on the one hand but also political and social on the other. The state exploited all possible policy measures to support export enterprises and the accumulation of capital. For describing this kind of the state's role, Amsden used such expression as 'getting the prices wrong' (Amsden 1989: 139). However, I would use such expression as 'getting all fundamentals wrong in favor of growth and export'. As is well known, it took the form of 'industrialization drive policy', especially 'export drive policy'. For this, the state intervened in the form of one-sided allocation of all economic resources towards export (e.g. allocation of credits to targeted industries and infant industries). It led the market, not merely followed it, especially through 'industry-specific' policies (Wade 1990: 233–236). The state actively led a strategic allocation of socio-economic resources to targeted industries and enterprises.

The statist mobilization was also done in relation to the money capital circuit. The state gave export enterprises easy access to internal savings and foreign loans. In the name of the so-called 'export-finance', export enterprises could receive subsidies and favors in getting bank loans easier than other enterprises. The fact that the banking system has been under the state's control made it easier for the state to channel the stream of credit in favor of export. In addition, the state supported the enterprises, especially big enterprises and public enterprises, to borrow money in the international financial market under the guarantee of the state to back up weak credit of the enterprises. In this sense, export enterprises could enjoy privileged status in access to both domestic savings and foreign loans.

However, the statist mobilization in favor of export-oriented industrialization extended beyond economic policy to 'getting the whole society wrong'. Here we can indicate diverse ideological interventions to inculcate social norms that fitted with incipient capital accumulation and that promoted new identities in its favor. The state has been an important agent in reproducing social norms to encourage obedience to a new order of capital. It also reproduced behaviors in favor of accumulation (e.g. savings rather than consumption). In addition, it endorsed a certain identity of the individual as a provider of low-wage labor, a production element and a provider of capital in shortage through voluntary savings. The state also promoted a new identity in the image of a self-sacrificial hard-worker in high labor intensity industries, as a self-employed worker and as a self-dependent breadwinner with self-responsibility to the individual and family security, not dependent on the state etc.

In addition, the state intervened significantly in the reproduction of a low-wage labor system. The state played an active role in keeping low-wage labor power in potential surplus and making a certain level of skill sustained, especially through legislation, e.g. new labor laws, or detrimental revisions of existing labor law.

This statist mobilization was supported by authoritarian integration. The pre-existing legal institutions (e.g. the law such as National Security Law) were crucial to the state's intervention in reproducing a stable production system based on low-wage labor, and suppressing the opposition to such a system. Compared to the 1960s when consensus was manufactured via the modernization project, the developmental regime in the 1970s tried to integrate the labor and whole society in the more authoritarian way. The Yushin regime in the 1970s was that of harsh authoritarian integration near to totalitarianism.

In summary, the developmental regime was based on the anticommunist regimentation. It means that anticommunism formed a kind of social basis for the

South Korean developmental regime. In this sense, the developmental regime in South Korea can be called the 'anticommunist' developmental regime. This means that anticommunism and developmentalism were combined and interacted with each other in the South Korean context. In addition, if we look at its mode of operation, we can see it has operated in the way of maximal statist intervention (statist mobilization) and authoritarian integration. The maximal statist intervention and authoritarian integration were basic characteristics of the operational mode of the Korean developmental regime. In this sense, the South Korean developmental regime was a statist one on the one hand and an 'authoritarian' one on the other. In the South Korean regime, developmentalism was combined with statism and authoritarianism. Therefore, we can say that the developmental regime is an anticommunist, statist and authoritarian one, in that political and social reorganization of South Korean society towards a growth orientation was made possible by anticommunism and was reproduced in statist and authoritarian mode. In other words, the South Korean developmental regime is characterized as the regime of statist mobilization and authoritarian integration based on the anticommunist regimented society.

Characteristics of the crisis of the South Korean developmental regime

Development of opposition to the developmental regime

The regime of statist mobilization and authoritarian integration in the anticommunist regimented social context gets confronted with crisis with democratization.

Despite the comprehensive intervention of the state, helped by the anticommunist regimented social situation, a crisis of the developmental regime began to be manifested in the mid and late 1970s. In the early stage, especially during the so-called 'economic take-off', the situation of the anticommunist regimented society channeled people into the voluntary accommodation to the developmental regime and the development itself.

However, from the early 1970s, opposition to such a developmental regime (statist mobilization and authoritarian integration) began to expand. The weakening of the regimentation effect of the anticommunism contributed to a revival of oppositional struggles, specifically opposition to authoritarian integration of the working class. In addition, opposition to diverse intervention of the state in one-sided favor of capital expanded. Diverse struggles began to be manifested around such issues as increasing inequality, preferential treatment of big business, corruption, environmental degradation, harsh and long-term dictatorship, restriction of freedom, exploitation of women etc., all of which have looked before as if they had been necessary for development. Opposition to these situations activated diverse social struggles and developed increasingly into political struggles, which had been restrained in the first stage of economic take-off.

What should be pointed out here is that direct and deep involvement of the state in the reproduction of the developmental regime resulted in a 'statization of struggles'. Struggles on various levels converged on the state, and had an implication of resistance against the state. This 'statization of struggles' gave a structural potential to the 'statization of the crisis', once struggles began to spread and develop.

Concretely, a disintegration of the developmental regime that existed hegemonically in the 1960s, began to take place in the 1970s. Contradictions in the industrialization process began to manifest themselves. The developmental regime started to show internal disintegration. Popular sector and oppositional activities and movements increased, and at the same time the developmental regime turned into a more rigid authoritarian regime in response to the deepening crisis. Accordingly, the previous developmental regime with a certain level of hegemony could not but transform itself to a 'more repressive one' that is a more authoritarian one. Ironically, it was the 'successful' growth that led to the creation of new social conditions for an internal rupture in the hegemonic order.

In South Korea, the developmental regime began to be confronted with serious conflict. This was because the all-out statist mobilization of the whole society for growth gave rise to a rapid industrialization, on the one hand, and more condensed structural contradictions on the other. Conflict originated from the structural condition that late industrialization by the developmental regime could not but relocate scarce resources into some targeted areas in extreme inequality in favor of the bourgeoisie in so short a time, and that it was inevitably accompanied by a higher alienation of the popular sector and more acute conflicts.

Opposition movements publicly began to crystallize, strengthening alliances in response to the deepening contradictions of the regime. The growth of the opposition and activation of the popular sector made the previous hegemonic status of the state impossible to preserve. As a result, statist mobilization could only be obtained coercively through external repression, in the authoritarian way. With the intensification and expansion of opposition movements, the hegemonic incorporation of the popular sector to the developmental regime, with the help of the anticommunist regimentation, which made possible the predominance of the state over the society, began to change. This provided a fertile condition for opposition alliances to develop more manifestly and with greater organization.

This meant that the developmental regime hasn't been able to sustain itself politically. The opposition alliance, called 'Minjung movement', which began to be crystallized in the 1970s and existed only as a loose horizontal network, developed into a more organized form in the 1980s. We can say that in the 1960s the developmental regime was still 'hegemonic', but in the 1970s it began to disintegrate, although it did not break down fundamentally. However, in the 1980s there was an oppositional alliance that was sufficiently developed to engage in 'strategic interactions' (Cheng and Kim 1994: 127–128). Such a development of the opposition necessitated the democratic change of the former developmental regime. It meant that the South Korean society entered the road of the democratic transition.

The important issue in the democratic transition is whether the transition occurs from the top-down in a conservative way under the initiative of the previous developmental alliance, or from bottom-up in a radical way under the initiative of the oppositional alliance (Cho 1998: 60–82). The process of political change until now shows that so far South Korea's experience belongs to the former form of transition. Even though the anticommunist regimented society and the developmental regime faced a major crisis, the oppositional alliance could not overcome it in a revolutionary way, and it was unable to dismantle the repressive state structure or to disrupt its dominant agencies. Therefore, oppositional forces had a limited leverage in rearranging the regime in its own way. In brief, political democratization during this period proceeded as a conservative democratization from above. In the conservative democratization from above, the developmental regime of statist mobilization and authoritarian integration undergoes a compromise-like transformation.

Two-faces of growth and the structure of crisis in South Korea

The issue here is whether the problems and contradictions of the developmental regime can be reformed in the democratic transition or not.

First, let's see the economic structural problems of the developmental regime. East Asian economic growth theories, including the developmental state theory, were based on the expectation of continual successful economic growth in East Asia. However, the sudden economic crisis, including the IMF's relief finance to South Korea, turned many scholars to consider the reality of East Asia from the point of view of crisis. Some scholars argue that the causes of the crisis are different from those of successful growth, and so try to find some unique factors to contribute to crisis. In my opinion, successful growth and economic crisis are different sides of the one coin. In my view, factors that contributed to growth, have converted to be causes of crisis, when they fell into the inertia of degradation and corruption. The problems that drove the South Korean economy into crisis should be regarded as inherent to statist mobilization and to the authoritarian integration regime.

The aforementioned regime of statist mobilization is characterized by the comprehensive role of the state in raising and allocating economic resources and concentrating those resources in a few selected areas and companies. A kind of selectivity in this state role has existed. In this mobilization and allocation, special relations were formed among the government bureaucrats, big companies, banks and other actors concerned. In the early rapid economic growth, this special relationship could save the 'transaction costs' among different economic actors. During that period, the special relationship has been a trade-off relation of subsidy on the side of the government, and economic performance on the side of capital (Johnson 1987; Weiss and Hobson 1995). A kind of tension between capital and government was there.

However, as the developmental regime degraded to become a long-term dictatorship, more authoritarian and politically more unstable, such a relation became a relation of political trade of corrupt political funds and economic subsidy. The government bureaucrats and politicians gave some companies economic preference, including banking loans, and the latter gave, in return, political slush money to the former. Here we can see the so-called 'crony' capitalism or 'corrupt' capitalism, which means the distorted, irrational relation among government, banks, entrepreneurs and so on. In the process of growth, this distorted relation has been more fixed and structured.

The special relation between the government and business has been expressed more seriously between the government and Chaebol. Through this collusion, the Chaebol could get favored access to the financial resources under the state's control, while politicians and bureaucrats could get access to political slush funds. A kind of closed circuit of corruption has been formed and reproduced.

Under this structured relation, big companies, especially Chaebol, could perform overinvestment and 'overdiffused' investment in unrelated areas. The Chaebol's monopolistic position in the distribution of credit has strengthened its monopolistic position in the market. In this structure, Chaebol could try debt-ridden diversification and expansion (Kim 1997). This is also connected to the poor and ineffectual management of banks. Chaebol's expansion-oriented management and the poor management of the banks reproduced each other. In this sense, the 'crony' relation which might have contributed to economic growth in the early stage, but transformed to its opposite, thus a fertile ground for economic crisis.

In order to explain this transformation, we should indicate that the statist mobilization and authoritarian integration which have been effective in organizing rapid economic growth have also been effective in repressing the counterforces against the subsequent degradation of the growth-oriented regime. In a one-sided growth-oriented society, it is very difficult to develop checking systems. Due to this, the economy, which rushed to rapid economic growth, rushed to rapid economic crisis too.

These kinds of problems have been expressed, in concentrated form, in Chaebol. In South Korea, where there has been a strong big-business bias in statist mobilization and in the allocation of resources, the problems became more serious and threatened the South Korean economy, when debunked. In South Korea, in which the policy bias was in favor of big companies, Chaebol continued to be strong and the monopolistic economic power of Chaebol has been greater than in any other economies, with the result that it brought a greater and more sudden crisis to South Korean economy.

The theoretical point here is that the simple distinction between the predatory and developmental state (Evans 1995: 43–50) does not make sense. In a sense, we have to talk about the 'predatory' characteristics of the 'developmental' state (Cho 1998: 53–58). The close connection itself among the government bureaucrats, entrepreneurs, banks and politicians, formed by the successful intervention of the state in mobilization and allocation of resources itself, could be inherently corrupt and always have the potential for such distorted relation. In reality, the

South Korean state has been a developmental one, on the one hand, and on the other, a state degraded to be a predatory, even rent-seeking, one. It is exemplified by the fact that former president Roh Tae-Woo collected as much as 600 million dollars in slush money from the big companies.

If there had been a checking system or countervailing power backing it, a certain level of the developmental regime could not be so easily reverted to a predatory one. Although there has been much critique and opposition against collusion among political and economic elites, this democratic reform or breakdown of such a collusion was not accepted by government bureaucrats as a reform agenda. As a result, the regime of statist mobilization and authoritarian integration, especially the Chaebol system, has been reproduced in inertia without the chance of reform.

The great imbalance between the state and civil society and between capital and labor, which enabled the functioning of the statist mobilization, prevented the development and institutionalization of the countervailing system against the degradation of the close relation among the main economic actors. We cannot find causes of successful growth and crisis separately. The causes of growth themselves are also ones of crisis. In this sense, we can say that the developmental regime of high growth is also one of potentially high crisis.

Confronted already with the development of the political opposition movement, the developmental regime couldn't but change to a post-developmental regime, precipitated by its economic crisis.

The transformation of the old developmental regime to the 'neoliberal neo-developmental regime'

Therefore, we can say that the 'old' developmental regime has changed to a 'new' one, that is, a 'neo-developmental regime', in the wake of democratization from the 1980s on, and economic crisis in the mid-1990s. This new regime has different characteristics from the old one in many aspects.

First, this developmental regime is new in that it has a democratic political form, changing its former authoritarian character. It can be said to be a 'democratic' neo-developmental regime.

The way in which a developmental regime is transformed might be different between countries, depending on the class relations, power relations and the type of democratization. The momentum of transformation for the South Korean developmental regime was created by the June democratic uprising in 1987. The military authoritarian government led by Chun Doo-Whan, which symbolized the anticommunist, statist and authoritarian developmental regime was confronted with people's strong opposition from the mid 1980s. As I mentioned, this critical political period saw the emergence of 'the conservative democratization from above' over 'the radical democratization from below', by way of division of the opposition forces, including opposition parties and dissident camps. After this, the South Korean developmental regime began to transform itself following the road of the conservative democratization from above.

While the struggle before 1987, which was characterized by the retreat of the military authoritarian government, aimed at the possible transformation of the developmental regime itself, the struggle after 1987 has developed around the direction of the transformation, i.e. whether the regime's reform is of any substance. With the retreat of the military authoritarian government in 1987, and the emergence of civilian government in 1993 (Kim Yong Sam's government) and an oppositional party government in 1998 (Kim Dae Jung's government), the 'authoritarian' developmental regime has changed increasingly to a 'democratic' developmental regime. People can now see a civilian-elected government rather than the past authoritarian 'un-elected' government.

In this process, the authoritarian integration has changed to the democratic. Under the democratic regime, social movements could enjoy relatively autonomous arenas of activities. Under the past one, there was exclusive repression of the institutional political arena and civil society by the authoritarian regime. The change has made it possible for diverse social groups to organize themselves and express their demands openly without fear of persecution. The people's movement could strengthen itself politically and organizationally. At the same time, the so-called citizens' movements expanded to include new areas with new issues. This was an important context, for the shift from authoritarian to democratic integration.

This political change means that the political form of the developmental regime has changed from an authoritarian to a democratic one. We can say that there is a 'democratic' neo-developmental regime after 1987. As said earlier, the South Korean regime has diverse aspects: statist, authoritarian, anticommunist, develomentalist. Although the 'authoritarian' character itself is one aspect of the reality of the developmental regime, the opposition of people to the regime focused on such political aspects as its authoritarian and dictatorial characteristics. The sharp opposition to the 'authoritarian' aspect of the developmental regime could develop into radical opposition to the developmental regime itself. The main thrust of opposition movement in the 1960s and 1970s was to criticize the long reign of the dictator, Park Chung-hee. However, the opposition movement in the 1980s had a radical orientation whose militant aim was to overcome the developmental regime itself.

This radicalization of the opposition was because of the increasing hardening of the authoritarian regime and the degradation of the regime to fascistic dictatorship. This 'revolutionization' ironically precipitated the transformation of the authoritarian regime to the democratic one.

Second, the neo-developmental regime should be defined as a 'neoliberal' one. The former statist character of the regime has transformed itself, as development proceeded. Statist mobilization meant that the state could keep a very strong state initiative in economic decision making, and that the state could 'mobilize' the population in a certain direction for development. The former was expressed in such phenomena as the economic planning agency playing the authoritative role over the individual entrepreneur or collective capitalist enterprises. A good example of the latter can be found in the 'New Village

Movement', which mobilized people, especially rural people, to renovate rural residential space and encouraged people to be committed to hard work. However, this type of statist mobilization was in effect no longer valid. It is because such a way of statist mobilization became increasingly perceived as out-of-date to the general population. Although a kind of 'state corporatist' organization in charge of such a mobilization, e.g. the Korean Samaeul-Undong Center (Association for the New Village Movement organization), still existed, it was not what it used to be.

In the pressure to change, state initiatives in the economy changed in the following way. First of all, business acquired more initiative in economic decision making and the relation between the business and the state became that of a 'collaborative symbiosis' rather than a 'hierarchical one' (Cho and Kim 1998: 152). The important characteristic of the statist mobilization was comprehensive intervention in business and the strong role of the state bureaucrat in economic decision making. Before, the state acted in a 'dirigiste' way in economic life. Economic decision-making policy in this one-side way has weakened, and the market and corporate sector, or capital in the broad sense, came to enjoy more autonomy. Collaboration and consultation now characterize the relation between business and the state (Doner 1992).

In addition, the decrease in state initiative is also seen in a much greater privatization of state-owned enterprises, which has been happening from the 1980s. In this aspect, global neoliberalism makes a favorable environment for a decrease in state initiative in the economy. In its early stage, the Chun Doo-Whan's government adopted both a privatization policy and a policy that opened South Korea to the global economy as an exit from the stalemate of the heavy-chemical industries in the late 1970s. Until the 1970s, the South Korean economy developed in a relatively closed environment, in which the domestic market was protected from the entry of foreign capital with the help of the 'umbrella of the Cold War' (Arrighi, 1996). The combination of the increase of the foreign debt and pressure for opening of the domestic market from abroad pushed Chun's government to open the economy, and, as a result, incorporation into the global economy proceeded rapidly. In this sense, we can say that the 'neo-developmental regime' is a neoliberal one.

This transformation of the 'old' developmental regime has been encouraged by neoliberal globalization stream, the dominance of which comes from diverse factors such as breakdown of socialism, rapid progress of information and telecommunication revolution and so on. Its core momentum is transnationalization of the capital movement, intensification of competition between businesses and, as a result, the national state is necessitated to adopt a new market-friendly policy and a new growth-encouraging policy (Cho, 2000: 164).

What is interesting is that civilian government, relatively free from the political burden of dictatorship, becomes a strong engine for a new developmentalism. The former authoritarian government lacked political legitimacy and popular support and has been, ironically, constrained to adopt the strong developmental drive in its late stage. Under the authoritarian regime, dictatorship and developmentalism were combined and perceived as the same. However, the Kim Yong-Sam's government was the first civilian-elected one, and so was not beset by political legitimacy issues. Because of this, the first civilian government could adopt a new growth-oriented economic policy strongly under the banner of 'strengthening the international competitiveness'. After it enforced a few anti-authoritarian political actions, including dismissing the former political military elite and taking corrupt politicians and public officials to court and so on, during the early stage (the year 1993–1994), it moved to enforce strong developmental policy packages. While the former economic policies were oriented towards supporting the incipient industries and helping business settle down, now they are oriented towards supplementing weak international competitiveness and providing the infrastructure and so on.

The aforementioned economic crisis and emergence of the opposition party government, the Kim Dae-Jung's government, has not contributed to reflection on, or fundamental change of, the developmental regime. Rather it has led to a new refreshment of the old developmental regime. The Kim Dae-Jung's government adopted policies aimed at a democratic reform of the old developmental regime, including reform of Chaebol, and, at the same time, enforced new developmentalist economic policies in the name of overcoming economic crisis and reconstructing a new successful 'trade state'.

This new developmental inclination was made possible by the separation of 'politics' and 'economy' that is the 'authoritarian' politics and 'growth-oriented' economic policies. The change from 'authoritarian' regime to 'democratic' one has weakened the dispute over the developmentalist character of the regime, and, as a result, political opposition to such a character has weakened. The civilian-elected government, free from controversy over political legitimacy, adopted neoliberal economic policies quite radically and such policies were met with a low degree of opposition. This curious combination of 'democratic' regime and neo-developmentalist economic policies, that is, promotion of the latter by the former, is exactly what the policy of so-called 'low-intensity democracy' strategy aimed (Graf 1995).

Third, however, this change does not mean that the state initiative has disappeared. Certain room for maneuver for the state can exist. For example, the Keynesian welfare state can move to purely neoliberal type of the state, or neocorporatist, or neostatist one (Peck 1996) under the influence of the global neoliberalism. The South Korean state moved towards a 'soft' statist type. It is a transformation of developmental regime, rather than overcoming the developmental regime. In South Korea, the neoliberal character of the state's activities and strong neostatist intervention is ironically combined.

The combination of the new soft type of statist intervention and market-friendly developmentalism survives intact. In South Korea, the success of the president's performance is evaluated still in terms of the economic growth rate. The state initiative functions strongly in a way to support the business activities in a different way intervening with the supply-side management by promoting innovation in product, process organization, market and so on. This state initiative is performed mainly in order to 'coordinate' the diverse economic activities and areas. Although the state initiative in such areas as the past 'micro' control of the economy and guidance of the market has weakened, such macro areas as making of rules for the new business area, selecting the macroeconomic guideline and so on, still exist intact. If the state initiative under the old developmental regime has been a kind of 'mobilizational' in the more vertical way, that under the new one is a kind of 'coordinational' in the more horizontal way.

This coordination role is necessitated by changes brought by globalization and informatization. The globalization and informatization bring with them new economic activities and new relations in new areas (e.g. electronic business). Therefore we can say that the state holds its initiative in a new 'coordination' role such as coordinating relations between new economic actors, making a new regulatory rule and channeling certain economic actors to new areas. The state plays still a vital role in 'the domestic mediation of international challenges' (Weiss and Hobson 1995: 187). In this sense, the state initiative in the form of mobilization has weakened, but its role in coordination or economic governance is still strong. Moreover, the state in South Korea is still playing an important role in amplifying the infrastructural base for development. This infrastructural base includes even the informational one. The state intervenes in encouraging and supporting innovation in supply side such as production process, technology (Jessop 1994: 263–264) and so on.

In addition to this general economic situation, the economic crisis in the late 1990s contributed to preserving state initiative. During the economic crisis, such urgent tasks as reforming big business (Chaebol), restructuring financial industries including banks, made the state initiative even stronger than before. In the process of the economic reform, the statist characteristic of the South Korean developmental regime was not considered a serious problem. The economic crisis was viewed as typical of 'market failure' and the moral hazards of big business, and so 'state failure' was overshadowed. The emergence of the first opposition party government in 50 years has given the general public a new expectation for the state initiative in removing the market failure and moral hazards of the Chaebol. Because of this, the state could keep its initiative in the form of state coordination in relation to business. What is more important is that the class character of the state did not change at all and the market-friendly intervention of the state in the economy continued to be the main characteristic of the state activities, although the 'pro-business' intervention was counterbalanced by the class and social struggles. For example, the 4 River Development Project of the Lee Myung-bak government, which amounts to more than 20 billion US dollars, can be an example of recovery of state initiative in the quite old form. In this sense, I would say that the neo-developmental regime is a kind of 'soft' statist type of neoliberal one.

Based on this discussion, we can say that the 'old' developmental regime has changed into a neo-developmental one. This is different from the former regime in that it takes a political form of democratic regime, based on democratic integration. However, it continues to keep the state initiative in a new 'soft' form' in such a way to coordinate the economy and intervening in the economy in the market-friendly way. However, the neo-developmental regime has not obtained a stable basis for public consensus. The struggle against the multi-faceted destructiveness of the neo-developmental regime is dynamically still underway even under the so-called 'neo-conservative' Lee-Myung-bak government (Cho 2008).

References

Amsden, Alice. 1989. *Asia's Next Giant: South Korea and Late Industrialization*, NY: Oxford University Press.

Arrighi, Giovanni. 1996. 'The Rise of East Asia: World Systemic and Regional Aspects', *International Journal of Sociology and Social Policy* 16(7).

Bonefeld, Werner. 1987. 'Reformulation of State Theory', *Capital and Class* 33.

Castells, Manuel. 1992. 'Four Tigers with a Dragon Head: A Comparative Analysis of the State, Economy and Society in the East Asian Pacific Rim', in R. Appelbaum and J. Henderson eds, *States and Development in the Asian Pacific Rim*, London: Sage Publications.

Cheng, Tun-jen and Eun Mee Kim. 1994. 'Making Democracy: Generalizing the South Korean Case', in Edward Friedman, ed., *The Politics of Democratization: Generalizing East Asian Experiences*, Boulder: Westview Press.

Cho, Hee-Yeon. 1998. *The State, Democracy and the Political Change in South Korea*, Seoul: Dangdae.

Cho, Hee-Yeon. 2000. 'Civic Action for Global Democracy: A Response to neo-liberal globalization', *Inter-Asia Cultural Studies* 1(1).

Cho, Hee-Yeon and Eun Mee Kim. 1998. 'State Autonomy and its Social Conditions for Economic Development in South Korea and Taiwan', in Eun Mee Kim ed., *The Four Asian Tigers: Economic Development and the Global Political Economy*, San Diego: Academic Press.

Chu, Yin-wah. 2009. 'Eclipse or Reconfigured? South Korea's Developmental State and Challenges of the Global Knowledge Economy', *Economy and Society* 38(2).

Cumings, Bruce. 1989. 'The Abortive Abertura: South Korea in the Light of Latin American Experience', *New Left Review* 173(January/February).

Doner, Richard F. 1992. 'Limits of State Strength: Toward an Institutionalist View of Economic Development', *World Politics* 44(3).

Evans, Peter. 1995. *Embedded Autonomy: States and Industrial Transformation*, Princeton: Princeton University Press.

Gereffi, Gary and Donald L. Wyman. 1990. *Manufacturing Miracles: Paths of Industrialization in Latin America and East Asia*, Princeton, NJ: Princeton University Press.

Graf, William. 1995. 'The State in the Third World', *Socialist Register*, London: Merlin Press.

Jessop, Bob. 1994. 'Post-Fordism and the State', in Ash Amin ed., *Post-Fordism: A Reader*, Oxford: Blackwell.

Johnson, Chalmers. 1987. 'Political Institutions and Economic Performance: The Government–Business Relationship in Japan, South Korea, and Taiwan', in Frederic Deyo ed., *The Political Economy of the New Asian Industrialism*, Ithaca: Cornell University Press.

Johnson, Chalmers. 1999. 'The Developmental State: Odyssey of a Concept', in Meredith Woo-Cumings ed., *The Developmental State*, Ithaca: Cornell University Press.

Kim, Eun Mee. 1997. *Big Business, Strong State: Collusion and Conflict in South Korean Development, 1960–1990*, Albany: State University of New York Press.

Lie, John. 1991. 'Review: Rethinking the "Miracle"-Economic Growth and Political Struggle in South Korea', *Bulletin of Concerned Asian Studies* 23(4).

Peck, Jamie. 1996. *Workplace: The Social Regulation of Labor Markets*, New York: Guilford Press.

Perkins, Dwight H. 1994. 'There are at least Three Models of East Asian Development', *World Development* 22(4).

Wade, Robert. 1990. 'Industrial Policy in East Asia: Does it Lead or Follow the Market?' in Gary Gereffi and Donald L. Wyman eds, *Manufacturing Miracles: Paths of Industrialization in Latin America and East Asia*, Princeton, NJ: Princeton University Press.

Weiss, Linda and John M. Hobson. 1995. *States and Economic Development: A Comparative Historical Analysis*, Cambridge: Polity Press.

World Bank. 1993. *The East Asian Miracle: Economic Growth and Public Policy*, Oxford: Oxford University Press.

2 Gender inequality and patriarchal order recontexualized

Uhn Cho

Introduction

Many studies assert that Korean society is gendered, from class structure to the state and labor market (Jo Ju-hyeon 2003; Cho and Jo 1994, Cho 2002; Moon 1998). Not only public space, but also cyberspace has been argued to be gendered (Chang 2003). Even silence is gendered (Yang 1998). The gendered representation of women's labor activism is further remarked in academic discourse (Kim Hyeon-mi 1999). Gender inequality is visible and ubiquitous in all areas, though gender discrimination is legally prohibited. Feminist scholars claim that gender equality is a mere myth in contemporary Korea, as it is shown that women are disadvantaged in the labor market, in terms of legal status, welfare and even love (Jeon Bang-ji 1998; Kang 1998; Kim Seon-uk 1998; Kim Yeong-ran 1998; Yi Bak 1998).

A growing number of studies that have tried to explain gender inequality have come to the realization that gender inequality is indeed unexplainable without tackling the fundamental question of patriarchal order. Conventional social and economic variables are limited in their ability to explain the gender inequality that is deep rooted in Korean society. For example, human capital variables such as education or working hours do not appropriately explain gender inequality in wage differentials (Jang 2000; Park 1988; Bai and Cho 1995). Furthermore, the relationship between class and gender in job mobility clearly demonstrates that determinants of job mobility for women are quite different from men, due to distinctively gendered employment regimes in Korea (Shin 2004). In other words, there should be specific mechanisms that systematically generate gender inequality. This begs the question as to what patriarchal order and mechanisms made females endure such inequality.

"One" working class overrides gender inequality

It is acknowledged that rapid industrialization has proceeded by positing gender as "a central axis of labor differentiation" (Lie 1998). As the Korean government initiated export-led industralization, males and females were differentially absorbed by corresponding industrial restructuring. In the period, the most distinctive gender issue had to do with working-class women, while the most distinctive class had not to do with working-class women. Workers are assumed to be males. Most studies remark that gender inequality was quite serious, but the issue was muted in the period when the Korean economy was transforming from an agricultural to a manufacturing one, and from an assembly economy to a high quality export producer (Jeon Sun-ok 2004; Yi 2001; Koo 2001).

Due to the expansion of the manufacturing industry female employment increased at a faster rate than that of males. In the period, young and cheap females were pulled into the manufacturing industries, while married women with low levels of education were also pulled into the paid labor force due to labor shortages. Further, the significance of marital status in the occupation of females can be shown more clearly by the proportion of single females in each occupational group: female labor absorbed differentially by marital status. The two major occupational groups containing the highest proportion of single females are clerical workers and production related workers. Almost 90 percent of clerical workers are single, as are about three-fourths of production workers. On the other hand, only about 20 percent of the urban married women in the labor force are paid employees. Even the clerical jobs, which absorb a considerable number of single females in the middle social strata, do not provide a cushion for married women in the middle class.

All through the period of light manufacturing and heavy-chemical industrialization, Korean women were included in the "development" process by a "hypermasculine state" as it has been labeled by some (Han and Ling 1998). The Korean government adopted a low wage policy with strong labor controls, exerting a disproportionate effect on female workers. Although state intervention in labor control and a low wage policy was not limited to female workers, the low wage policy and the ban on labor union activities in export industries adversely affected females, as they were concentrated in extra-cheap labor.

Female workers experienced tremendous gender inequality and oppression not only in the workplace, but also in their everyday lives. Women's wages were less than half that of males, though the former worked longer than the latter. As Lie (1998) points out, the legacy of agrarian patriarchal ideology facilitated the construction of cheap female labor, mediated by male workers who struggled for autonomy and patriarchal status in gender-segregated households and workplaces. Male power became reified and institutionalized in offices, factories and the state, capitalizing on the cultural practice of patriarchal authority. In spite of such adverse effects, gender equality was not an issue for women workers until the mid 1980s (Yi 2001; Koo 2001). Even then they did not protest against gender inequality or discrimination itself but against general exploitative working conditions and repressive labor policies.

The Korean government did not provide child care centers in spite of the rapid increase of working mothers. The child care issue was not raised until several left-alone children were victimized. Gender equality or improving working conditions for women were not accounted in terms of policy. State policy towards working women was literally non-existent in the development period; until the 1987 Great Workers' Struggle that gender-related laws were enacted – the Sex Equality in Employment Act (1987), the Employment Security and Promotion Act (1989), the Mother–Child Welfare Act (1989). All through the period, "developing" women for "the development of the society" was what mattered in social policy. For example, a law for gender equality is named as Basic Law for Developing Women, which was renamed as Basic Gender Equality Law and it was about ten years later, 2007.

According to the accounts of women labor activists, at the time they did not regard these gender issues as serious problems, as the labor problems they faced at the time, by men and women, were so overwhelming. They thought of "gender problems" only in terms of the working class as a whole, while labor unions often work only for male workers. Sometimes labor unions prevented female workers from organizing their own voice (Koo 2001; Jeon Sun-ok 2004). Some women unionists were bothered at the fact that they had to leave the labor movement when they got married. They came to become aware of patriarchy and gender inequality as a serious problem unto itself, apart from class inequality. But they did not link this to a greater women's movement that advocated the achievement of gender equality as a central goal. "Caught between capitalism and patriarchy," as Seung-Kyung Kim (1997) describes it, women workers did not know whether they had to struggle against family or class. They did not dare to attack patriarchy in the midst of class struggle.

The ideology of the male breadwinner in economic crisis

The arrival of global pressure represented by the International Monetary Fund (IMF) bail out has shown more explicitly how gender inequality is reproduced in the period of "economic crisis." If agrarian patriarchy included women in the workforce during the development era, the interests of mobile global capital has tended to utilize local patriarchy to exclude women from the workforce. Under the IMF guidelines of maintaining a low-growth economy, transparency in financial management and so forth, layoffs spread throughout all sectors.

Women workers were more quickly dismissed though all workers were dismissed, making popular the expression "IMF" to stand for "I Am Fired." From computer operators to hospital and research staff, women of all occupations were asked to leave the workplace for one reason or another. Pregnant women were highest on the priority list of workers to be laid off, followed by married women with spouse. Some women tried to maintain the appearance of being single or postpone official reporting of their marriage registration. The term "IMF *cheonyeo*" (IMF maiden) was coined to describe this predicament.

As the "ideology of the male breadwinner," works alongside the interests of global capital, the IMF crisis had immediate effects on women's employment, as well as on gender relationships in Korean society (Cho 2002; Jo Sun-gyeong 1998). In almost all industries, rates of female layoffs were higher than males', as shown in Table 2.1. Furthermore, larger companies tended to lay off females more than males. In large firms with over 500 employees, the layoff rate for females was almost 1.5 times higher than males (PCWS 1999).

Table 2.1 The reduction rate of employees by occupation, 1997–1999

	Reduction rate (%)			
	July 1997 to July 1998		*July 1998 to March 1999*	
	Male	*Female*	*Male*	*Female*
Total occupation	–5.3	–8.2	–7.9	–10.8
Professional and administrative managerial	0.1	1.2	2.9	0.0
Clerical	6.9	–18.4	–7.5	–21.1
Service, sales	2.4	–6.5	–1.0	–4.9
Agriculture and fishing	5.5	3.2	–12.9	–33.1
Production	–15.3	–14.8	–14.6	–5.6

Source: PCWS (1999).

During the period, the number of employees for males decreased by 5.3 percent, while for females it was 8.2 percent over the year between July 1997 and July 1998 (Table 2.1). The change reflected the initial impact of IMF policies on the employment status of males and females. In the later period between July 1998 and March 1999 the rate was 7.9 percent for males, while it was 10.8 percent for females. Of particular note was the fact that the reduction rate of female clerical workers reached as high as 18.4 percent in the first period and then the later period it peaked as high as 21.1 percent. More specifically, the reduction rate for regular employees in the manufacturing industry was as high as 20.9 percent during one year of IMF era. The rate of counterpart males was 12.9 percent, as shown in Table 2.2. As much as one-fourth of regular clerical female employees were laid off during that period.

Labor unions easily agreed to the layoffs of women workers in order to maintain the status of the male breadwinners. The male-dominated unions bartered away the rights of female workers in the interest of male workers. In this situation the Korean Women Workers Association United (KWWAU) was founded in 1998. As a nationwide women's labor union, it purported to overcome the limited opportunities for women in labor unions.

Table 2.2 Reduction rate of regular employees in manufacturing industry over one year of IMF era year, 1997–1998

	Number of employees	*Reduction rate (%)*	
		Male	*Female*
Total manufacturing	2,402.2	–12.9	–20.9
Production	1,487.2	–13.1	–18.9
Clerical	914.9	–12.5	–25.3

Source: reconstructed from PCWS (1999).

The case of the National Agricultural Cooperative Federation (NACF) offers a good example of how the ideology of the male breadwinner fits well into the interests of global capital. The NACF is one of the largest public enterprises in Korea, employing more than 3,000 workers. As soon as the NACF was forced to "restructure," it identified 762 working couples throughout their various branches, asking them to choose which spouse should leave their job. Out of these working couples, the female employee was called upon first to leave the workplace. If the woman was reluctant to leave the job, then her husband was called in. As a result, as much as 91.2 percent of the layoffs in the NACF were female. The NACF insisted that wives "volunteered" to leave, claiming that it never forced women to leave, but rather it had been their decision between spouses.

The case of the NACF was merely one example. There were many other public and private firms that forced female employees to leave the workplace under different pretenses such as "honorable retirement" or "early retirement with incentives." The NACF case received widespread publicity, as it was brought into court by enraged female workers determined to get their jobs back. Two of those who had been forced to leave their jobs filed suit with the help of women's movement organizations. Besides the two litigants, 28 female professors and activists joined in the suit as complainants. But the court decided that the NACF was not guilty of gender discrimination, stating that "during the IMF era," it was necessary for major public enterprises to ask employees of "relatively stable livelihoods" to leave the workplace. Women's organizations filed an immediate appeal against the lower court's decision, and lost again in the higher court. The case eloquently demonstrates how the ideology of the male breadwinner continued to display its strong and deep roots in Korean society.

The ideology of the male breadwinner has exercised power in everyday discourse. During the IMF period, employers openly said that it was unavoidable to lay off women workers since they were not primary breadwinners. Newspapers, broadcast and television programmers were eager to start the "campaign to restore the husband." *Gi* (energy or self-esteem), or to be more exact, the male breadwinner's *gi* was a central concern. The purpose of the campaign was to raise men's diminished *gi* that had been damaged due to unemployment and other economic stressors. Some feminist scholars claimed that "Confucian" patriarchal ideology was utilized in order to justify the discharge of women from the labor market (Jo Sun-gyeong 1998), while some other feminist scholars argued that global capital had utilized the local gender system in Korea for its own purposes, that of "mobile" global capital cooperating with a "immovable" patriarchy to extend and reproduce gender inequality (Cho 2002; Yoon 1998).

What is important to note here is not the extent, but the ways through which the economic recession worked in the interests of patriarchy to get women back in the home while making women conscious of gender status. As women were pushed into the labor market at lower wages on behalf of unemployed husbands, the issue was problematized in terms of the question of whether these women workers would disrupt or strengthen the patriarchy at family level (Shin 2000).

Since IMF bailouts, so-called "birth strikes" and "marriage sabotage" were coined as birth rate and marriage rate were on the abrupt decrease. However, they were rarely linked to the predicament of female layoff. Moreover, the ideology of the male breadwinner worked to increase female-headed households under the poverty line, as male-headed households were the primary recipients of pensions and employment insurance, while female-headed households were the main beneficiaries of livelihood protection and other government aid (Lee 2002).

Hojuje: patrilineality, gendered citizenship and gender inequality

The most current and controversial issue for gender politics in Korea was the abolishment of the *hojuje*. The *hojuje* system has institutionalized the legal order of succession of family headship as something passed down a line of sons. When there is no male heir, the first daughter can assume the domestic authority of the family head, but only on a temporary basis, until she marries. It has not only protected men's dominance over women in terms of maintaining patrilocal marriage, the patriarchal family, patrilineage in kinship and the inheritance of property, but also underlain the nationalist discourse around Korean tradition, obscuring inequality behind the name of family. Some argued that the abolishment of the *hojuje* challenges official nationalism by undermining the patrilineal family as the basic unit of the nation. As Seungsook Moon argued, the refusal of abolishing *hojuje* was ultimately a conservative response with a modern twist, a backlash against the swell of women's voices demanding equality (Moon 1998: 55).

Though there were several organized efforts to reform family law, the patrilineal family law was enforced for more than four decades. *Hojuje* remained intact in spite of steady and fast women's organizing effort. The attempts of feminist groups to abolish *hojuje* were always met by hostile reactions from self-proclaimed Confucianists, and received lukewarm responses from the legislature, who were concerned about the reaction of a conservative electorate. Yet feminist scholars and activists continued to appeal for its removal to abolish it in 2005.

The outdated system creates myriad problems, such as a preference for sons, discrimination against women and negative effects on children of divorcees, not to mention gendered citizenship. A distorted male/female sex ratio reflects the stubbornness of a patrilineal patriarchal order. In 1975, the sex ratio was 122.4. It kept on going about the same. As of 2000, the sex ratio stands at 110.2 in favor of males; but the ratio tips in favor of male children as each additional child is added to a family; the male/female sex ratio for the first child is 106.2, 107.4 for the second, 141.7 for the third and 166.9 for the fourth child (Table 2.3). In 2005, the ratio stepped down to 107.8. Even for the fourth child, the sex ratio marked down to 132.4.

Accordingly, the Korean marriage market suffered from the lack of supply of bridegrooms since 2000. So called marriage migrants have increased rapidly

Table 2.3 Sex ratio by birth order

Birth order	*Year*						
	1975	*1980*	*1985*	*1990*	*1995*	*2000*	*2005*
Total	112.4	106.4	109.4	116.6	113.4	110.2	107.8
First child	120.0	106.0	106.0	108.6	105.9	106.2	104.8
Second child	109.8	106.5	107.8	117.2	111.8	107.4	106.5
Third child	110.8	106.9	129.2	190.8	179.4	141.7	128.5
Fourth child	105.5	110.2	146.8	214.1	213.9	166.9	132.4

Source: KNSO, *Annual Report on Vital Statistics*, relevant years.

since 2005. As of 2006, there were 36,960 cases of marriage to a foreign spouse in Korea (Korea National Statistics Office 2007). This accounts for 11.9 percent of the total marriages registered in that year, out of which more than 75 percent (30,208 cases) were marriages between Korean men and Asian women, mostly South East Asian or Chinese Korean (Kim 2008). Even though international marriage migration of women from and within Asia has been on the increase over the last few decades, the Korean case represents somewhat different stories embedded with patriarchal order; in the sense that lower class males have rare chance to find their mates due to the sex–ratio imbalance resulted from son preference in their birth days.

And, further, Korean society is vexed by a high divorce rate and remarriage. The former is even lower than most OECD countries, and the latter has increased quite rapidly, and is the highest, next to the United States, in the world. As shown in Table 2.4, the divorce rate jumped from 5.9 percent in 1980 to 35.9 percent in 2000. As of 2002, one in two marriages ended in divorce and the rate of female remarriage have increased from 4.1 percent in 1980 to 14.5 percent in 2000. As divorce and remarriage rates increase, the patrilineal family system and the abolishment of the *hojuje* has become a sensitive and immediate issue over which everyday Koreans are concerned. The disadvantages that the family-head system imposes on women have been considered primarily within concrete and

Table 2.4 Divorce rate and remarriage rate (%)

	1980	*1985*	*1990*	*1995*	*2000*
Raw divorce rate	0.6	1.0	1.1	1.5	2.5
Divorce rate	5.9	10.3	11.4	17.1	35.9
Female remarriage rate	4.1	5.7	7.1	10.0	14.5
Male remarriage rate	6.4	7.7	8.4	10.0	13.1

Source: Korean National Statistical Office, *Annual Report on the Vital Statistics* (1989, 1995, 2001), Recited from KWDI 2000a and 2000b.

Notes
1 Divorce rate refers to numbers of divorces/marriages per 100.
2 Raw divorce rate refers to numbers of divorces per 1,000 persons.

detailed legal disputes, such as a mother's relations with her children in cases of divorce or remarriage; however, the impact of *hojuje* abolishment would be far reaching. More than anything else, children of a remarried mother have not necessarily kept on the patrilineal family name. And also children of Korean women and foreign husband could get Korean nationality if they want. As international marriage increases, patrilineality and *hojuje* could not be kept on.

Conclusion: gender inequality faces a new phase of gender politics

The ideology of the male breadwinner has worked very closely with the state, global capital and class ideology to support the patriarchal order in contemporary Korea. Besides the ideology of the male breadwinner, patrilineality is another generative mechanism that facilitates the production and maintenance of gender inequality. They have co-worked in various and subtle ways, depending on differing social contexts.

The chapter recontextualizes the way in which the ideology of the male breadwinner and the patrilineality facilitate to generate gender inequality that results in the cleavages of patriarchal order. It shows that the ideology of the male breadwinner and the patrilineality of *hojuje* have been two pillars that directly support the patriarchal order are at stake. The ideology of male breadwinner could not keep on the gendered division of labor without dismantling the basic patriarchal order. In the same vein, *hojuje* could not go on in the global and post authoritarian regime of the marriage and family.

It is clear that gender inequality cannot be mitigated unless gender politics directly intervene to tackle and reform the major principles of patriarchal order. The Korea experience demands that gender inequality will have no choice but face a new phase of gender politics in the coming era.

References

Bai, Moo Ki and Woo Hyun Cho. 1995. "Women's employment structure and male-female wage differentials in Korea." In *Women and Industrialization in Asia*, edited by Susan Horton. London: Routledge.

Chang, Pilwha. 2003. "Cyberspace and Sexuality." *Korea Journal* 43.3.

Cho, Uhn. 2002. "Global Capital and Local Patriarchy: The Financial Crisis and Women Workers in South Korea." In *Women and Work in Globalising Asia*, edited by Dong-Sook S. Gills and Nicola Piper. London: Routledge.

Cho, Uhn (Jo, Eun) and Jo Sun-gyeong. 1994. "Nodong sijang-eseoui seong bulpyeong-deung-ui siltae-wa geukbok bangan" [A Report on Gender Inequality in the Labor Market]. Seoul: KWDI.

Han, Jongwoo and L. H. M. Ling. 1998. "Authoritarianism in the Hypermasculinized State: Hybridity, Patriarchy, and Capitalism in Korea." *International Studies Quarterly* 42.

Jang, Ji-yeon. 2000. "Jeonggyu/bijeonggyu jeonhwan-eul jungsim-euro bon chweomnyeok-gwa saengae gwajeong" [Work History and Life-Course Examined through Conversion between Regular and Irregular Employment]. *Nodong gyeongje nonjip* [Korean Journal of Labor Economics] 23 (special issue).

Jeon, Bang-ji. 1998. "Gukje jipyo-wa hanguk-ui seong bulpyeongdeung" [International Index and Gender Enequality in Korea]. *Yeoseong-gwa sahoe* 9.

Jeon, Sun-ok. 2004. *Kkeunnaji anneun sida-ui dorae–1970 nyeondae hanguk yeoseong nodong undong-e daehan saeroun jarimaegim* [They Are Not Machines]. Seoul: Hankyoreh.

Jo, Ju-hyeon. 2003. "Gun gasanjeom je nonjaeng-gwa jende jeongchi–ganeungseon jeopgeunbeop-ui gwanjeom-eseo" [Veterans' Extra Point System and Gender Politics: From the Perspective of Capabilities Approach]. *Hanguk yeoseonghak* [Journal of Korean Women's Studies] 19.1.

Jo, Sun-gyeong. 1998. "Minjujeok sijang gyeongje-wa yugyojeok gabujangje" [Democratic Market Economy and Confucian Patriarchy]. *Gyeongje-wa sahoe* [Economy and Society]. 38.

Kang, I-su. 1998. "Tonggye-ro bon hanguk yeoseong-ui jiwi" [Women's Status seen through the Statistics]. *Yeoseong-gwa sahoe* 9.

Kim, Cheong-Seok. 2008. "Features of International Marriage of Korean Men to Women from Four Asian Countries". In *Cross-Border Marriage: Process and Dynamics*, edited by Doo-Sub Kim. Seoul: The Institute of Population and Aging Research: 141–164.

Kim Hyeon-mi. 1999. "Hanguk nodong undong-ui damnon bunseok-eul tonghae bon seongjeok jaehyeon-ui jeongchihak" [The Politics of Gender Representation seen through the Discourse Analysis of the Korean Labor Movement]. *Hanguk yeoseonghak* [Journal of Korean Women's Studies] 6 (autumn/winter).

Kim, Seon-uk. 1998. "Yeoseong-gwa beop, irun geot-gwa iruji motan geot" [Women and Law Success and Failure]. *Yeoseong-gwa sahoe* [Women and Society] 9.

Kim, Seung-Kyung. 1997. *Class Struggle or Family Struggle? The Lives of Women Factory Workers in South Korea.* Cambridge: Cambridge University Press.

Kim, Yeong-ran. 1998. "Bin-gon-ui yeoseonggwa sahoe bokji segyehwa" [Feminization of Women Social Welfare, and Globalization]. *Yeoseong-gwa sahoe* 9.

Koo, Hagen. 2001. *Korean Workers.* New York: Cornell University Press.

Korea National Statistical Office (KNSO). 2007. Daejeon: KNSO.

Korea Women's Development Institute (KWDI). 2000a. *Blueprint for Women's Development.* Seoul: Korea Women's Development Institute.

Korea Women's Development Institute (KWDI). 2000b. *Statistical Yearbook on Women.* Seoul: Korea Women's Development Institute.

Lee, Hyekyoung. 2002. "Women in Poverty, Public Assistance, and Welfare Services in Korea." *Korea Journal* 42.2.

Lie, John. 1998. *Han Unbound: The Political Economy of South Korea.* Stanford, CA: Stanford University Press.

Moon, Seungsook. 1998. "Begetting the Nation: The Androcentric Discourse of National History and Tradition in South Korea." In *Dangerous Women: Gender & Korean Nationalism*, edited by Elaine H. Kim and Chungmoo Choi. London: Routledge.

Park, Saeil. 1988. "Labor Issues in Korea's Future." *World Development* 16.1.

Presidential Commission on Women's Affairs (PCWS). 1999. *The Presidential Commission on Women's Affairs Report.* Seoul: Republic of Korea.

Shin, Gwang-yeong. 2000. "Economic Crisis and Patriarchy." Paper presented at the fourth conference of Asian Pacific Sociological Association at Nishinomya, Japan, September 14–16.

Shin, Gwang-yeong. 2004. "Gyegeup seong-gwa iljari idong" [Class, Gender and Job Mobility]. *Hanguk sahoehak* [Korean Journal of Sociology] 38.1.

Yang, Hyunah. 1998. "Remembering the Korean Military Comfort Women: Nationalism, Sexuality, and Silencing." In *Dangerous Women: Gender & Korean Nationalism*, edited by Elaine H. Kim and Chungmoo Choi. London: Routledge.

Yi Bak, Hye-gyeong. 1998. "Sarang-i uri-reul pyeongdeung hage harira?" [Love will Set You Equal?] *Yeoseong-gwa sahoe* 9.

Yi, Ok-ji. 2001. *Hanguk yeseong nodongja undongsa* [History of Female Worker's Movement in Korea]. Seoul: Hanul.

Yoon, Bang-Soon. 1998. "Korean Women in the Global Economy: Industrialization and Gender Politics in South Korea." *Yonsei Journal of Women's Studies* 4.

3 Regionalism

Its origins and substance with competition and exclusion

Wang-Bae Kim

Why regionalism today?

Since the end of the twentieth century, scholars all over the world have grappled with the impact of globalization in creating new ways of life. While there haven't been many substantial points of convergence in various understandings of globalization, one viewpoint that has garnered increasing attention is understanding globalization as comprehensive transformation in politics and culture that goes beyond mere transformation of economic order alone. Proponents of political globalization assert that international government agencies have acquired more influential powers while autonomous powers of individual countries have been eclipsed (see Castells, 1997: p. 269). On the contrary, some predicted that states will be neither undermined nor weakened and that globalization will collapse in the face of nationalism. On the other hand, cultural globalization is so complicated and diversified that it has provoked contradictory arguments (see Mittleman, 1997; Scott, 1997; and Ross and Trachte, 1990). Some argue that the unique third "Global Culture" which differs from all existing ones, is being generated. Others hold that global culture, being nothing more than the Americanized culture, means homogenization of diverse cultures at the expense of individual nation states with distinct cultural traits (see Featherstone, 1996; and Sklair, 1995).

In spite of these variations in perspectives on globalization, one common conclusion is that globalization is the process of erasing regional boundaries. However, it is worth noting that the "regionalization" which redraws the lines of territorial borders, occurs at the same time as globalization is eliminating national borders. In the current wave of globalization, new regional blocs such as the European Community (EC), Asian Pacific Economy Cooperation (APEC), and North American Free Trade Agreement (NAFTA) have simultaneously replaced previous national boundaries.

Whether regional boundaries consist of sets of several nation states or small communities, it is clear that regionalization (and regionalism) is regarded as a phenomenon that confronts globalization (and globalism). The term "glocalization" appropriately reflects dialectical process of the two tendencies: globalization and regionalization (see Wilson and Dissanayake, 1996; for correspondence of local economies to the world capitalist system, see Stallings, 1995).

Recently we can find various "symptoms" which are implicitly or explicitly related to regionalization (or regionalism). First, post-modernistic epistemology, which emphasizes a relativistic view at the micro level, denies totalistic thought and ontology in macro discourse and asserts recognition of local as the locus of meaningful life in post-industrial society (see Warf, 1995).

Regionalism as an anti-discourse to globalism has become closely related with nationalism. Anti-hegemonic discourse, resisting hegemony of a few powerful countries, the United States in particular, poses political and cultural questions; national sentiments regarding *who we are*, and *how to identify our forefathers and descendants*. While race-related nationalism has formed historically beyond regional boundaries, regionalism may compound within specific, spatial boundaries. Nonetheless, both are closely related to each other, and also to post-colonialism which criticized globalization's tendency to reinforce a biased Western centered viewpoint. Post-colonialism, which emphasized the restoration of subjects in locales, now accentuates the local area (region). As political, economic, and cultural importance of China, Japan, and South Korea have increased, closer attention is now being paid to this region, urging us to reconsider its changing status.

Post-modernism, post-colonialism, and discourse on East Asia have suggested an entirely new way of thinking about locality, regionalism, and especially "regional settings" as the locus of individual life. Regionalism in a more comprehensive sense refers to the entire range of characteristics historically formed in a specific space through all interactions of political, economic, and cultural factors. It is fluid and formed in the context of time and space.

Then what are the characteristics of regionalism in South Korea today? How do we approach and evaluate its substance? Regionalism in South Korean society is typified by the term *Jiyeokgamjeong* (regional sentiment), is more closely defined as discrimination toward a specific region. This "regional sentiment" has been lamented as a "ruinous national disease" (*mang'gukbyung*) that has exerted a powerful and persistent negative influence throughout Korean history, particularly on people's attitudes and political behavior. *Jiyeokgamjeong* has driven people to vote for candidates and political parties based merely on their regional background (see Kim, Wook, 2004). It caused long-lasting divisions that have undermined national solidarity by provoking political cleavages and economic alienation among regions. In South Korea, *Jiyeokgamjeong* has led to unequal distribution of resources in politics and economic development. It affects one's job opportunities and promotions, marriage prospects, social relations, and other aspects of everyday life.

Although *Jiyeokgamjeong* is regarded as the most common form of regionalism, regionalism has other facets as well, including disparity between the capital city Seoul (metropolitan area) and local areas (*jibang*), which became a stark reality. Under South Korea's "growth first, distribution later" strategy of economic planning, rapid industrialization in 1960s and 1970s was predicated on specific groups, class, industries, and regions. Thus, industrialization has brought about so-called "spatial polarization." Seoul has occupied the supreme position in the country with the most educational, medical, and other public facilities as well as the lion's share of South Korean national administrative entities and businesses (see Kang, 2007; Kim and Young-Jin, 2008).

We also observe another form of regionalism. Under a highly centralized regime, Korean society had never possessed a regionally dispersed power structure. In the mid-1990s, "age of the local" was introduced as a symbol of increasing democratization, restoring local self-governments with local elections for organizing local councils. Local self-government is now regarded as laying building blocks of grass-root democracy and civil society, and establishing a space for local inhabitants to improve quality of life (see Lee, Shin-Haeng, 2006). Consequently, through various images on local spaces (for instance, through local feasts or banquets), movements to construct peculiar "local" characteristics have arisen and, as a result, a new form of regionalism has emerged (see Kim, Baek-Yung, 2007; Lee, Moo-Yong, 2006).

In South Korea, regionalism is commonly regarded as a harmful and negative attitude because of the social deformities and impediment it creates for overall development of Korean society. It has been frequently argued that *Jiyeokgamjeong* has undermined national integration, rational consensus, and sound political development. Also, polarization (or regional disparities) between Seoul (metropolis) and other local areas is contrary to the principle of resource distribution justice. However, regionalism does not only entail negative elements. Currently it has been witnessed in Korean society that newly formed regionalism including local self-governance may imply positive motives for restoration of abolished subjects in the course of globalization, and improving quality of life.

The formation of regionalism in South Korea reveals complicated issues. This chapter attempts to examine regionalism in South Korean society in three dimensions: (1) *Jiyeokgamjeong* as a typical regional sentiment, (2) intra-regional disparities (polarization between Seoul and the local), and (3) emergence of a new kind of regionalism (locality).

The substance of *Jiyeokgamjeong*

Jiyeokgamjeong as a form of regional sentiment and one constituent of regionalism in general, may be described as a social attitude toward a certain region. In Korean society, it refers to a socio-psychological state that is manifested through prejudice, discrimination, and pervasive stereotypes of a specific region. *Jiyeokgamjeong* also refers to confrontational and hostile attitudes toward people in other areas. Clearly, in this context, the term *Jiyeokgamjeong* is associated with negative connotations. For the last 30 years, *Jiyeokgamjeong* has been perceived as a pathological condition that afflicts Koreans.

One of the frequent criticisms of *Jiyeokgamjeong* is that it undermines national solidarity and impedes rational debate and critical consciousness on policies or ideology. Also as seen in Jeolla province case, *Jiyeokgamjeong* manifests itself by adversely affecting social relations such as employment, promotion, associates, marriage, and so forth (see Kim, Man-Heum, 1987; Kim, Jin-Guk, 1984; Kim, Hye-Suk, 1988).

How, then, is it possible to explain *Jiyeokgamjeong*? I will broadly categorize the existing interpretational approaches into "historical approach" and "political behavioral approach," examine each in detail, and suggest "social mobility framework" as a more viable and alternative approach for analysis.

Historical interpretation

Historical interpretation approach regards regional sentiment in Korea as a historical phenomenon and seeks its origins in the past. Today the typical spaces experiencing *Jiyeokgamjeong* are Jeolla and Gyeongsang. Historical origins of the regional conflicts may be traced as far back as the Three Kingdoms period, which consisted of three independent kingdoms: Goguryeo, Shilla, and Baekje. Jeolla province was Baekje's territory and Shilla established itself in where now is Gyeongsang province. Historical interpretation presents that prejudices reflecting historically built hostility between the two areas (or once countries) has been inherited through Koryo (918–1392) and Joseon Dynasty (1392–1910) (Lee, Ki-Baek, 1977; Lee, Ee-Hwa, 1983).

Such an approach, however, has limitations. It can be a subjective, arbitrary interpretation without historical documentation, reflecting merely the pervasiveness of popular stereotypes. Historical incidents in and of themselves, are inadequate for explaining today's *Jiyeokgamjeong.* In regards to the political factionalism during the Joseon Dynasty, some point out that groups from modern-day Gyeongsang and Jeolla provinces were not involved in regional conflicts or discriminations, but allied together in their mutual suffering (see Song, 1994).

Political behavior approach

Jiyeokgamjeong reveals its most definite features in election behaviors in contemporary South Korea. Voters still tend to support candidates and political parties related with their own region of origin, even though voters no longer reside in the area (on *Jiyeokgamjeong* and political behavior, see Bae, 1992; Shin, 1992; Cha, 1988).

Jiyeokgamjeong exerts a powerful influence on election behavior regardless of generation, occupation, and class. It not only hinders establishment of political parties based on a particular social agenda or common class interests but also paralyzes rational political choice. For example, a disproportionate number of people from the Gyeongsang area have been appointed and promoted in government administrative offices during most of Korea's modern history since Park Jeong-hee (who was from Gyeongsang province) seized power in 1961, while those from Jeolla area have been excluded. The so-called Gyeongsang group continued to appoint personnel from their area to high social and political positions to secure their power, forming a network of cronyism, to reduce risk and maximize the efficacy of ruling (Kim, Yong-Hak, 1992).

In every election season, most candidates state "regional integration" and "eradication of regional sentiment" as their campaign pledges. However, many critics hold that *Jiyeokgamjeong* has been "strategically" invented by politicians. *Jiyeokgamjeong*, in this sense, is an irrational, knee-jerk mechanism to exclude prominent political rivals. On one hand, the Gyeongsang power group urges that "we must maintain power, because if radical Jeolla rivals seize power, they will cast our nation into chaos and disorder." On the other hand, the Jeolla power group exhorts its supporters to "stand together to elect a candidate from our region, otherwise our region will continue to be excluded from economic growth and political power."

During the regime of former President Park Jeong Hee (1961–1979), regionalism was subdivided so that the influence of *Jiyeokgamjeong* of the Chungcheong area (the central region of the Korean peninsula) had come to be reflected on political behavior. As Kim Jong-pil (representative politician of the Chungcheong area) announced his candidacy for president in the late 1980s, he vehemently denounced the so-called "Chungcheong bumpkin" stereotype. He established his power base by asserting that "People in Chungcheong are not ignorant fools."

Even aside from discourse of mass media inciting regionalism, regional sentiment is clearly an established and diffused phenomenon. From Jeolla to Gyeongsang to Chungcheong, a common political tactic is to exploit sentiments of regional chauvinism in order to artificially incite *Jiyeokgamjeong*. In sum, *Jiyeokgamjeong* today is not a spontaneous phenomenon, but a blind prejudice fabricated by politicians who merely seek to consolidate their political foundations (Ahn, 1992).

Political behavioral approach is persuasive in that *Jiyeokgamjeong* in Korea clearly reveals its distinctive features which undermine national integration, rational judgment, and rational political culture. *Jiyeokgamjeong* has always been identified and cited as the core reason for aberrations, idiosyncrasies, and distortions in the electoral process. However, granted that *Jiyeokgamjeong* may be clearly identified in political process of election behaviors, it still fails to explain exactly how it was generated and internalized in so much of the Korean populace.

"The social mobility" interpretation

To explore *Jiyeokgamjeong* and its ensuing conflicts as a more comprehensive social phenomenon, we need to understand that *Jiyeokgamjeong* basically arises from conflicts around resource distribution (such as power, wealth, reputation), acting as a mechanism that excludes specific groups from the distribution process. That is, in situations where heterogeneous groups gather in a specific space for resource distribution, coalitions and exclusions occur to win resources, and in the process, prejudice against a specific group is acted upon.

Korean society has experienced tremendous social mobility. In the 1960s, the first industry sector laid the foundation for the national economy and secondary and tertiary industries comprised less than 30 percent of total industries. However in the 1990s, the portion of industries became totally reversed. Along with the transformation, most of the population from the agricultural sector became concentrated in Seoul and its suburbs. By the 1990s, the majority of Seoul's population came to be composed of migrants from other areas in the country. The number of Seoul's original inhabitants made up less than 20 percent of the total population in Seoul. For those people, "pies" were too few to share. To enlarge the limited number of "pies" within a short period, conflicts and tensions regarding resources production and distribution were inevitable. Given the context, the struggles for resources were understandably more fierce and intensive than in other societies.

Jeolla region, based mostly on agriculture, underwent the most drastic structural changes in population upheaval and relocation during the industrialization. Thus, it is all the more likely that people from Jeolla were regarded as the most bellicose in struggles for resources from the perspective of other inhabitants. Therefore, those from other areas began to make defense coalitions to maintain their resources and exclude the "outsiders" from the Jeolla region. The exclusionary mechanism stimulated socio-psychological defense mechanism (strategy of creating and disseminating stereotype and negative prejudice). Stereotypes are propagated and become fixed as "facts." At the same time, people from Jeolla share a common "persecution consciousness" (sense of "victimization" known as *pihaeuishik*), which strengthens their own cohesion and makes them wary of people from other areas. Sometimes political groups play a leading role in utilizing the exclusionary mechanism in conflicts over resource distribution.

Spatial division of labor and uneven regional development

Industrialization and regional structuration

In South Korea, unequal regional development shapes another type of regionalism that exacerbates regional tensions and conflicts. The industrialization of South Korea centered in certain regions, particularly in Seoul, under the direction of the state, which created wide disparities in regional development. The regional disparities produced by this vertical division between Seoul and other local areas suggest another dimension of regionalism different from the regional sentiment discussed above. I briefly summarize the changes in regional structures during the rapid industrialization.

In the 1960s, South Korean industrialization actively focused on simple labor-intensive, light industries based on a cheap labor force. Industrial areas were located in traditionally large, metropolitan cities such as Seoul, Busan, Daegu. However, the southwestern region of Jeolla was almost completely bypassed in the development strategy. In the 1970s, the industrialization of South Korea switched from light industry to heavy industry. New, large-scale industrial complex areas were formed on the eastern and southern coastal areas. Regional structures changed dramatically (Korea Development Institute, 1987; Kim,

Youn-Jeong, 1997). However, the development was still concentrated in metropolitan areas of the southeastern coast.

In the mid-1980s to the 1990s, facing protective trade policies of advanced countries and increasing competition from developing latecomers, the South Korean economy entered a new phase. The state began to shift away from declining industrial sectors that could not compete with the low wage latecomers such as China, Indonesia, Thailand, etc. Instead, South Korea was driven to the "intensification of industrial structures" to stimulate investment in technology research and development in order to make inroads into new high-tech industries. Areas of declining industries such as coal mining (e.g. Taebaek), textile, shoes, and electronic assembly (e.g. Guro and Masan), were severely deindustrialized and other regions intensified their existing production systems and transformed into newly competitive sites. These areas featured peculiar characteristics of "enterprise city" in which large corporations wielded tremendous influence in the political, cultural, and educational spheres of life, virtually managing residents' everyday life in general (Yeom, 1998). The R&D aspect of high-tech industries became concentrated in the metropolis and brand new industrial spaces were structured in the central regions, which have been described as "technopolis."

As manufacturing industries involved with information technology, engineering and fashion underwent a sudden dramatic development, which were heavily dependent upon market changes and active in developing new products, consumer product service business grew rapidly in Seoul (Jeong and Song, 1993: pp. 132). Seoul, as the primary metropolis in South Korea, came to be the "information metropolis" (Park, 1993: pp. 236–241).

Spatial division of labor and class structure

Changes in industrial structures by region created spatial differentiation of labor market and classes that resulted in regional disparities in life opportunities (see Massey, 1984). In the mid-1980s the metropolitan area already occupied over half (51.9 percent) of the total manufacturing occupations and 55.5 percent of the total expert skill occupations. Administrative management and office occupations accounted for 64.3 percent and 63.9 percent (Kang, 1990). This shows that the "white-collar" class was concentrated in the metropolitan center of Seoul. Industries which require specialized skills and training for R&D are centered in metropolitan areas. Seventy percent of the total R&D institutes in all industries and related specialized labor force are located in metropolitan areas.

Metropolitan areas have a high concentration of the upper class labor functions such as management while enjoying economic rights of possession and ownership. In industrial areas of Youngnam, by contrast, white collar executives who perform the functions of management and control on middle and lower level, and direct production workers are predominant. Meanwhile in other areas, peasant and old middle classes (engaged in agriculture and independent, small-sized enterprises) are dominant. Given that classes are immense groups involving the distribution of wealth, spatial differentiation of class may mean a spatially differentiated distribution of wealth (Hadjimichalis, 1984).

The emergence of regional politics and the new regionalism

A series of discourses on local autonomy and regional politics in South Korean society has now emerged. With the revival of local elections exploring the possibilities of recent democratization for the first time in 50 years (with the exception of a few years) and with the environment, traffic, housing, and so forth emerging as pressing social issues, the "local" is receiving increasing attention. Mature capitalist states in the West have begun a post-modern focus on the locus of local life, paying attention to "the local" as a legitimate object of study. With the emergence of a neo-liberal system accompanying the restructuring of world capitalism, more attention is being placed on each unit of regional space rather than an analysis of space at the level of the nation state. As neo-liberal governments curtailed their spending on national welfare, local governments began a significant transformation in their functions and status, producing a more spontaneous and active role in the areas of production and consumption (on post-modernism system of social welfare and relationship between the local and state, see Burrows and Loader, 1994).

Local politics under the advanced capitalist system of these times is also powerful, influenced by the process of capital accumulation and its restructuring at the global level. Policy formulations involving changes of local governments in advanced capitalist states like the US and the United Kingdom are caused by the changes in capital accumulation structures at the world level. For example, a flexible accumulation system concentrates new skilled labor and technology within a specific space to establish brand new policies for local autonomy that is markedly different from pre-existing ones. When capital flees from existing industrial areas local governments are called upon to cope with the after-effects. Thus, local government steps in to establish various policies for coping with unemployment and revitalizing the local economy. As part of the urban development strategy of local governments for reviving declining spaces, real estate capitalists and financiers are tapped to take a leading role in the redevelopment and the revitalization of the local economy. Thus local government takes the initiative to redevelop market and create new spaces for consumption.

It is premature to discuss the substantive effects and consequences of local government's new role in South Korea, a process which has just recently begun. However, the expectation that local government is an inevitable part of a progression toward democracy will coexist with criticism that the political process is being abused to ensure the vested interests of certain people. The criticism stems from the objection that national or central authority politics unduly influence and exploit local politics. In addition, there arise voices warning of the impracticality or ineffectiveness of local councils and the "NIMBY (Not in My Back Yard)/PIMFY (Please in My Front Yard)" phenomena. The concerns about local autonomy focus on the administrative aspects of the political process such as election behavior and distribution of centralized powers. In that the local autonomy may lay the foundation for democracy through the distribution of power, most concerns revolve around political processes such as agencies of local government and the constitution of local council and local elections. To be sure, the discourse on local autonomy in South Korean society originated from the existing structures of politics. Local politics appeared as a symbolic slogan for the realization of democracy by political transactions among institutionalized political groups which had clear interests in power distribution (see Kim, Wook, 2004).

However, current local politics cannot be appreciated only from political and administrative perspectives. Local politics is a presupposition and consequence of civil society. That is, the realm of civil society extends to local autonomy, and, in turn, the extension of civil society renders local autonomy possible. As the index on the expansion of middle and working classes, the expansion of markets, and the expansion of other private spheres reflects for civil society grow rapidly with rapid industrialization (Kim, Seong-guk, 1992). Industrial society to the extent that it is a pluralistic society starts to reveal the depth and scope of its conflicts in the various ways, that the central government attempts to manage and control it with its limited powers. As citizens call for social justice and the equitable distribution of wealth, power, and the enjoyment of life, more and more importance is laid on the buffering function of local government. At present, civil society's capabilities far exceeds the central government's managing capability. Because of these political and economic considerations, discourse on local autonomy and local politics are becoming increasingly prevalent in South Korean society (see Lee, Shin-Haeng, 2006).

Local politics is a systemic reflection of the larger economy, culture, and politics. It is not constrained to the political sphere of classical perspectives, but generates through the overall process of regional structuring. That is, the context of local politics is formed in local industrial structures, the local composition of population and classes, local history and culture, and within the mechanism itself which gives birth to the very context. Therefore, to understand local politics, an approach to the complex and various "total social process" embedding local politics is necessary, beyond the political spheres such as election administration, council organization, and the processes of power distribution (see Kim, Wang-Bae, 2000).

Needless to say, the accumulative mechanism acts as the driving force of regional structuring in capitalist society, is the decisive condition for local politics. Regionally differentiated development is a point of debate on the level of local politics, and matters related to life spheres such as the problems of taxes and the distribution of collective means of consumption like environment, traffic, housing, and other social/public services, are embedded in specific local situations, and appear as the spatial result of uneven capital accumulation.

Local politics entails the politics of place. Place is the spatial foundation for life where individuals give and take reciprocal actions with each other and shape their own identities (see Michael and Pile, 1993; Hwang, 2011). The politics of place is the process of subjective self-reflection of regional residents. "What is the meaning of this space where I live? What are the problems of this space? And what might be the spatial actions for establishing my identity?" Likewise, self-reflections about place inspire participation which may lay the foundation for local politics (Jeong, 1997).

Above all, the politics of place highlights events within a specific space and resolves them through communication and debate among various constituents. Therefore local politics as the politics of place points to the politics of "contextualization" based on local specificity. That is, the politics of place recognizes and embodies the detailed differences of spaces, as opposed to politics emerging without distinction to place or time.

The politics of place reflect the dynamics of regionalism, which is composed of identities, consciousness, and specific lifestyles. Regionalism is constructed through the residents' conscious participation in making decisions regarding place and the creation and mobilization of symbols for these contexts. Regionalism in its current form is taking place on a relatively small scale and is different in its dimension from *Jiyeokgamjeong* and regional disparity in Korean society created by regionally differentiated development.

Conclusion

Regionalism, corresponding to globalization's disintegration of people's unique cultures and identities (therefore causing the disorder in individual identity), receives recognition as a specific endeavor to secure one's own spheres of life. In spite of the positive aspects of regionalism in ideal type, *Jiyeokgamjeong* is pejoratively regarded as a negative symbol of pervasive regional discrimination and stereotypes in Korea, which has undermined social integration.

However, regionalism in Korea has more complex and multi-dimensional features. One feature is the exchange of *Jiyeokgamjeong*'s regional stereotypes between Jeolla province and other areas. The pre-existing debates on this divisive topic broadly distinguish two approaches. One is the historical perspective that finds the origins of regional discrimination as far back as the Three Kingdoms period, and the other is political behavior perspective that finds its origin in the political utilization of popular incitement and mobilization by politicians to obtain or secure their interests. A third and alternative approach, however, is the perspective that seeks the factors which produce regional discrimination in the conflicts that arise among specific groups competing for resources created by South Korea's traumatic social and regional dislocation during rapid industrialization. This view is gaining increasing plausibility. People in southwest Jeolla recorded the highest regional transfer, i.e., social mobility, to newly established urban industrial centers. Such a massive and conspicuous relocation, this perspective argues, raises the ire, wariness, and suspicion of people from other areas. Therefore, negative and simplistic fixed stereotypes are generated, and politicians exploit these myths and stereotypes to consolidate *Jiyeokgamjeong*. Likewise this perspective understands that regional sentiment contains a complex series of intensifying factors. Still, *Jiyeokgamjeong* in South Korea now is gradually declining as the frequency of regional transfers within the country has decreased, communication and transportation networks have closed regional gaps, and as social movements have made efforts to resolve negative aspects of the *Jiyeokgamjeong*.

At the same time, we observe possibilities of another kind of vertical division between metropolitan areas, especially Seoul, and other local areas. This produces regional disparities as a result of the specific space based-industrialization and spatial division of labor. As a humorous euphemism for the nation, “Seoul Republic,” reveals, most political, economic, and cultural resources are concentrated in the capital of Seoul, which plays and serves as the nation’s headquarters covering and controlling all the other local areas. These regional splits deepened to the point where they have been deemed an “internal colony.”

With the recent formation of local politics, the establishment of regional identity at the local level based on the quality of life in each area, and participation in the decision-making process another kind of regionalism emerges as I introduced briefly.

In sum, regionalism in South Korea is multi-dimensional, multi-formed, and complex. The historical formation of regionalism is produced in the conflicting and tension-filled process of “competition, defense, and exclusion” of resource distribution. For a long time, regionalism in South Korea has been lamented as a tenaciously persistent “national disease.” Therefore, it is required for the Korean people to dissolve the negative aspects of regionalism and rather to shift it as a dynamic means for developing a progressive democracy and a stable civil society in South Korea.

References

Ahn, Byeong-Man. 1992. “Chiyuk Kaldeung-ui Haesochaek: Jeongdang Jeongchi” [Resolutions to Regional Conflicts: Politics of Political Parties]. In Korea Sociology Association ed., *Hanguk-ui Chiyukjooui-wa Chiyuk Kaldeung* [Regionalism and Regional Conflict in Korean Society]. Seoul: Seongwon Publishing Co.

Bae, Gyu-han. 1992. “Seongeo Gwajeong-gwa Chiyuk Gamjeong” [Election Process and Regional Sentiment]. In Korea Sociology Association ed., *Hanguk-ui Chiyukjooui-wa Chiyuk Kaldeung* [Regionalism and Regional Conflict in Korean Society]. Seoul: Seongwon Publishing Co.

Burrows, R. and B. Loader eds. 1994. *Towards a Post-Fordist, Welfare State?* ch. 2. London: Routledge.

Castells, M. 1997. *The Information Age: The Power of Identity*, vol. II. New York: Blackwell Publishers, p. 269.

Cha, Jong-Cheon, 1988. “Chiyukjuuijeok Seongeo-wa Yugwonja: Je Sipsamdae Daetongryeong Seongeohubo JiJi-e Daehan Logit Bunseok” [Regionalistic Election and Voters: Logit Analysis of Supports for Candidates in the 13th Election for the President]. *Korean Sociology* 22: 143–159.

Featherstone, M. ed. 1996. *Global Culture.* London: Sage Publication Ltd.

Hadjimichalis, C. 1984. “The Geographical Transfer of Value,” *Environment and Planning* D, 2: 329–345.

Hwang, Jin-Tae. 2011. "Analysis of Politics of Agora in the Right to the City," *Space and Society* 35: 42–70.

Jeong, Guen-sik. 1997. "Chiyuk Jeongcheseong-gwa Doshi Sangjing Yeongu" [For the Research of Local Identity and City Symbol]. In Social Science Institute ed., *Chiyuk Sahoe Yeongu Bangbup-ui Mosaek* [Search for Researching Method of the Local Society]. Gwang-Ju: Jeonnam University Press.

Jeong, Jun-ho and Woo-gyeong Song. 1993. "Giup Gujo-ui Byeonhwa-wa Saengsanja serviceup-ui seongjang" [Changes in Enterprise Structures and Growth of Producer Service Business]. In *Seoul Yeongu* [Seoul Research]. Korea Space and Environment Institute: 132.

Kang, Hee-gyeong. 1990. "Shinheung Gongup Gukga-ui Gyegeup-ui Gongganjeok Bunhwa" [Spatial Division of Class in Newly Industrialized States], PhD Sociology, Seoul National University.

Kang, Hyun-Soo. 2007. "Guk'ga Gyunhyung baljeon eul uihan Seoul jiyucky jeongchaek Jeian" [Suggestions on Seoul Metropolitan Area Policy for Promoting Mutual Concern with Other Areas and Balanced National Development], *Gonggan-kwa Sahoe* [Space and Society] 27: 52–80.

Kim, Baek-Yung. 2007. "Modification of Symbolic Spaces and Invention of Collective Memories: How the National Places in Seoul were Reconstructed through the Colonial Experiences," *Space and Society* 28: 189–221.

Kim, Hye-Suk. 1988. "Chiyukgan Gojeonggwannyeom-kwa Pyeongyeon-ui Silsang" [Real Substance of Fixed Ideas and Prejudices between Regions]. In Jin-Guk Kim ed., *Shimlihak-eseo Bon Chiyukgamjeong* [Regional Sentiments on the Psychological Perspectives]. Seoul: Seong-Won Publishing Co.

Kim, Jin-Guk. 1984. "Chiyuk Mingan-ui Pyeongyeonjeok Taedo Yeongu" [Research on the Discriminal Attitudes to the Local People]. In *Haksaeng Saenghwal Yeongu* [Research on Students Life] Vol. 16. Gwang-Ju: Jeonnam University Press.

Kim, June-Woo, and Young-Jin Ahn. 2008. " 'Regional Development Think-tank Capacity' as a New Dimension of Regional Disparity: A Case Study of a Metropolitan City Located in a Non-Capital Region," *Space and Society* 29: 94–115.

Kim, Man-Huem, 1987. "Chiyukmingan-ui Pyeongyeonjeok Taedo Yeongu" [Research on the Discriminal Attitudes to the Local People]. In *Hanguk Sahoe Chiyuk Galdeung Yeongu* [Research on Regional Conflicts in Korea Society]. Seong-Nam: Contemporary Society Institute.

Kim, Seong-guk. 1992. "Hanguk Jabonjuui Baljeon-gaw Shimin Sahoe-ui Seonggyeok" [Development of Korean Capitalism and Characteristics of Civil Society]. In Korea Sociology Association and Korea Politics Association ed., *Hanguk-ui Gukga-wa Shimin Sahoe* [State and Civil Society in Korea]. Seoul: Hanul Publishing Co.

Kim, Wang-Bae. 2000. *Dosi, Gonggan, Seanghwalseogae* [City, Space, Lifeworld: Interpreting the Text of the Class and State Power]. Seoul: Hanul Publishing Co.

Kim, Wook. 2004. "The 17th National Assembly Election of Korea and the Political Changes in the Chungchung Region: With Particular Focus on the Weakening and Change of Regionalism," *Journal of Political Science and Communication* 7: 69–87.

Kim, Yong-Hak. 1992. "Elite Choongwon-eseoui Chiyukgyukcha" [Regional Gaps in Elites Recruits]. In Korea Sociology Association ed., *Hanguk-ui Chiyukjooui-wa Chiyuk Kaldeung* [Regionalism and Regional Conflict in Korean Society]. Seoul: Seongwon Publishing Co.

Kim, Young-Jeong. 1997. "Hanguk Chiyuk baljeong-ui Siltae Bigyo" [Comparative Research on Regional Development in Korea]. In Kyeong-Ryung Seong *et al.* eds.,

Chibang Jachi-wa Chiyuk Baljeon [Local Self-Governing and Regional Development]. Seoul: Mineum Publishing Co.

Korea Development Institute. 1987. *Chibang Gongup-ui Teukseong-gwa Yukseong Jeongchaek* [The Characteristics of Local Industry and its Fostering Policy]. Seoul: Korea Development Institute.

Lee, Ee-Hwa. 1983. *Hanguk-ui Pabeol* [The Factions in Korean Society]. Seoul: Eomun-gak Publishing Co.

Lee, Ki-Baek. 1977. *Minjok-gwa Yuksa* [Nation and History]. Seoul: Iljogak Publishing Co.

Lee, Moo-Yong. 2006. *Jiyoekbaljeon-ui Saerowoon Paradigm, Jangso-marketing Jeon-ryak* [The New Paradigm of Local Development, Location Marketing Strategy: Club Culture in Hongdae-Area and Cultural Politics of Location Marketing]. Seoul: Non-Hyeong Publishing Co.

Lee, Shin-Haeng. 2006. *Pulbburi Jeongchi-wa Saheojeok Jeongdangseong* [Grassroot Political and Social Legitimacy]. Paju: Bubmoon Publishing Co.

Massey, D. 1984. *Spatial Division of Labor.* London: Macmillian.

Michael, K. and S. Pile. 1993. "The Politics of Place." In K. Michael and S. Pile eds., *Place and the Politics of Identity.* London: Routledge.

Mittleman, J. 1997. *Globalization: Critical Reflections.* Boulder, CO: Lynne Reinner Publishers.

Park, Young-Min. 1993. "Seoul Chiyuk Jeongbohwa Gwajeong-ui Jeongchigyeongje" [Political Economy on the Process of Regional Information]. In Korea Space and Environment Institute ed., *Seoul Yeongu* [Seoul Research]. Seoul: Hanul Publishing Co.: 236–241.

Ross R. and K. Trachte. 1990. *Global Capitalism: The New Leviathan.* New York: State University of New York Press.

Scott, A. ed. 1997. *The Limits of Globalization.* London: Routledge.

Shin, Gwang-Young. 1992. "Tupyo Hangwe-was Chiyukjuui" [Election Behavior and Regionalism]. In Korea Sociology Association ed., *Hanguk-ui Chiyukjooui-wa Chiyuk Kaldeung* [Regionalism and Regional Conflict in Korean Society]. Seoul: Seongwon Publishing Co.

Sklair, L. 1995. *Sociology of the Global System.* Baltimore, MD: Johns Hopkins University Press.

Song, Bok. 1994. "Chiyuk Kaldeung" [Regional Conflict]. In *Hanguk Sahoe-ui Kaldeung Kujo* [Social Conflicts in Korean Society]. Seoul: Hyundaemunhak.

Stallings, B. 1995. *Global Change, Regional Response: The New International Context of Development.* Cambridge: Cambridge University Press.

Warf, B. 1995. "Postmodernism-kwa Chibangseong nonjaejaeng," trans, by Son Myungcheol, in *Gonggna-kwa Sahoe* [Space and Society] 5: 153–170.

Wilson, Rob and W. Dissanayake eds. 1996. *Global/Local.* Durham, NC: Duke University Press.

Yeom, Mi-gyeong. 1998. "Research on Restructuring of Enterprise City in Japan: On the City Policy in Kitakyushu," PhD sociology, Jeonnam University, Gwang-Ju.

4 Economic development and women's status in Korea

Mee-Hae Kong

Introduction

With rapid economic development and the advent of the women's movement, the changing status of women received much attention around the world. The status of women has been defined as women's access to public resources that are open to everyone (Ward, 1984). The status of women, in this sense, reflects the level of social justice which plays a critical role in distributing these resources to each gender in a society. Justice is equality for equals. Women's inferior status means injustice. Injustice, here, is the unequal treatment of the members of the two genders.

Although Korea has achieved remarkable economic development within a relatively short span of time, gender disparity seems to be problematic. Compared to the West, the newly developed countries of East Asia show a high negative percentage difference between the overall HDI (Human Development Index) and gender-disparity-adjusted HDI. For example, Hong Kong indicates the highest negative figure in this (–28.3), followed by Singapore (–23.8) and Korea (–22.2) (Chang, 1996). In addition, GEM (Gender Empowerment Measure) of Korea in 2005 indicated 59th position out of 80 countries (UNDP, 2005).

Is gender disparity inevitable for the national economic growth in the East Asian countries, including Korea? What kind mechanism plays a critical role to maintain women's lower status?

Scholars have paid attention to the effects of the "economic miracle" on gender relations in the basic social unit of Korean culture (Chang, 1996; Cho U., 1996; Kim, 1995). They argue that Korean families on the basis of the Confucianism create different social relations and ideologies, including gender relations and family ideologies. That is, the traditional familism (family centered ideology) in Korea reacts to the exigencies of the nation's intense industrialization in different ways from western familism. This exclusive familism provides survival strategy that enables the families to protect their members from the relative weakness of the national policy.

This chapter is to provide global explanation about following inquiry: to what extent has economic development led to the improvement of women's status compared to the general development of society in the last couple of decades? In the following section, the effect of development on women's employment, family, and gender role, and women's political empowerment will be reviewed.

Segregation of female labor

Along with an export-oriented growth strategy, Korea created the rapid incorporation of female labor which dominated in export industries such as textiles, wearing apparel, electronics, and footwear. These four industries were assessed to provide over half of all export earnings in the early 1970s (Seguino, 1995).

In the beginning of industrialization, Korea preferred young unmarried female supply for labor-intensive export industries. Table 4.1 indicates the labor force participation rates for women and men for selected years for the period 1970 to 2008. According to Table 4.1, women's labor force participation has steadily risen since 1970, while men's labor force participation has slightly declined until 1985 and is fluctuating. After economic crisis occurred in 1997, women's labor force participation has dropped around the level of 1990 and is rising up to now. However, the gender gap is over 23 percent.

Korean women's labor participation rate forms a typical M-shaped curve. It shows high participation in women's late 20s, drops in their early 30s, and rises again from the late 30s in 2005 (Korea National Statistical Office, 2007). This means that Korean women's economic participation is heavily affected by their life-cycle stages and that marriage and child rearing are important factors to reduce women's participation in the labor market.

Moreover, Korean women tended to be marginalized in the process of development and industrialization. The majority of women who participate in the labor force are still working in the informal and subcontracting sectors (firms employing fewer than five). Out of the employed women, according to Table 4.2, 59.1 percent are in the informal and subcontracting sectors in 1990 (Cho U., 1996). Again, informal worker rate for women has rapidly risen after 1997,

Table 4.1 Labor force participation rates by gender, 1970 to 2008 (%)

Year	*Female*	*Male*
1970	39.3	77.9
1975	40.4	77.4
1980	42.8	76.4
1985	43.1	72.3
1990	47.0	74.0
1995	48.3	76.5
1999	46.9	74.4
2002	48.9	74.6
2005	50.3	74.1
2008	50.0	73.5

Sources: Korea National Statistical Office (2007); Statistics Korea (2011).

Table 4.2 Informal worker rates by gender, 1980–2010 (%)

Year	*Females*	*Males*
1980	42.5	53.7
1985	50.2	42.8
1990	59.1	45.4
1996	59.3	33.3
2000	69.7	40.8
2005	43.7	31.5
2010	41.6	26.8

Sources: Cho U. (1996); Korea Women's Development Institute (2011).

reached up to 69.7 percent in 2000, and is decreasing recently. The gap between genders in informal sectors is still around 15 percent in 2010.

Gender segregation by occupation indicates another aspect of women's lack of power in the labor market. According to Uhn Cho's chapter in this book, only small portions of female workers occupy the prestigious sectors such as professional and managerial/administrative positions. The proportion of women in sales positions is relatively high from 1990s, because of the transition of industrial structure in Korean society. However, the case of managerial/administrative positions shows more severe gender disparity. The proportion of females in these sectors was 0.3 percent in 2000, 0.4 percent in 2005, and 0.5 percent in 2008. In addition, women's economic status does not seem to have improved because of the feminization of cheap labor. Let me turn to the wage disparity between genders.

In spite of the relatively strong demand for female labor, women's relative wages have not improved substantially since the late 1970s, although the earning ratio is increasing steadily. For example, the female/male earning ratio was 44.8 percent in 1981, 53.5 percent in 1990, 63.2 percent in 2000, and 63.4 percent in 2006 (Korea National Statistical Office, 2007).

Table 4.3 indicates the ratio of female to male earnings in selected industries in the manufacturing sector for the period 1975 to 1990. Overall, the female/male earning ratio in manufacturing sector has risen from 47.0 percent in 1975 to 50.5 percent in 1990. This trend was more prominent in the female-dominated export industries – textiles, wearing apparel, and electronics. On the contrary, the wage gap has widened in the transport industries (Seguino, 1995).

Table 4.3 Ratio of female to male earnings in selected industries in the manufacturing sector, 1975–1990 (%)

Year	*Total*	*Textiles*	*Apparel*	*Electronic*	*Transport*	*Machinery*
1975	47.0	N.A.	N.A.	N.A.	N.A.	N.A.
1980	45.0	46.3	48.9	44.7	50.9	49.5
1985	47.0	48.6	56.8	48.0	48.0	53.1
1990	50.5	52.0	58.4	57.6	50.4	54.4

Source: Seguino (1995).

The slight increase in the ratio of average female to male wages in manufacturing sectors is partly due to labor union activity (Seguino, 1995). During pro-democracy movement of the 1980s, women began to organize labor unions in response to dangerous work conditions, discriminatory work rules, and low pay. Widespread strikes in 1987 and 1988 resulted in substantial wage increases for workers, particularly in female-dominated industries.

Nevertheless, Seguino (1995) argues, gender-based wage differentials remained wide during three decades of rapid economic growth in Korea. Based on the assumption that growth of earnings is driven by productivity growth, she explains the wage gap between genders resulted from women's concentration in industries with slow productivity growth. This trend continued after the national policy of social service sector for women has been focused on women-dominated jobs such as household helpers, nursery teachers, and sick care-givers.

Maintaining family centered ideology and traditional gender roles

Since kinship solidarity has been the single most important structure of Korean society, the family is considered as the basic social unit. Confucianism exercised great influence on family and overall society in Korea. Especially the rules guiding the relationship between husband and wife were based on severe prejudice toward women, resulting in lower status of women. According to Confucian virtues, a woman was required to obey to her father, husband, and son. In addition, a woman in the patriarchal family was regarded symbolically as an outsider from her biological family once married and also an outsider from her husband's family until producing a son. Because a woman's place was supposed to be at home, a "virtuous" woman should not deal with outside world and should not get ahead of her husband (Kong, 1992).

With a rapid increase of women's education and labor participation outside home, feminism also has influenced to change the family over the past decades. The traditional extended family was transformed into the nuclear family and women had more control over the decision-making process within the family, although it does not mean that each individual woman obtained the actual power over her partner in the home. In addition, women in Korea became enlightened with the concept of equal rights between genders, educational opportunity, social participation, and individualistic value.

As a result, Korean women, on the one hand, are trying to develop new social roles with progressive and active attitudes, improved education, and social participation. On the other hand, they still maintain the traditional gender roles in the family because of widespread and deep-rooted acceptance of gender inequality based on a powerful legacy of Confucianism (Kim and Han, 1996). Accordingly, distorted thinking about gender roles leads Korean women to be placed in a lower position consistently: being treated as less important than men, excluded from prestigious occupations, alienated from politics.

Marriage and family is a system that holds traditional patriarchal gender roles. Married women with jobs are facing the deep conflict between their intentions and reality, because they have to pursue their career and take care of their family at the same time. The majority of Korean women do not have positive self-concepts and opportunities to exercise their potentials (Kim and Han, 1996).

According to Kim and Han's study (1996), however, Korean women have gradually tried to escape the patriarchal system, involving social participation. In their survey, 84.3 percent disagree with the notion "women need not try to succeed in careers as men do", and 82.7 percent oppose that "women should undertake household chores and child-rearing even when they have jobs". But still those in their 50s and older and those with lower education (below middle school) seem to have traditional gender role attitude.

In a recent study by the Ministry of Gender Equality (2008), Korean women were asked if "women should have priority to marriage and family over her career". Among respondents, 70.2 percent agree (including agreement and strong agreement) and 12.3 percent disagree (including opposition and strong opposition). In response to the question "husband should be a representative of the family", 64.1 percent women answered as agreement, while 19.2 percent as disagreement. These statistics imply that Korean women still have strong traditional gender role attitudes.

In spite of drastic social change, enlightened notion of equality between genders, transformed family structure, and weakened parental authority over their children, both traditional and new concepts of family coexist in Korean society. For example, the majority of Korean parents want their son to be successful in a public domain and their daughters to have good spouses while expecting high education for both sons and daughters. This conflict between new values and the established ethical system becomes more clear when the tendency of son preference and gender ratio of newly born babies are reviewed.

As presented in Table 4.4, the ratio of newly born boys in 1990 is almost 117 per 100 girls, indicating 9 percent increase rate compared to 1980. The overall gender ratio stood at 106.4 boys to 100 girls in 2008. The imbalance of gender ratio especially becomes severe in the case of the third and the fourth born infants in 1990 and continues to in 2008. This means that married Koreans still hope for a son. In Kim and Han's study (1996), as many as 13.2 percent of women said that they would feel guilty if they did not bear a son. This feeling is

Table 4.4 Ratio of boys to girls (100 persons) by birth order (%)

Year	*Total*	*First born*	*Second born*	*Third born*	*Fourth born*
1980	105.6	106.0	106.5	106.9	110.2
1985	109.4	106.0	107.8	129.2	146.8
1990	116.6	108.6	117.2	190.8	214.1
1995	113.4	105.9	111.8	179.4	213.9
2000	110.2	106.2	107.4	141.7	166.9
2005	107.7	104.8	106.4	128.2	–
2008	106.4	104.8	105.6	116.7	–

Sources: Korea National Statistical Office (2007); Korea Women's Development Institute (2011).

more common among married women, those in their 40s and older, and the under-educated. What does this tell us ultimately?

In her study "Male Dominance and Mother Power: The Two Sides of Confucian Patriarchy in South Korea", Hae Joang Cho (1996) discussed the two sides of Confucian patriarchy; extreme suppression of women on the one hand and extreme idealization of motherhood and encouragement of mother's accomplishments on the other. She argues that patriarchy legitimizes mother power as a way of incorporating women in a male-dominated social system. That is, instead of excluding women from the public and political domains, patriarchy institutionalized mother power since it is the most unthreatening source of power to the patriarchal system.

Mother power is based on their son or sons' well-being. As a result, mother power basically places at the personal level within the family. On the surface, institutionalized mother power enables women to be independent from their husbands. This independence, however, is limited within the symbiotic nature of mother–son relationships. Without the mother–son relationship, women barely establish their identity as autonomous individuals. Thus, Hae Joang Cho (1996) contends, "The heavy emphasis on the identity of women as mothers is, in fact, the major stumbling block in the women's rights movement in Korea today. It is not motherly to feel oppressed" (p. 97).

Furthermore, after experiencing the long-lasting socio-political instability from events such as Japanese occupation and the Korean War, exclusive familism became the core value that protected the family itself (Cho H., 1996; Kong, 1992). The tendency of exclusive familism seems to have strengthened through the rapid industrialization of Korea. As contemporary capitalism developed the division between the public and private domains, the family assumes a nuclear form based on a particular gender division of labor: the breadwinner husband and the full-time wife (Kim, 1995).

The separation of public and private domains legitimizes the separation of the official economic sphere from the domestic sphere. Women who are alienated at home lose their identity and try to compensate for their loss by pursuing the well-being of their family. Also, Korean women pay little attention to community welfare programs, compared to the middle-class housewives in Western societies. Korean women instead tend to focus their time and energy on immediate family interests (Cho H., 1996).

In short, mother power and sequent "overdependence" between mother and son and exclusive familism play a critical role in maintaining an extremely conservative social system in Korean society. As Cho H. (1996) suggests, the fundamental social change and women's empowerment cannot be obtained until mother power is deconstructed and reconstructed exclusive familism and the disctinction between the dual public/private domains.

Lack of women's political empowerment

In general, political activities are correlated with social education, work experience, and group membership. Women in newly developed countries have fewer opportunities in these areas. Because of the lack in education and work experience, the ability to organize political actions is also limited. Although women's educational and work opportunities have increased in Korea, these are not critically effective in enhancing women's political status at more powerful levels of government (Kong, 1990).

Women's political status has been categorized into two indicators: women's political participation, and equal rights legislation (Ward, 1984). Korean women gained political rights through suffrage. However, there are still several constraints on women's political participation: (1) women's perception of their public role; (2) cultural norms and social prejudices; and (3) lack of active women's political organizations.

First, women's political issues are closely related to their domestic maternal role. Even women tend to view their public roles as extensions of their traditional tasks of mothering and nurturing. Since women in political power have mostly involved "soft" issues (such as health, welfare, or education), their impact on government and whole society is little visible. Second, cultural norms and social prejudices are more important factors than women's socio-economic determinants in defining women's political roles and status. Thus, increasing women's economic independence has not yet transferred to increasing their political power. Finally, obstacles in the socio-cultural superstructure are so strong that women cannot develop their political organizations. Women's political strength can grow in terms of women's organizations, women can hardly mobilize themselves to integrate into political institutions. Although their educational and employment opportunities are increasing, women are continually excluded from political elite tracts.

Fundamental changes in politics and gender relations in daily life are possible by the organizations of women. Women's organizations, however, have been strongly discouraged by national politics within the world-system. With intrusion of the world-system, women's organizations in the process of development became marginalized by the insufficient credit for members. Moreover, since multinational industries are looking for a cheap and docile labor force, women's unionization has been deliberately disrupted by national governments (Kong, 1990). Techniques of hierarchical organization and control seem to be closely related to the gender division of labor.

Men had enough opportunities to develop organizational structure, since men have had a head position both in the household and in the workplace, while women's subordinated position at home and work did not provide women with the ability to organize into groups as wage workers. Further, during the process of industrialization, male unions played a role in excluding women from gaining skills. Because the main policy of male unions was to keep women less efficient, women received lower wages and remained in segregated jobs.

Let me turn to the point of women's political participation in Korea regarding to women's three roles: as voters, decision makers, and political activists (Chun, 1996; Kim and Chun, 1996). First, voting is the most common method of political participation for women. Although voting is relatively simple compared to other political activities, women are able to access political power and clarify eligibility for leadership through voting. In the National Assembly election, 67.0 percent in 1992, 71.9 percent in 2000, and 74.8 percent in 2004 of female electorate participated in voting (Korea Women's Development Institute, 2011). This partly indicates women's active political participation.

Women's political participation became more active with reinstatement of local autonomy in Korea from 1991. Many changes have been made in repeated elections up to the local elections of 1995. The recognition that local politics is the politics for daily life enabled several women to win in the local elections. Despite the fact that women became more active about election activity, discussions about politics, and membership in political parties, women are not likely to participate in the democratic process in a direct way.

Second, the Korean political situation does not allow women to be representatives at the elite level. Political elites include legislators, governmental officials, political party officials, and other opinion leaders from diverse public and private sectors who influence the policy-making system. According to Table 4.5, the number of women in the National Assembly was slightly increasing: two (0.8 percent) in 1996, five (2.2 percent) in 2000, ten (4.1 percent) in 2004, and 14 (5.7 percent) in 2008. Although local autonomy was expected to provide women with more opportunities, the result was disappointing. Only 41 won out of 124 women (0.9 percent of the total) in the 1991 local election, 71 won out of 206 women (1.6 percent) in 1995, 56 won out of 140 women (1.6 percent) in 1998, 77 won out of 222 women (2.2 percent) in 2002, and 110 won out of 391 women (4.4 percent) in the 2006 election (KWDI, 2011). This result implies that Korean women failed to achieve a breaking-through into the male domain of political power.

The highest rank of government positions that women have reached is the minister level. There have been fewer than 15 women cabinet ministers since 1948. The proportion of female ministers is below 5 percent in 1997, 14.3 percent in 2004, and 13.3 percent in 2011. The higher the decision-making positions, the lower the percentage of women. At the end of 1999, only 3.0 percent were women above the fifth class of national government employees. Now the rate of women above fifth class has been reached 8.4 percent in 2005, and 10.8 percent in 2008 (KWDI, 2011). In spite of the increasing number of women in the government, the majority of them belong to the lower ranks.

Table 4.5 Number of women candidates and women elect in the national assembly

Total candidates	*Women candidates*	*Total*	*Elect*	*Women elected*
1996	1,339	22	253	2
2000	1,040	33	227	5
2004	1,175	66	243	10
2008	1,113	132	245	14

Source: Korea Women's Development Institute (2011).

Third, women's participation in high level positions in the political parties is disappointing, although women's active participation in party activity is growing. There are few women members (less than 10 percent) in the decision-making posts (such as party advisor, party affairs committee, the central standing committee, party chairs) in the existing political parties in Korea. This reflects the patriarchal idea that women are merely assistants. Because of the bureaucracy of political parties, women hardly get the position of candidacy. On the other hand, it is also true that women have been too passive in claiming their rights to share the high level decision-making positions.

In general, Korean women have been excluded and alienated from politics. There are several obstacles in empowering women: first of all, cultural ideology effectively prevents women from participating in the public domain; women lack self-consciousness of gender equality; the national policies are not balanced for women; the distribution of power is determined by the rule of the dominant ideology, that is, male power holders.

Conclusion

The purpose of this study is to review the effect of economic development on women's employment, the family and gender role, and their political empowerment. Economic growth has been the primary concern for power elites in Korea for several decades. Although Korea achieves a certain level of economic growth, those who have suffered from the developmental process are the powerless people, including women. As we have seen, despite increasing women's participation in the labor force, they tended to be marginalized in the process of development and industrialization. Gender segregation by occupation and sector indicates another aspect of women's lack of power in the labor market.

Marriage and family in Korea is a mechanism that maintains traditional patriarchal gender roles. Married women with jobs are facing the deep conflict between their intentions and reality, because they have to pursue their career and take care of their family at the same time. Thus, the majority of them do not have positive self-concepts and opportunities to exercise their potentials.

Political activities are correlated with social education, work experience, and group membership. Women in Korea have fewer opportunities in these areas than men. Because of the lack in work experience, the ability to organize political actions is also limited. Although women's educational and work opportunities have increased recently, these are not critically effective in enhancing women's political status at more powerful levels of government.

In order to construct a new society, women need to have systematic knowledge about the world. In addition, an understanding of women's oppressive condition or women's present status needs a call for change and participation in altering power relations. Knowledge based on concrete personal experiences in particular settings will provide women with institutional identities. The institutional identities are important to develop national resources for women.

References

Chang, Pilwha. 1996. "A Feminist View of Social Policy in Some East Asian Countries", *Asian Journal of Women's Studies* 2: 7–37.

Cho, Hae Joang. 1996 "Male Dominance and Mother Power: The Two Sides of Confucian Patriarchy in South Korea", *Asian Women* 2: 77–104.

Cho, Uhn. 1996. "Female Labor in Korea: Economically Active but not Empowered", *Asian Women* 2: 55–75.

Chun, Kyung Ock. 1996. "Women's Political Empowerment in Korea: Legitimacy and Prospects", *Asian Women* 2: 17–53.

Kim, Myung-Hye. 1995. "Gender, Class, and Family in Late-Industrializing South Korea", *Asian Journal of Women's Studies* 1: 58–86.

Kim, Young Hee and Jeong Shin Han. 1996. "Korean Women's Consciousness of Sex-Roles, Marriage and Child-Rearing", *Asian Women* 2: 149–172.

Kim, Young lan and Kyung Ock Chun. 1996. "A Study of the Political and Social Consciousness of Korean Women", *Asian Women* 2: 117–147.

Kong, Mee-Hae. 1990. "The Status of Women and their Quality of Life Korea in Developing Countries", Unpublished PhD Dissertation, Ohio State University.

Kong, Mee-Hae. 1992. "A Feminist Critique of the Selfish Familism in Korean Society", *Journal of Family Studie*s 4: 1–19 (in Korean).

Korea National Statistical Office. 2007. "Women's Life Reviewed by Statistics" (in Korean).

Korea Women's Development Institute (2002) http://gsis.kwdi.re.kr/gsis/ko/main.html.

Korea Women's Development Institute (2011) http://gsis.kwdi.re.kr/gsis/ko/main.html.

Ministry of Gender Equality. 2008. "National Domestic Violence Survey" (in Korean).

Seguino, Stephanie. 1995. "Gender Wage Inequality and Export-Led Growth in South Korea", *Women's Studies Forum* 11: 187–210.

Statistics Korea (2011) www.kostat.go.kr/portal/english/resources/1/index.statistic.

UNDP. 2005. "Human Development Report 2005".

Ward, Kathryn. 1984. *Women in World-System: Its Impact on Status and Fertility*. New York: Praeger.

5 Social class and income inequality in Korea

Kwang-Yeong Shin

Compared with other East Asian countries such as Taiwan and Singapore, as well as other developing countries, South Korea is considered to have the lowest level of economic inequality. While there is still controversy over the relationship between the degree of income inequality and economic growth, which was a question raised in other East Asian countries, the low level of economic inequality in Korea is regarded as the key factor to Korea's economic success (UNDP 1996, 52–53). Korea has been cited as an exemplary case for economic growth with relatively equal distribution.

However, social inequality in contemporary Korea remains the most understudied issue in Korean academia in the 1990s. While most Koreans believe themselves to be sensitive to social contradictions or inequality and also for having a strong sense of egalitarianism, there have been few empirical studies of social inequality in Korea in either Korean or Western social sciences. Some empirical research on income inequality in Korea has reported the Gini coefficients that have indicated the degree of income inequality in its gross term.

The financial crisis that began in late 1997 significantly transformed the structure of income distribution as well as the production system, altering employment structures, job opportunities, and economic compensation mechanisms. While the immediate consequence of the financial crisis resulted in massive unemployment with more than a recorded one million unemployed in 1998 and a rapid rise of irregular workers, the long-term effect of the crisis was a worsening of economic inequality and a polarization of income and asset ownership. In addition, the government, faced with the aggressive demands of the IMF, adapted a high interest rate policy, which contributed to the unexpected increase of wealth for the rich and consequently widened the gap between the poor and the rich. The long-term consequence of the economic crisis was a social crisis as well by increasing inequality and the number of the working poor. While South Korea was appraised as a successful case for its fast recovery from the economic crisis, its disruptive social impact could not be immediately nullified by the fast economic recovery.

In this chapter, I will address the issue of class inequality, exploring the extent to which class inequality exists and how class inequality is associated with education and gender in South Korea. An empirical analysis of income determination provides an understanding of income inequality generated by social classes, proving that social classes play a most significant role in shaping economic life in contemporary Korean society.

Social class and income inequality in Korea

With the demise of the Eastern European states, the utility of social class as a concept became a topic of hot debate among not only Korean sociologists, but sociologists in the West as well. While the debate in the West has focused on the declining explanatory power of social class on political behavior and economic inequality, the debate in Korea has mainly focused on the decreasing relevance of social class in understanding politics in South Korea, and on new social movements since the 1990s. The core issue of the debate is not class inequality but the destiny of class politics associated with the relationship between class position and political attitude or action of social class (Clark and Lipset 1991; Pakulski 1993; Evans 1999). Empirical studies of class inequality, however, suggest that class inequality persists even in post-industrial societies such as America and Britain (Hout *et al.* 1993; Gordon 1996; Cotter and Hermsen 1999).

Class inequality can be described by economic inequality based on the social division of labor. Wright (1985 and 1997) argues that inequality of income and wealth is one of the central factors underlying the formation of social classes and social conflict. Economic inequality in industrial capitalism is an outcome of the structure of the inequality-generating mechanisms based on different types of ownership: ownership of capital assets, ownership of organization assets or simply authority, and ownership of skill assets or credentials. Owners of capital assets hire other employees or can be self-employed without hiring other employees. In industrial capitalism, those who own productive property and hire other people can monopolistically appropriate outcome of economic activities of employees as profit. Those who do not have productive property are employed to get material resources as a different form of wages. However, there is class differentiation among employees associated with the different types of productive asset ownership. Those who have authority, scarce skills, and expertise can get monopoly rent which refers to premium, which is beyond the market wage. Monopoly rent is social surplus by scarcity in the labor market because there are systematic barriers in the way of increasing the supply of scarce resources to meet the demand of employing organization.

Employees with authority are able to appropriate surplus because "the strategic position of managers within the organization of production enables them to make significant claims on a portion of the social surplus" (Wright 1997, 20). Employees who possess professional skills and knowledge are able to appropriate surplus due to the scarcity of those skills and knowledge, which is sustained by systematic obstacles to the access to those skills and knowledge (Wright 1997, 22–23). Those who own authority or possess scarce skills and knowledge can be called the middle class. Those who do not own productive skills or authority, or scarce skills, belong to the working class.

According to another matrix of ownership, those who participate in economic activity can be classified into different social classes (Wright 1997, 24). Table 5.1 shows the basic class map of industrial capitalism.

While class inequality might be the most salient structural property in an industrial capitalist society, the extent to which class determines social inequality might vary across time and space. As many researchers argue, institutional features such as the seniority wage system or the collective bargaining system significantly affect the process of wage determination and the level of wages. Other labor market institutions and cultural factors might also affect the effect of class on individual income (Dore 1973; Esping-Anderson 1992; Freeman 1998; Rueda and Pontusson 2000). Furthermore, the importance of class in determining individual income and wealth can also be strongly correlated with gender or age. Nevertheless, class division still remains as the most important structural factor in determining one's economic status in an industrial capitalist society. Although gender is an important determinant of income inequality, it is not an independent factor of income inequality. Gender inequality is always correlated with class inequality, as articulated through patriarchy and capitalism.

Class and income inequality: measurement and analysis

Data and variables

Data was collected in August and September of 2003, with 1,831 cases across the country, excluding Jeju-do province. Based on proportional probability sampling (pps), the sampling framework was designed to represent the significant proportion of the population in South Korea. The original number of interviewees according to the research design was 2,200, the interviewees having been between the ages of 20 and 65 at the time of interview. It excluded housewives and family workers who did not receive wages. The information from respondents was obtained by interviews conducted by professional interviewers.

To explore class inequality, we utilized monthly wages and income as indicators of the economic returns of individual's economic activities. While inequality of assets such as housing and financial assets might be better indicators of class inequality, we used the wage indicator in order to compare the results of our research with that of others. Additionally, since it is difficult to obtain reliable and available information about an individual's wealth, in this analysis

Table 5.1 Basic class typology

	Owning class	*Non-owning class*		
Employers	Capitalists	Expert managers	Non-expert managers	Authority
	Small employers	Experts	Workers	No-authority
Non-employers	Petty bourgeoisie	Scarce skills/ credentials	No-skills/credentials	

we use monthly income to measure economic inequality. In addition, class inequality in housing and education is also included in the analysis in order to capture the different dimensions of social inequality based on class.

In this study, we follow the classification of social class with respect to the factors of ownership, authority, and credentials suggested by E. O. Wright (1985 and 1997). Property ownership, authority within an organization, and credentials are major sources of class division in modern capitalist societies. First of all, according to the ownership status of means of production, the economically active population is divided into two categories: owners and employees. Owners are classified into three class locations so as to explore income variation with the owning class: the capitalist class that owns the means of production and hire of ten or more employees; small employers who own the means of production and hire less than ten but more than one employee; and the petty bourgeoisie who work alone or employ only one employee. According to the type of ownership of productive assets, employees are divided into four classes: expert managers who own authority, scarce skills, or expertise; non-expert managers who only own authority; experts who do not own authority but possess scarce skills or expertise; and workers who have neither authority nor scarce skills. In other words, those who have supervisory control over other employees in the process of work or have discretionary power to determine other employees' wages and promotion are classified as managers. Employees who completed professional education in a university or graduate school and have professional occupations are considered to possess scarce skills or expertise.

Other independent variables are defined and measured in conventional ways. Education is measured by the number of completed years of education. For those who drop out from the various levels of education, one year is added to the completed years of education of the previous level of education. Age is measured by itself and squared. Industry is classified into four sectors, those being agriculture, manufacturing, the service industry, and the government.

Class and class distribution

For the last four decades, Korean society has experienced tremendous structural change in terms of industry and occupation as well as the economy in general. Rapid industrialization transformed the agrarian class structure into an industrial one. The industrial class structure constitutes the largest proportion of wage earners among the workforce, whereas the agrarian class structure makes up the largest proportion of the rural petty bourgeoisie including small peasants. The working class makes up 52.8 percent of the labor force, while the petty bourgeoisie is 24.7 percent of the force. The proportion of petty bourgeoisie is continuously declining mainly due to the reduction of farmers in rural areas. The proportion of farmers in the total workforce diminished from more than 60 percent in 1960 to almost 10 percent in 2003 (KNSO 2003, 189).

Table 5.2 presents the distribution of the labor force into seven class locations. At first glance, it appears that the working class comprises the largest

Table 5.2 Class distribution in Korea

Class	*Total*	*Male*	*Female*	*Proportion of females*
Owners				
Capitalists	0.9	1.1	0.6	31.3
Small employers	8	7	9.1	51.7
Petty bourgeoisie	24.3	25.9	22.3	41.7
Non-owners				
Expert managers	3.4	5.8	0.5	6.5
Non-expert managers	5.8	9	2.1	16
Expert non-managers	2.8	2.9	2.7	43.1
Workers	54.8	48.1	51.9	62.7
Total	100	100	100	45.3

proportion of the labor force, while the capitalists comprise the lowest proportion of the labor force. While the proportion of the working class is quite similar to other industrial countries, the proportion of the capitalist class is relatively lower than in any other industrial country. The proportion of the capitalist class is 1.6 percent in Japan, 1.8 percent in the United States, and 2.1 percent in the United Kingdom (Wright 1997, 47). The small Korean capitalist class (0.9 percent) might be a consequence of the concentration of capital into a small number of large capitalists.

The distinctiveness of Korean class distribution lies in the proportions of the petty bourgeoisie being much higher than in any other industrialized country. With the proportion of petty bourgeoisie in Korea standing at 24.3 percent, which is three or four times as high as that of the US, Canada, Britain, or Sweden, this is considered an exceptional case in comparison to most other industrialized countries, except for Japan (23.2 percent) (see Wright 1997, 47–49).

Table 5.2 also presents unequal class distribution by gender, revealing that female employees are extremely small in number among the social classes with authority (within organization). The proportion of women (within class) is the lowest among the managers. The ratio of women among expert managers is only 6.5 percent, far below the proportion of women in the total sample, 45.3 percent. Women make up only 16.2 percent of non-expert managers. On the other hand, the proportion of women is greater than that of men in the working class. While there is only a small difference between men and women as owners, there is a striking difference between the genders among the ranks of employees.

Class and income inequality

Table 5.3 displays income inequality across the social classes in South Korea in 2003. In general, the owner class earns a far higher income than the non-owner class. This indicates that ownership status and types of employment significantly affect the level of an individual's income. As we might expect, the monthly

Table 5.3 Earnings difference across classes (10,000 Korean won)

Classes	*Mean earnings*	*Standard deviation*
Owners		
Capitalists	3,118.13	3,280.29
Small employers	459.04	490.56
Petty bourgeoisie	230.82	1,537.78
Non-owners		
Expert managers	232.13	82.87
Experts	212.80	83.28
Non-expert managers	198.45	79.76
Workers	124.78	71.30

earning of capitalists is highest among seven classes with 3,118 million won. But there is a large standard deviation of 32.80 million won, implying that there is a significant internal variation of income among capitalists. Small employers also show a high monthly income of about 4.90 million won. The average monthly income of the petty bourgeoisie is about 2.30 million won. In sum, Table 5.3 shows that owners of means of production enjoy much larger income than non-owners and the size of monthly income among owners is strongly correlated with the number of employees.

Table 5.3 also indicates that there is a systematic variation of income among employees. While expert managers display the highest monthly income of 2.32 million won, workers display the lowest monthly income with 1.25 million won. Those who have authority, such as expert managers and non-expert managers, earn much higher monthly income than those who do not have authority, such as experts and workers. The mean of monthly earnings of both managers (expert managers + non-expert managers) is 2.11 million won and that of non-managers (experts + workers) is 1.29 million won. The difference of the mean monthly earnings between managers and non-managers is 0.83 million won. Furthermore, those who possess scarce skills and expertise, such as expert managers and expert non-managers, earn much higher monthly income than non-expert managers and workers. The mean of monthly earnings of experts, 2.23 million won, is larger than that of non-experts, earning 1.32 million won. The difference of the mean monthly earnings between experts and non-experts is 0.91 million won. When we compare the effect of authority on income with that of scarce skills and expertise, we can see that the skill dimension is much more important in determining monthly wage of the employees.

Class and education

Class cleavage reflects not only income inequality but also social inequality. While class mobility is possible, class membership is not randomly achieved by anyone who wants to be a member of a particular class. While the ownership of the means of production or property determines the choice of members of the economy, employer, or employed, educational achievement has been perceived as the most distinct factor affecting one's economic status. Table 5.4 displays the distribution of class by levels of educational achievement. It reveals that there is a close association between educational achievement and class position in South Korea. This strong association suggests that the large investment in education is a rational choice made by Korean parents in order to provide their children with a better chance to become members of the upper class.

Class and gender

The Korean class system is a highly stratified according to gender, with a strongly patriarchal labor market in which women are concentrated among occupations with low wages and limited possibilities for promotion. Women are not only overrepresented in the less privileged classes, such as the petty bourgeoisie amongst owners, or workers amongst employees, but are also less rewarded than men within the same class. Table 5.5 displays the distribution of monthly wages or income by social class and gender.

There are two points especially worthy of note – the first, that there is an income difference between males and females within classes, and the second, that within each class, the monthly income of women is far lower than that of men. When two exceptional cases are included in the analysis, they significantly changed the analysis results: specifically, these were two female leaders of

Table 5.4 Completed years of education by class

Class	*Middle school*	*High school*	*College*	*University*	*Graduate*	*Total*
Capitalists	8.3	20.8	25.0	33.3	12.5	100
	1.2	0.8	1.6	1.3	4.5	1.3
Small employers	10.0	37.1	12.9	40.0	–	100
	4.3	4.3	2.4	4.7	–	3.9
Petty bourgeoisie	19.5	41.1	13.3	24.6	1.5	100
	56.1	31.9	17.0	19.3	10.4	26.1
Expert managers	–	7.3	8.0	73.0	11.7	100
	–	1.6	3.0	16.6	23.9	7.6
Managers	3.6	46.1	33.9	15.2	1.2	100
	3.7	12.5	15.1	4.2	–	9.1
Experts	0.7	1.7	1.4	84.1	12.2	100
	1.2	0.8	1.1	41.4	53.7	16.3
Workers	8.5	45.3	34.2	11.6	0.5	100
	33.5	48.1	59.7	12.5	4.5	35.7
Total	100	100	100	100	100	100

Note
The numbers in the upper rows refer to the distribution of completed years of schooling by row and the numbers in the lower rows refer to the distribution of completed years of schooling by column.

Table 5.5 Monthly income by class and gender (Korean won)

Class	*Male*	*Female*	*Ratio (female/male)*
Capitalists	3,118.13	286.67	0.09
Small employers	529.11	292.11	0.55
Petty bourgeoisie	293.06	151.14	0.52
Expert managers	234.75	197.06	0.84
Non-expert managers	198.78	197.70 (172.44)*	0.99 (0.87)
Experts	233.93	183.75	0.79
Workers	147.17	103.27 (99.09)*	0.70 (0.67)

Notes
Numbers in parentheses indicate the mean monthly wage, excluding five outliers; * refers to the average monthly wage, excluding five outliers.

insurance sales teams who received extremely high incomes due to the extremely successful sales performance. While they belonged to the lower rungs of the supervisory ladder, they enjoyed an exceptionally high level of income for their class position. The second significant point is that while there are gender differentials within class, systematic class differentials persist within either gender. In each gender, the owner classes have much larger monthly income than non-owner classes. Within the owner classes, the capitalist class has a much larger monthly income than the petty bourgeoisie, i.e., the self-employed. While the average monthly income of the capitalist class is 3,170 won for men and 286.67 for women, the income of petty bourgeoisie is 246.16 won for men and 184.86 won for women. Even the male working class receives a larger monthly income than the female supervisor or female professionals. This strongly supports the assertion that the Korean stratification system is highly structured according to social class and gender.

Gender differences of income within classes indicate that there is also a systematic pattern in determining monthly wages or income with respect to gender. For owners of the means of production, the monthly income difference between men and women becomes smaller with the decrease in number of employees. For employees, the difference in wages between the genders is smaller among those who have authority or scarce skills. The ratio of the mean wage of women to that of men is highest for expert managers and lowest for workers. Working-class women are the mostly underprivileged social group in Korea owing to their working-class membership as well as gender.

Determinants of income inequality

In our analysis, class inequality in Korea is salient in terms of economic rewards or returns, but the relative importance of class in determining income has not yet been analyzed. Table 5.6 provides the outcome of regression analysis showing the extent to which class is an important structural variable to determine an individual's income. Model 1 is a model that comprises individual variables, including education, as human capital. Because the lifetime income profile shows an

Table 5.6 Regression analyses of logarithm of individual income on various variables

Variables	*Model 1*	*Model 2*	*Model 3*	*Model 4*
Individual variable				
Education	0.0613***	0.0608***	0.0498***	0.0359***
Age	0.123***	0.119***	0.127***	0.096***
Age*Age	–0.0018***	0.0013***	–0.0014***	–0.0012*
Industry				
Agriculture	–	–0.123*	–0.155*	–0.263***
Service	–	–0.024	0.058	0.003
Government	–	–0.015	–0.018	0.022
Manufacture (0)	–	–	–	–
Gender				
Female	–	–	–0.448***	–0.356***
Male (0)	–	–	–	–
Class				
Capitalists	–	–	–	1.159***
Petty bourgeoisie	–	–	–	0.244***
Middle class	–	–	–	0.341***
Workers (0)	–	–	–	–
Adjusted R-Square	0.111	0.112	0.210	0.339

Notes
* p<0.05, ** p<0.01, *** p<0.001.

inverse U-shape curve, age and squared age are included in Model 1. Both education and age are significant variables that affect an individual's income. It explains almost 11 percent of the variance of income, which is measured by an adjusted R-square. Comparing the adjusted R-squares of Model 1 with that of Model 2, we observe that Model 2, which adds industrial sectors to Model 1, does not improve much. Controlling for individual variables, those who work in the agricultural sector earn less income than in manufacturing sector by 12.3 percent.

Model 3 indicates that gender is the significant variable in income determination in Korea. Controlling for education, age, and industry, Korean women's monthly income is almost 45 percent less than that of Korean men. Model 3 displays that the explanatory power of Model 3, 0.210, is also almost twice that of Model 2, remaining low, at 0.112. To identify the net explanatory power of gender, we compared the R-square of Model 4, and Model 4 without the gender variable. The difference of R-squares of Model 4 and Model 3 in Table 5.7 showed an almost 6 percent income variance that can be explained by gender.

Model 4 shows the effect of class on an individual's income. It indicates that even after we control for education, age, gender, and industry, there are clear-cut class differences in monthly income. Improvement of the explanatory power by Model 4 is 12.9 percent, as shown in Table 5.7, which is the largest variance of income explained by a single variable. Compared with the working class, the class advantage in terms of monthly income is largest for the capitalists and

Table 5.7 Comparison of the explanatory power of each model

Model	*Adjusted R-square (ARS)*	*Net ARS*
A. Model 4 – individual variables	0.297	0.032
B. Model 4 – industry	0.332	0.007
C. Model 4 – sex	0.280	0.059
D. Model 4 – class	0.210	0.129

Note
Net ARS=(ARS of Model 4)–(ARS of each model).

lowest for the petty bourgeoisie. Class inequality expressed as structural inequality exerts a significant effect on income determination and contributes to the reproduction of economic inequality in general.

Conclusion

This chapter explores economic inequality by social class in Korea using survey data. While the concept of class has been challenged by postmodern theorists, class cleavage still exerts a significant effect on economic life in industrialized countries. This study strongly confirms that class is still the most significant factor generating economic inequality in Korea. While other factors such as gender and education are also significant factors in generating economic inequality, social class plays the most powerful role in shaping economic inequality in Korea.

Korea had been appraised as a case of economic success with a more equitable distribution of wealth than any other industrialized nations. However, economic inequality has become a socially and politically volatile issue after the economic crisis in 1997. Neo-liberal economic reform, guided and enforced by the International Monetary Fund, drastically transformed the labor market and income distribution in the 2000s. Income distribution has continuously deteriorated for the last decade, as confirmed by government statistics and social critics. Indicators of inequality provide fairly consistent trends of worsening distribution of income in Korea.

This study also explores income inequality as an outcome of class relations. By analyzing determinants of income, this study identifies to what extent class locations affect individual income. This study also suggests that class inequality is positional equality and that positional inequality is the most significant source of economic inequality in Korea. We can conclude that social class directly affects income determination and indirectly affects it through education.

Unfortunately, we cannot analyze the trend of economic inequality because of a lack of reliable data that is suitable for the analysis of class inequality. The next step in a broader study of the issue will include an analysis of the trend of class inequality and the effect of the interaction of class and gender on income with time series data. As we observe, the effect of gender on income is also striking and requires more thorough exploration. In addition, we need to analyze wealth inequality among social classes, which plays a much more pertinent role in reproducing class inequality in capitalist societies. Class inequality in Korea can be fully understood when wealth inequality among social classes is fully explored. Surely.

References

Clark, Terry N. and S. M. Lipset. 1991. "Are Social Class Dying?" *International Sociology* 6.3: 397–410.

Cotter, David A. and Joan M. Hermsen. 1999. "Systems of Gender, Race and Class Inequality: Multilevel Analysis." *Social Forces* 78.2: 433–460.

Dore, Ronald. 1973. *British Factory, Japanese Factory.* Berkeley: University of California Press.

Esping-Anderson, Gosta. 1992. *Changing Classes*. London: Sage.

Evans, Geoffrey (ed.). 1999. *The End of Class Politics? Class Voting in Comparative Context*. Oxford: Oxford University Press.

Freeman, Richard. 1998. "War of the Models: Which Labour Market Institutions for the 21st Century?" *Labour Economics* 5.1: 1–24.

Goldthorpe, John H. and Gordon Marshall. 1992. "The Promising Future of Class Analysis: A Response to Recent Critiques," *Sociology* 26.3: 381–400.

Gordon, David M. 1996. *Fat and Mean: The Corporate Squeeze of the Working Americans and the Myth of Managerial "Downsizing."* New York: Free Press.

Hout, Mike, Clem Brooks, and Jeff Manza. 1993. "The Persistence of Classes in Post-Industrial Societies." *International Sociology* 8.2: 259–277.

Korea National Statistical Office (KNSO). 1988–2003. *Social Indicators in Korea.* Seoul: KNSO.

Krieger, Nancy, Jarvis T. Chen, and Joseph V. Selby. 2001. "Class Inequalities in Women's Health: Combined Impact of Childhood and Adult Social Class – A Study of 630 US Women." *Public Health* 115.3: 175–185.

Pakulski, John. 1993. "The Dying of Class or of Marxist Class Theory?" *International Sociology* 8.3: 279–292.

Park, Hyung-joon. 1991. "Gaegub bunsuk jiwie gwanhan jaeron" [Reconsideration of the Status of Class Analysi] *Changjakkwabipyung* [Creation and Critique] 74: 367–388.

Rueda, David and Jonas Pontusson. 2000. "Wage Inequality and Varieties of Capitalism." *World Politics* 52.3: 350–383.

Shin, Kwang-Yeong (Sin, Gwang-yeong), Jo Don-mun, and Jo Eun. 2003. *Hanguk sahoe-ui gyegeumnon-jeok ihae* [An Understanding of Korean Society from the Perspective of Class Analysis]. Seoul: Hanul.

UNDP. 1996. *World Development Report*. Oxford: Oxford University Press.

Wright, Erik Olin. 1985, *Classes*. London: Verso.

Wright, Erik Olin. 1997. *Class Counts*. Cambridge: Cambridge University Press.

6 Changes in social movements in the post-dictatorship context in South Korea – focused on three dimensions

Hee-Yeon Cho

Theoretical considerations

This chapter aims at analyzing new features of change in the social movements in the wake of democratization, based on the case of South Korea. The transition to democracy has been made possible by the driving force coming from social movement struggles against dictatorship. However, such a transition brings with it a new context. Therefore, the social movements themselves cannot but change in the process of democratization. This chapter tries to analyze this change, accepting this ironic fact as its starting point.

Social movement change in studies on democratization: 'multi-dimensional differentiation'

In the political and sociological analyses on democratization in the Third World and Southern Europe, the phases of the process of democratization are generally divided into two: the phase of democratic transition in the narrow sense, in which the so-called 'liberalization' policy is adopted and democratic institutions, including free election, are introduced, and, based on this free election, the 'plural' competition among diverse political parties happens. In this phase, the democracy becomes irreversible rule of competition and, within this rule, the chance of alteration of dominant position from one party to another is realized. The other phase is of the expansion of the democratic principle to political and social arenas. The so-called 'democratic consolidation'[1] comprises a main part of this phase, in which the democratic norm takes root as a dominant in most political and social areas.

The transition from the earlier to the later phase can happen in diverse ways. For example, in some countries there is a wide democratic insurgency making for democratic breakthrough, while, in other countries, there is not. In addition, in some countries, the dictatorial regime breaks down and loses power in a discontinuous way, while, in other countries, the transition continues under the hegemony of the former dictatorial forces. In South Korea, in June 1987, the Great Democratic Struggle caused the harsh dictatorial government to break down.

In this kind of phase change, we can see a new change in the social movements in terms of their main tasks. The main task of movement changes from the overthrow of the dictatorship to the democratic reform of the old dictatorial regime and furthermore the political and social establishments, greatly influences the directions of social movements and differentiation. During the dictatorship and at the early phase of democratization, the tendency of convergence within social movements predominates, despite the differences in issues, orientation, strategy and so on. A kind of centripetal force of diverse movements converges into one common issue that is anti-dictatorship in nature.[2] The overthrow of dictatorship as the main task overshadows other issues of social movements and defeats dictatorial regime.

However, this kind of centripetal trend begins to change as the democratization process moves forward. After the dictatorial regime gives way to a democratic one, the social movements, which aimed at defeating it, are put in a kind of post-dictatorship situation, which in turn provides social movements with a different context resulting in change in the social movements themselves. As the monopoly of the state power by dictatorial forces gives way, the social movements begin to pay attention to new agendas in post-dictatorship. Considering this, I can say that this chapter aims to analyze the change in social movements in the later phase of democratization.

If so, what kind of change does social movement experience in the post-dictatorship context? How do the dynamics of social movements change? One argument is that because the main target of social movements disappears, they will lose their dynamics and will be reduced in their capacity of popular mobilization. P.L. Hipsher's paper is one example of such an argument. He concludes in his study on urban social movements in Chile and Spain that 'transitions from authoritarian rule not only provide opportunities for grass roots social movements to mobilize in protest but may also place constraints on their ability to remain insurgent'.[3] The latter aspect especially is believed to come from that fact that the fear and threat of an authoritarian regression remain foremost in the thoughts of political leaders and the radical parties pursued a strategy of non-confrontation. J.J. Ryan analyzed the impact of democratization on the revolutionary movements with a focus on the guerilla movement. He differentiated it into three different types: 'destruction of the movement', 'negotiated surrender', 'negotiated settlement' and 'overthrow of the regime'.[4] Except for 'overthrow of the regime', the other three types show us a different picture during the dictatorship, in which social movements do not keep their mobilization capacity or ability to drive the government from below, although he focused only on the guerilla movement. Concerning this argument, I think that whether social movements can keep their former dynamics or not is not a proper question, because the democratization, which social movements have fought for, brings with it a new context in which they should be accustomed to and subsequently change their movement strategies. In my opinion, the social movements become more popularized. However, the way their dynamics are expressed changes. In a sense, the democratization process, ironically, should be thought of as re-contextualization and re-arrangement of social movements, resulting in the expression of the dynamics of social movements in different aspects. I think that change in social movements in democratization should be viewed as 'multi-dimensional differentiation', which means not that the main feature of social movements is a centripetal convergence over one main task and all the capacity of mobilization by social movements are expressed around such a task, but that because such a main task is achieved, the dynamics and capacity of mobilization of social movements are dispersedly expressed over various new agendas and therefore show a trend of multi-dimensional differentiation. Based on the consideration above, here in this chapter, I try to analyze the overall picture of such a dynamic differentiation of social movements, presupposing differentiation as the main characteristic.

This analysis of mine is based on South Korea, which shows us a very dynamic model of change in social movements in a post-dictatorship context. As is well known, social movements in South Korea have been a strong driving force for democratization not only under the dictatorship but also in the post-dictatorship context. The social movements in South Korea could keep their popularity and dynamics enough to diversify their activities in the process of democratization, in this sense, I think that the South Korean case will be a rich resource for analyzing the change in social movement in post-dictatorship context. For this, I will differentiate three horizons of social movement change first, and then analyze the characteristics of change.

Three dimensions of changes in social movements in democratization

In order to show the multi-facetedness of social movement change in the post-dictatorship context, here I will differentiate three dimensions of change in social movements and, thereafter, describe the concrete phenomena on these dimensions in the main part of this chapter. First, concerning the ideological aspect of social movements, we can differentiate diverse movements by a continuum of the ideological spectrum, which spans from conservative through liberal to progressive. The ideological content of three such ideological orientations can be different, depending on the historical period and countries. The meaning of the concept 'liberal' is different between the US and South Korea or Asia. In the US, liberal implies partly progressiveness. However, in South Korea or in Asia, liberal is a kind of middle position between conservative and more radical ideas. It is more so in the so-called neo-liberal globalization, which goes along with the democratization promoting liberalism. In addition, such ideological orientation can be differently expressed over different issues such as homosexuality, same sex marriage, patriarchic practices, conscientious rejection of military service, migrant labor, abortion, pornography, individualism, environmental issues and so on. In reality, the boundary between different ideological orientations is not fixed and one individual can have different orientations over different issues. For example, in the 1980s, some feminists criticized very progressive activists for being so patriarchal in family life. In the South Korean context, conservative movements have been characterized as ultra-right and anti-communist under the influence of 'the anti-communist regimented society'.

Second, concerning objects of social movements, I want to divide system-centered movement and lifeworld-centered movement, which is based on the differentiation of system and lifeworld by J. Habermas. The former is focused around reform of the political and economic systems, while the latter is focused around diverse issues within the quotidian world.[5]

Third, there are different attitudes concerning the relation of social movements and institutional politics.[6] As the democratization proceeds, there continues to be a change in the relation between the institutional politics and movements and in such an attitude.

The aforementioned dimensions of social movements can be illustrated by Table 6.1.

The structural and subjective changes emerging in democratization

Comparatively speaking, some countries in Asia have been successful in industrialization and others have not. South Korea belongs to the former. Social movements in South Korea have developed themselves in opposition to the developmental dictatorship which has quite successfully driven industrialization. It is quite difficult for a dictatorship to be able to sustain its legitimacy in the case of failure of industrialization, because a poor economic performance gives an impetus for development of social movements. However, despite a successful economic performance of dictatorship, social movements can develop in confrontation with it. South Korea will be such a case. The successful economic

Table 6.1 Three dimensions of changes in social movements in democratization

Dimensions	*Categories*	*Content*
Ideological character	Conservative, liberal, progressive orientation of movements	Diverse ideological differences show up among social movements in the democratization: diverse in terms of ideological content. And different orientations, depending on issues.
Objects of movements	System-centered and lifeworld-centered movements	There are movements aimed to change political-bureaucratic and economic systems, on the one hand, and the lifeworld, on the other hand.
Political character	Institutional politics-oriented and de-institutional politics-oriented movements	There is difference in movements in terms of attitude to institutional politics. There is institutional politics-oriented movement to enter it and change it, on the one hand, and anti-institutional politics movement, on the other hand, which has orientation to keep away from the institutional politics and de-link from it.

performance driven by dictatorship might have put social movements in a marginalized and unpopular position. However, they have been able to organize a quite successful opposition, despite of a successful performance by the dictatorship.[7] Under the developmental dictatorship, social movements are characterized as 'anti-dictatorial' movements that are main and dominant. What we could see during the dictatorship was oppositional mobilization of civil society.[8] According to reduction of consent on dictatorship, South Korean civil society increasingly mobilized itself in an oppositional manner. In the early stage of dictatorship, the civil society remained quite passive. The developmental dictatorship mobilized people to be obedient followers of the modernization policy with the aid of existent nationalism and statism. People were ordered to be hard workers to achieve modernization of the nation as anti-communist warriors. However, they changed themselves more and more to be self-empowered subjects with oppositional consciousness. Ironically, the middle class, which has been the main beneficiary of modernization and gave strong political support in trade with their beneficiaries, began to defect from the dictatorship. With the help of changes in the political and social climates coming from this oppositional mobilization of the civil society, social movements as organizer of active part of it, could find a fertile land for anti-dictatorship to be popularized. Based on this oppositional mobilization of the civil society and anti-dictatorial movements' leading role, the South Korean June Democratic Breakthrough became the climax of the anti-dictatorial movement in June 1987, also known as the Democratic Great Struggle (*Yuweol Minju Daehangjaeng*). It became a turning point for the breakdown of the military dictatorial government to and for military forces to retreat from the grip of state power. Impressively enough, social movements have been a driving role for democratization from below not only in the struggle for South Korea's democratic transition, but also in the conflicts over democratic reform of the dictatorial regime in the post-dictatorship context.

The active roles in the early and later phases of democratization, including the democratic consolidation, could be different. In some cases, social movements which have kept their dynamism in the earlier stage of democratization could not keep it up in the later stage. However, in South Korea, social movements continued to remain as strong driving forces all the way through democratization, sustaining their own dynamism. In this sense, we can define South Korea's case as one example of 'democratization by social movements'.

Expansion of autonomous free spaces and emergence of modern subject of rights

For understanding the change in social movements, we have to understand those engendered by the Democratic Great Struggle of June 1987. It brings with it two changes: structural and behavioral. First, we could see expansion of autonomous free spaces of political and social activities. With the help of popular struggle against the dictatorship, the military regime had retreated, and the formal democracy, including free press and free election, recovered. As a result, the former repressiveness of the dictatorial state apparatuses was weakened. People were able to enjoy expanded freedom of diverse political and social activities. Second, the aforementioned oppositional mobilization of the civil society developed toward to a new 'self-empowered revitalization of the civil society', enjoying the expanded new freedom of activities. With this self-empowered revitalization of the civil society, I mean two phenomena. One is that people get self-empowered and become different from what they used to be. The other is that diverse group actors, including class, occupational groups, minority groups and so on, get self-empowered to become different from what they used to be during the dictatorship.

The former means that the people had changed from a kind of obedient 'pre-modern people' (*baekseong*) to modern individual citizens in the process of opposition against dictatorship, having a new awareness of civil and political rights and political consciousness. The civil and political rights, guaranteed formally by the first Constitution legislated in 1948, had been disregarded and not protected in real political life. Many students and the general populace had been tortured and arrested without due legal protection in the dictatorial period. Now legal protection of such rights had national consensus, which any post-dictatorship government could not but respect. We can say that, in a sense, the former obedient people had been 'reborn' as a modern public in the process of overcoming the dictatorship through a kind of individual self-empowered subjectification. The self-empowered revitalization of diverse group actors means that diverse social groups, including classes, minority groups, women and so on, organize diverse collective behavior and make organizational associations, demanding their interest openly and more aggressively. Before the democratic breakthrough, the civil society mobilized in opposition against a unified battlefront against dictatorship. However, it is diversely mobilized along the diverse lines of cleavage, interest diversification or majority–minority. Many minority groups made their own identities clear and demanded equal treatment against formerly unproblematized discriminations. These structural and behavioral changes in the civil society made a new base for social movements to organize their public action in diverse ways, and this contributed to dynamic differentiation of social movements.

Differentiation of the moderate civil movement from the progressive grassroots people's movement

Based on the remarks above, I want to analyze in detail the phenomena which happened on three dimensions of change in social movement in the post-dictatorship context. First, under the influence of expansion of autonomous space of political and social activities, a new emergence of so-called 'civil movement' (*Simin undong*) occurred.[9] It meant that the moderate groups differentiated themselves from the progressively oriented grassroots people's movement, which has led the anti-dictatorial movement, and established themselves as a kind of new movement with its own independent identity. This new movement is characterized as 'liberal' in its main ideological orientation. During the dictatorship, liberally and progressively oriented figures and groups united to fight against the common goal of breaking down the dictatorship. Especially because the anti-dictatorial movement had relied on the leading and militant struggles of the progressive movement against dictatorship, different groups with liberal or progressive orientations could not but unite themselves in a common battlefront. In addition, even liberally oriented figures and groups became more radicalized in their struggle against dictatorship. In the 1980s in South Korea, after the Kwangju massacre, the student movement and other social movement activists became more ideologically radicalized to arm themselves with Marxism, Juche-ism, Maoism, Leninism and other radical ideologies. In a sense, ideological radicalization and militancy in struggle was increasingly intensified in the harsh repression of dictatorship and the struggle against it. The anti-dictatorial movement called itself a 'people's movement', which has a radical or progressive connotation in the South Korean context.

However, these two orientations which remained united in the anti-dictatorial movement began to divide. This was especially evident with the moderately oriented figures and groups, who differentiated themselves from the progressive grassroots people's movement independently, stating different identities such as moderate, not radical orientation, institutionally permitted action program and so on to the public. Differentiating themselves seemed necessary in that the expansion of political and social spaces removed the former condition in which even a simple political opposition act had become illegal and subject to punishment, making opposition actions a huge sacrifice.

The emergence of the civil movement and its diversification

Against this situation, many civil movement organizations emerged and expanded their popular base.[10] If the grassroots people's movement, which has led the militant opposition against the dictatorship, could be defined as a progressively oriented one in the dictatorial context, the civil movement could be defined as a non-radical, mostly liberal one, aimed at driving the democratic reform and rationalization of the post-dictatorship regime. Although the ideological spectrum spanned from moderate conservative to moderate progressive, the dominant ideological orientation was liberal. The civil movement in its early stage in the late 1980s and early 1990s identified itself as using legal and institutionally guaranteed methodology, heading for liberal and plural democracy, and having support mainly from the middle class, while the progressive grassroots people's movement had been using a militant illegal or semi-legal struggle strategy, heading for a socialist or anti-capitalist regime, and trying to mobilize the working class and lower classes such as peasants and the urban poor. The early identity of the civil movement was defined in this way. This might be the ideological content of the liberal movement, or civil movement, in the South Korean or Asian context.

The civil movement developed through two stages. The first was from the late 1980s to the early 1990s, and the second after the mid-1990s. The former was a period of 'constitutive emergence'[11] of the civil movement, while the latter was one of differentiation and diversification. The Foundation of Citizen's Coalition of Economic Justice (CCEJ) in the name of extermination of land speculation, realization of economic justice and so on, signified the start of the first stage of the civil movement in July 1989, when the military candidate Roh Tae-Woo tried to perform a kind of 'transformative' reform of the post-dictatorship from above after winning the presidential election in 1987. After the retreat of the military dictatorship, diverse issues, which did not get proper attention from the movement community and the populace, have been brought to the front. For example, housing prices skyrocketed.

Thereafter, diverse movement organizations were founded in this period. In South Korea, the YMCA, YWCA, Young Korean Academy: Heungsadan, Consumers Union of Korea, and Korean Womenlink have been main organizations arising during the civil movement. Some women's movement organizations changed in identity from the former grassroots people's movement to the new civil movement. This meant that the political situation, whether dictatorship or post-dictatorship, influenced the identity of the movement. During the dictatorship, progressive or radical orientation had been strong, and moderate or liberal orientation became stronger under the post-dictatorship.

In the second period from the mid-1990s, the civil movement began to be diversified in terms of its orientation and its identity, accordingly, as the citizen's movement expanded to various issue areas and the number of its organizations increased. In April 1993, the Korean Federation of Environmental Movement was founded when seven local environmental organizations and the Association for Anti-Pollution came together. In April 1994, Green Korea was founded based on a combination of some local organizations. In September 1994, People's Solidarity for Participatory Democracy emerged with a new identity as a progressive civil movement. Some human rights organizations refused to be identified as civil movements with a liberal orientation rather than a progressive one.

In addition, the diversification of the civil movement is evidenced by its issues. We see the foundation of diverse organizations such as the Citizen's Coalition for Better Government in December 1997, Civic Solidarity for Open Society in April 1998, Global Civic Sharing in December 1998, Citizen's Alliance for Consumer Protection of Korea in July 1997, Civil Network for Cultural Reform in September 1999, Citizen's Network for Educational Reform in May 1998, Korea Waste Movement Network in October 1997, Networks for Green Transport in March 1993, Joint Committee for Migrant Workers in Korea in July 1995, and Lesbian and Gay Human Rights Federation in September 1997. This stream expanded to diverse local areas. Other examples include Citizen's Solidarity for Participation and Self-Governance of Busan in May 1991, Jeju Solidarity for Participatory Self-Government and Environmental Preservation in September 1991 and People's Solidarity for Kwanak in March 1995. In this process of the expansion of the civil movement, new movement organizations emerged for enhancing local autonomy and grassroots self-rule. In the local and grassroots level, diverse movement organizations emerged, which were based upon rank and file's self-organization and problematizing their local and provincial issues. Typical cases are as follows: Movement for Keeping Ujang Mountain Alive in 1994, Movement for Regulating Cigarette Vending Machine around youth zones at Buchon in 1991, a movement for legislation of municipal ordinance of information freedom at Chongju in 1991, revision of municipal regulation for day nursery at Kwachon in 2001, impeachment of Sungnam mayor by grassroots people in 2001 and Movement against Approval of Love-Hotels at Il-san in 2000, among others.

Organizational development of the grassroots people's movement in the post-dictatorship context

Now, let's see change in the formerly radically oriented people's movement in the aftermath of democratization. The grassroots people's movement could develop itself in terms of organization and its popular base, enjoying newly expanded political and social spaces of free activities. The grassroots people's movement, which had comprised the main force of the anti-dictatorial movement, could not expand its popular organization because of the harsh repression of the dictatorship. However, in the post-dictatorship context, the grassroots people's movement rapidly began to expand its local branches and new sub-organizations. This was most remarkable in the labor movement. Just after the Great Democratic Struggle of June 1987, thousands of new democratic trade unions began to organize nationwide, and former government-patronized unions began to democratize from inside. For example, there was a change of leaders to a democratic one during the so-called 'Great Labor Struggle' in July/August/September of 1987.[12] This new surge also swept over white-collar workers across various areas. Based on this emergence of new democratic trade unions, the National Council of Trade Unions was organized in January 1990 and, thereafter, the Korean Confederation of Trade Unions came into being, covering such areas as Korean Big Conglomerates, white-collar workers, public service workers and blue collar workers.

In addition, the peasant movement, teacher's movement, urban poor and other grassroots people's movements could expand themselves organizationally. For example, national organizations such as the Korean Farmers League in April 1990, National Alliance of Street Vendors in October 1988, National Alliance of Urban Poor in November 1989 and National Alliance of the Displaced in 1994.

The grassroots people's movement has covered diverse professional organizations with progressive orientation. In diverse areas, such professional movements expanded their organizational and popular bases. We could see also foundation and re-organization of diverse progressively oriented movement organizations in diverse sectoral areas such as professors, lawyers and in diverse issue areas such as anti-American military base and information rights: Association of Physicians for Humanism, Network for Healthy Society in November 1987, the Joint Committee for Migrant Workers in Korea in July 1995, Minbyun: Lawyers Association for a Democratic Society in May 1988, Minkahyu Human

Right Group: Political Prisoners' Family Association in December 1985, National Reconciliation Self-reliance and Reunification in May 1999, Korean National Congress for Reunification in July 1994, National Campaign for Eradication of Crime by US Troops in Korea in October 1993, Association of Korean University Students in 1993, Korean Teachers and Educational Workers' Union in May 1989, National Professors Association for Democracy in June 1987, Korea Progressive Academy Council in November 1988, Jinbo Network in November 1998 and others.

These network organizations have driven the democratic reform of the former dictatorial regime and have done reform movement, including campaign for overcoming the dictatorial legacy and correcting economic and social structures distorted during the dictatorship.

Popularization of the system-centered movement and de-marginalization of the lifeworld-centered movement

Here I want to show the second characteristic, discerned in the wake of democratization.

Popular support of the system-centered movement

The object of opposition of the anti-dictatorial movement was a totalitarian political and economic system, in which the military forces kept state power in its hands. Although the military forces retreated from the grip of state power after the democratic struggle, it did not mean automatic emergence of the democratic system itself. The creation of a democratic system demanded another long struggle for democratization, or democratic rationalization of the post-dictatorial. In this sense, reform movement for democratization or democratic rationalization of political and economic systems was brought to the fore in the post-dictatorship context. Such a movement implied the democratic reform of the political system on the one hand, and that of an economic system, including a reform of Korean Chaebol and so on, on the other hand. In this chapter, I define them together as the system-centered movement.

This system-centered movement was popularized differently from the vanguard-like movement during the dictatorship, which was never popularized except during the last stage of dictatorship because of harsh repression and the presumably expected large sacrifice made by the anti-dictatorial opposition. Such popularization of the democratic reform movement was helped by the fact that people achieved a higher political consciousness and the political arena of political and social activities had expanded. As a result, the democratic reform movement of political and economic systems was supported widely by the general populace. The system-centered democratic reform movement got public attention, especially because the democratic reform performed by the government had been very incomplete and short of people's expectations, and also because the status-quo forces, which had a stake in the former system, seemed to resist the reform.

Political lag and proxy representation

Concerning the reform movement of the political system, the important area of reform was political, including political party reform and parliament. This is because in every society, politicians are a social group having strength in their decision making abilities, which hugely impacts other social areas. Political reform received attention from the people. Social movements including the citizen's and grassroots people's movements continued to strongly campaign for political reform and to change the party constitution of the parliament, which was in favor of the former dictatorial forces.

Because the civil society has been mobilized oppositionarily and people had changed into a public with a modern consciousness of rights and critical political consciousness, there was a huge discrepancy between the political party area and the civil society after 1987. Although the civil society has already changed much during the democratization process, the political parties did not change as rapidly as the civil society had expected. As a result, the discrepancy remained huge and the politics and parties as a whole continued to be distrusted very much. This situation can be defined as the 'political lag'. Because of this political lag, people demanded a driving force and momentum from social movements for a strong democratic reform of politics. This situation resulted in a special situation, in which the civil society movement organizations played the role of alternative or supplementary parties, which created political reform agenda and pressed political parties to undertake certain kinds of reform. The situation in which political reform oriented organizations undertook the role of not only watch-dog but also that of a kind of proxy-party can be called 'proxy representation'.[13]

The climax of this kind of proxy representation as a political reform movement was the Blacklisting Campaign against Corrupt Politicians in the general election of April 2000, which was led by Civic Action for the General Election in 2000 (CAGE). This campaign comprised two phases. In the first, the political reform movement made a blacklist of corrupt politicians who had been involved in bribe taking, fraud and other corruption cases and demanded that the political parties not nominate them for candidates. In the second phase, its campaign appealed to voters not to vote for the blacklisted candidates in the election campaign period. The first was called the 'Nakchon movement' and the second the 'Nakson movement'. These campaigns meant that civil society movement organizations intervened in the process of a party's nomination. Those movement organizations are said to be doing a kind of proxy-party role.

Political reform movement has been expressed in diverse forms such as monitoring for free and fair elections, monitoring the parliamentary regular inspection of the administration, summoning of corrupt politicians, organizing public pressure for revision of former bad laws related to dictatorial repression or new legislation of a new law in favor of people's interest, denunciation of improper persons or incumbent persons involved in fraud and corruption or misuse of their power and so on.

Economic reform movement for democratization of the economic system

The economic reform issues have been very much diverse. CCEJ, which led the economic movement in the late 1980s and early 1990s, raised quite successfully such issues as regulation of land speculation in the name of the public concept of land ownership. It brought to the front such reform issues as the independence of the Korea Central Bank from the political control of the government, more public provision of public housing, change of tax policy in favor of the lower class rather than business, the introduction of Real Name Financial Transaction System, reform of Korean Chaebol including disintegration of its over-diversification, increase of the inheritance tax, public regulation of big business and so on.[14] Such agendas as the independence of the Korea Central Bank and Real Name Financial Transaction System and larger provision of public housing have been adopted as government policies, although not fully satisfactory.

As is well known, the developmental dictatorship went along with a corrupt or the so-called 'crony' coalition of the state and business. The dictatorial government gave various subsidies to big business, Korean Chaebol in South Korea, in trade-off for providing political support and political slush money. The economic reform movement tried to problematize this unjust coalition and raised various policy measures to publicly regulate the Big Conglomerates. As is well known, East Asian economies, including South Korea, fell into economic crisis in 1997. South Korea rushed to an IMF bailout.

The period of economic crisis was identical with that of the emergence of the first new opposition party government in nearly 50 years, the Kim Dae-jung government. The new government could not but adopt a broad range of economic reform policies. The civil society movement, including the citizen's and grassroots people's movements for economic reform, regarded this period as having a very high chance of success, because economic crisis implied the necessity of economic reform to renovate structural problems which had been accumulating and never had the chance for reform during the dictatorship. On the one hand, the Kim government adopted reform policies from above in such areas as industry, finance, public service and labor; and, on the other hand, the civil society movement tried to organize strong pressure for economic reform from below. During this period, the Economic Reform Committee of People's Solidarity for Participatory Democracy (PSPD) had exerted quite an influential role in the drive for economic reform. It tried to raise agendas of economic reform and directly pressed Korean Chaebol to restructure them reformatively. It adopted a minority shareholders' movement as a methodology to push diverse reform agendas.[15] From the standpoint of the minority shareholders, PSPD tried to problematize un-transparent management, corruption, fraud, illegal behaviors and so on. Its members attended general meeting of shareholders, of for example Samsung, as minority shareholders and criticized distorted management at the meeting. Sometimes it organized class action against corruption or misuse of managerial power.

In addition, it tried to heighten legal responsibility for corrupt or misused managers of improper management, especially in public litigation. The best example of shareholders' action against improper management was a lawsuit brought against former officers of the Korean First Bank (KFB) on 3 June in 1997. PSPD sued on behalf of 61 minority shareholders. The plaintiffs won 40 billion won in compensation against the former president and directors of KFB. It was alleged that the bank's officers had received bribes in return for providing credit to the broken Hanbo conglomerate, causing huge losses to the bank and finally to the interest to the shareholders. On 24 July 1998, the Seoul District Court ruled in favor of the minority shareholders and gave them a decision of a historic 40 billion won penalty.[16] In addition, PSPD also sought criminal or administrative investigations to raise management accountability. For example, PSPD filed a criminal complaint with the Prosecutor's Office on 11 June 1998, charging Samsung Electronics, Samsung Display Devices, Samsung Electro-Mechanics, Samsung Motors and the board members of each company for violating laws regulating the introduction of foreign capital, foreign currency management laws and securities transaction laws. PSPD also sought investigations by the Free Trade Commission into Samsung Electronics, which was suspected to have illegally transferred assets and business licenses to Seoul Commtech at a price below market value between 1998 and 1999 to the chairman's son, who became the largest shareholder of Commtech by purchasing convertible bonds issued by the company. In addition, PSPD filed a complaint that the lawyers representing Hyundai Electronics aided the officers of Hyundai companies in concealing their criminal behavior, in connection with Hyundai Electronics' illegal manipulation of stock prices.

In 1999, PSPD ran campaigns known as the 'Minority shareholders' movement against the five largest conglomerates' and the 'movement for betterment of corporate governance'. In 2000, it campaigned for new legislation for class suits in securities and bonds transactions. PSPD adopted a targeting strategy, which problematizes the most symbolic case in diverse ways such as lawsuit, request of investigations by the public agency concerned, raising criminal or administrative complaints, campaigns for legislation and so on. In addition, a taxpayers' movement for budget watching was attempted as a form of economic system reform movement. This movement meant that economic reform agendas were being raised from the perspective of the taxpaying public. In this movement, diverse actions such as monitoring state budget spending, opening budget information to the public, tax system reform and so on, were undertaken as movement strategies. An agenda of the tax system is the demand that the government introduce the integrated comprehensive taxation of one's whole transaction.

A main monitoring point was whether the citizens' hard-earned tax money was well used or not. Even the expediency fund of the provincial mayor has been monitored by a local movement organization to be debunked, not to become private confidential money. As a symbolic campaign strategy, Citizen's Action Network tracked representative examples of budgetary waste and awarded the most egregious offenders with 'pork prizes', starting from 1999. In addition, quite exemplarily and successfully, PSPD and the Democratic Labor Party have campaigned to legislate a new public regulation of lease contracts for commercial buildings in order to protect the rights of tenants.

Diverse campaign strategies have been adopted by the movement for pressing the economic reform forwards and raising public attention, institutional, outer-institutional, professional or popular methods. In the institutional method, we could see public lawsuits, sending a public letter to agencies or persons involved, and participation in general meetings of shareholders. We could see, for outer-institutional methods, sit-in demonstrations, picketing for professional methods, press releases, making declarations, providing professional reviews or comments to newspapers, holding seminars or organizing discussions, providing information, contributing essays to the media; for popular methods, demonstrations and rallies, campaigns and so on.

Bottom-up struggle to speed up the democratic reform

The grassroots people's movement from below has struggled to speed up the democratic reform, get it more radicalized and to make the terrain of reform itself broader in order to cover people's livelihood issues. As aforementioned, the democratic reform from above has been distorted and lagged behind due to the political consideration of the government and political forces and resistance from the status-quo forces. In this possible stagnation, the grassroots people's movement has organized popular pressure on to the democratic reform toward more progressive direction, using mass-demonstration, diverse confrontations and so on. This kind of campaign of the grassroots people's movement has given stronger leverage to the civil movement, which used to act within an existing institutional arrangement. For example, the peasant movement contributed to making a united system of health insurance covering rural areas, self-employed and employed, which has been one of the main agendas of it with other pro-democracy and human right movement organizations. In addition, the labor movement has performed the so-called 'Struggle for Social Reform' including reform of health insurance, basic livelihood, pension and so on, contributing to reform of the pension system. This kind of grassroots people's movement gave larger momentum to the civil movement for driving the government to adopt social reform policies of their own.

Expansion of the lifeworld-centered movement

Behind or along with the popularization of the system-centered movement, we have seen the expansion of the lifeworld-centered movement after 1987. Here, the lifeworld-centered movement is a new movement which focuses on diverse issues within everyday life, the resolution of which cannot be reduced to struggle against exterior power, including the state power or economic power. Speaking in sociological terms, this movement has the character of a value-oriented movement rather than a power-oriented one. The boundary between system-centered and the lifeworld-centered movements is variable, and one movement might imply both characters. For example, aims of the environmental movement are to change the anti-environmental government policies on the one hand, and to change people's everyday consumptive life style on the other.

This movement differentiates itself from the system-centered movement in that it expands accordingly as the basic material and political issues such as absolute poverty and dictatorship are overcome, and the critical awareness of importance of lifeworld issues are increased enough to look at them as no less important than political or economic issues. We are able to see this kind of change in terms of people's attitudes and perspectives. The importance and positiveness of the lifeworld-centered movement can be found in trying to expand the democratic principle to other social life areas, in which unequal power relations are taken for granted and are not problematized, such as patriarchal gendered relations in family life, repressed diversity of sexuality, reproduction of obedient culture and knowledge accustomed to the status-quo, and stigmatized minorities, among others. Given that the political and economic power relations of all society are reproduced on the basis of unproblematized culture, knowledge, attitude and consciousness, the expansion of this lifeworld-centered movement can be viewed as a kind of deepening of social movements. At the same time, the expansion of the lifeworld movement means an increase in the multi-dimensionality of the progressiveness. Before, I divided ideological orientations such as conservative, liberal and progressive, mainly along the lines of political ones. However, ideological differentiation over diversified issues arise, such as the family head system (*hojoo-je*), homosexuality, pornography, education, ecology, crime of adultery, right of information, conscientious refusal of military service and so on.

De-marginalization of the lifeworld issues

If we see a change in the lifeworld movement, it surely has existed before the retreat of the anti-dictatorial movement. For example, as an environmental movement, there has been a struggle by the victims of the 'On-san disease' in On-san region in the late 1970s. There have been the efforts of the women's movement, refusal of the military service by Jehovah's Witnesses for their religious conviction not to commit murder and the campaign of the disabled for the right to freedom of movement. These movements have been done mostly by victims. However, they were overshadowed by the urgent anti-dictatorship issue and largely dismissed as movement agendas. This marginalization of the lifeworld issues began to change in the wake of democratization. A kind of de-marginalization came up and certain issues became hot and mainstream sometimes, depending on a conjuncture. Of course, this change has been helped by the expansion of the political and social spaces and self-empowered subjectification of the citizen. This change was precipitated after the emergence of the opposition party that is Kim Dae-jung's government, because people under the Kim regime were of a higher level of critical political consciousness than those under the Roh Tae-woo and Kim Yong-Sam governments, which had kept the former repressive grip on civil society and people in a transformative state. After the opposition party government, the lifeworld issues began to receive more attention from the people and movement community: e.g. social and economic human rights, homosexuality, foreign workers' rights, culture, education and environmental issues. As a case in point, pollution in Nakdong River in 1991 became a national and popular issue, in which most movement organizations came together despite their differences in agendas. In addition, conscientious refusal of military service has been regarded as a very exceptional and radical action or confined to specific religious fundamentalist group such as Jehovah's Witnesses. However, it began to be accepted as a movement that fought against the existing militarist order by the mainstream student movement activists from around the early 2000s.

Pressed by and responding to this change, the opposition party government changed its attitude toward these kinds of issues by trying to accept them as policy issues. The setup of the National Commission of Human Rights in November 2001 signified a positive effort by the government to further the institutional guarantee of civil and political rights, driven from below by the social movement. The Institutionalization of the Presidential Commission on Sustainable Development, Republic of Korea in September 2000 serves as another example.

De-materialist value orientation

In the expansion of this lifeworld-centered movement, we can see alternative values and thoughts which go against current ones. New value orientation, including a kind of 'de-materialist values' as coined by R. Inglehart, which is different from existing values which focus on increasing levels of material life and acquisition of political power, began to spread. This change in values can be expressed in diverse phenomena such as endorsing a slower simpler life, return-migration/refarm movement to the rural community, life co-operative movements, organic farming, vegetarianism and more focus on spirituality movements. Such diverse ideas as eco-communitarianism, ecological fundamentalism, eco-feminism, radical communitarianism, idea of non-ownership (*moosoyoo*), life thought of poet Jee-ha Kim, among others, have spread among some communities and activists which had wanted to keep their eyes on untouched aspects of life by existing social movements which were aimed at changing current political and economic power relations. In the case of the communitarian stream, diverse efforts such a San-an communitarian farm, Gandhi School, Da-il Community, Hanmaeum Community, Mil-al Labour Family in San-seong province in Muju, Pool-moo Eco-Co-op, Kong-saeng Nong-Dure as a movement for Symbiosis of city and rural community, and Ho-jeo Eco-Co-op have been tried. Some radical groups in this kind of lifeworld-centered movement are determined to direct themselves toward an 'exit' from the existing establishment system. The lifeworld-centered movement shows us diverse features such as this in the post-dictatorship context.

Transformation of the movement into institutional politics

The way in which the political orientation of the social movement is expressed varies as the political situation, including the relation between the political parties and social movements, changes. In the wake of democratization, we could see a 'transformation of the movement into the institutional politics', which means re-positioning of the political element of the movement to the institutional political arena.

Return of the formerly excluded politicians and an individual move of radical activists from the movement to politics

During the dictatorship, the institutional political arena was contracted in such a way to exclude political figures who exhibited any hint of anti-governmental oppositional acts or consciousness. This resulted in a special situation, in which the institutional political arena is seen as an area open only for political coverts coopted by the dictatorship, not the oppostitional politicians or activists.

Under the late phase of the dictatorship, in particular the Yushin System from 1972 to 1979, the opposition parties have been repressed in various ways, and therefore only government-patronized politicians could survive with smiling faces and obedient attitudes toward the dictatorship. As a result, many politicians were expelled from the parliament and joined the anti-dictatorial movement. A kind of union of excluded politics (*jaeya*) and social movements occurred. Accordingly, as the dictatorship changed to a harsher repression regime in 1972 when the Yushin System started, and in 1975 when Emergency Act 9 was proclaimed, many politicians with critical attitudes toward the dictatorship were expelled from the parliament. Sometimes they were personally escorted to information agencies such as KCIA and tortured and coerced until they were accustomed to the dictatorship. Some aspects of the institutional political figures and activities became those of the movement. We can define this situation as a 'transformation of the [institutional] politics into the movement or movement politics'. However, aided by the expansion of the institutional political arena after the democratization, a reverse trend emerged, that of a transformation of the movement or movement politics to institutional politics. This can be discerned in two phenomena. First is the return of formerly excluded politicians to the institutional political arena. With the new policy to unfreeze the regulation of oppositional political figures, they came back to the institutional political arena, running in the national election as candidates in 1985. This can be called 're-politicization of the expelled politics',[17] which became the first road of the transformation of the movement to politics.

Along with this, the oppositional movement activists with radical political orientation, who fought against dictatorship with the excluded politicians and made alliances with them against it, moved their area of activities from the street to the political party or parliament. Because these figures have moral and political symbolism, many of them won their elections to become national assembly persons with the political prestige coming from their anti-dictatorship movement career. By the help of this new recruit, the mistrusted politics could re-legitimize itself to a certain level, representing changed political opinions and demands of the people successfully. This is the second road of the 'transformation of the movement into the politics'.

This kind of re-positioning of movement activists to politicians was defined as 'co-optation' from radical factions of the social movement.[18] However, this recruitment of movement activists as politicians meant the narrowing of the distance between the movement and political party activities. Given that prior activities within the political arena have been interpreted as conversion from the movement to 'dirty' politics, this meant a big change.

Movements for establishment of themselves as an alternative political force

Second is the emergence of new political parties or political groups to represent movement agendas into the institutional arena. These came from a 'movement for establishment of themselves as an alternative political force', a kind of a new political empowerment, in order to represent new political agendas and needs. This kind of new political movement was attended by several civil society movement forces such as progressive or labor movements, environmental movements for the green party, women's movements or grassroots activists for local politics. This second is exemplified when movement activists form specific political groups and move their position in the form of the political group, whereas the first is exemplified when movement activists change their position on the basis of individuals.

This means that the political element which has been expressed in the anti-dictatorial street movement during the dictatorship separated itself from the movement in the narrow sense and moved to the institutional political arena. This is another road of the 'transformation of the movement into the politics' on a group basis. This can be defined as a 'new politicization of the movement'. This also means that it became possible to 'do politics' as an extension of movement activities, not as a political conversion. In the view of the boundary between the institutional politics and the movement, this change means, on the one hand, that the social movement extended its arena of activities to institutional politics and, on the other hand, that institutional politics expanded its arena of activities to cover the former activists, which has given some re-legitimizing effect to the institutional politics.

Diverse forms of the new politicization of the social movement

In relation to the second stream, we have seen first of all, the movement for progressive or labor party formation from the mid-1980s, just after the democratic breakthrough. This movement was an expression of the growth of progressive or labor forces. Within the progressive people's movement camp, there have been two groups. One tried to make an alliance with the relatively progressive liberal party in the institutional political arena, such as the Democratic Party, New Democratic Party or National Council for a New Politics, to let it represent the progressive agendas on behalf of a progressive grassroots people's movement. The other tried to make its own progressive or labor party independent of the other liberal political parties, albeit while being relatively progressive. The latter thought that a relatively progressive but basically liberal political party could not fully function as a political representative of the progressive 'social' forces. As time has passed, the first group lost its voice within the movement community and the second group became mainstream within the progressive social and labor movements. This stream for an independent progressive party was expressed as the People's Candidate movement in the presidential election of 1987, the Party of the People in the general election of April 1988, the People's Party in 1990, the Candidate of People in the presidential election in 1992, People's Victory 21 for Democracy and Progress in 1997, and the Democratic Labour Party in January 2000. The Democratic Labour Party received 8.1 percent proportionate votes in local elections, and its candidate in the presidential election of 1997 garnered 957,148 votes, or 1.6 percent of the valid votes. In the national election in 2004, it became a third major party with ten seats among 299, including two local seats and eight proportionate representation seats, based on the support of 2,066,072 voters in the proportionate voting. This entry of the labor party to the National Assembly means a important step for the new 'politicization of the movement'.[19] However, it was split into two parties in February in 2008 into the DLP and Progressive New Party, and now there is a campaign for making a new united progressive unified party.

Efforts of other social groups for entry to the institutional politics

In addition, other social forces tried to enter the institutional political arena. First of all, there was the effort of the women's movement, based upon the presupposition that the institutional political arena had been monopolized by men and structured in a gender-biased way to systematically exclude women. Interestingly, the effort of the women's movement has been expressed not as the making of an alternative party, but as making a space for a women's candidate for politics, notably in the quota of proportionate candidates or in nomination for local constituencies. Aided by this kind of effort, from the year 2002, the local election, a quota system was introduced that guaranteed a 50 percent proportionate for women candidacy in national and local elections.

In addition we see attempts by the environmental movement to create the green party. The Korean Federation of Environmental Movement (KFEM) and Green Korea have been at the forefront. Some activists from KFEM and other organizations created the Green Political Committee to promote the political entry as an independent party with ecological agendas. However, this group is now trying to make itself a stepping stone for an environmental political party, including environmental political education and propaganda among its agenda, based on the supposition that it will take a long time for the Green Party to take a root in the South Korean context. In the general election of 2004, it focused on supporting the environment-friendly candidates. It renamed itself 'Chorok Political Group' to cover more potential participants. In addition, a group of Green Koreans made a preparatory committee of the Korean Green Party in the early 1990s. This group made a Green Peace Party in 2003 with other groups and later re-made the Green Social Democratic Party in alliance with the former government-patronized Korean Federation of Trade Unions, but failed to get seats in the national election in April 2004. In November 2011, a Green Party was re-formed newly.

In the case of grassroots movements in local communities, many movement activists adopted a kind of participatory strategy with running candidates. After the recovery of the local self-government system, many activists ran for election as candidates for provincial or municipal councilors or mayors and some of them won the election. In the local elections of 1996 and 2002, 2006 and 2010 we could see many candidates with backgrounds of grassroots activists and many of them entered the provincial or municipal governments and parliaments and tried to realize their agendas as policies, which they wanted to push the local government to adopt. This kind of 'the politicization of the movement' does not mean that the movement can be reduced to institutional politics, because a new surge of movement having more radical agendas emerged to fill up the vacant spaces left after the activists' move to the politics. However, this change brought with it a more flexible boundary line between the movement and institutional politics and more openness toward each other, on the one hand, and on the other, a new surge of new radical movement groups in diverse areas such as radical young feminists, more radical socialist party-oriented groups.

In the Seoul provincial by-election in June 2011, Park Won-Soon, who has had a representative symbolic status within the civil movement, ran for the mayor, and succeeded in being elected. Because he has been the founder of one of the most influential watch-dog organizations, this new phenomenon seemed to blur the clear dividing boundary between the institutional politics and social movements. The civil movement in Korea, which has kept a popular support for its watch-dog activities, is confronted with a new challenge to keep its influence and autonomous space for its activities.

Notes

1 The so-called 'democratic consolidation' can cover the second and third phases of democratization. 'Democratic consolidation can thus only be fully understood as encompassing a shift in political culture.' Here political culture means that 'the norms, procedures, and expectations of democracy become so internalized that actors routinely, instinctively conform to the written (and unwritten) rules of the game, *even when* they conflict and compete intensely' (Diamond, L., 1999, *Developing Democracy: Toward Consolidation*, Baltimore: Johns Hopkins University Press, p. 65).

2 I called this phenomenon 'deepening of social movement', by which 'such phenomena as the development of the militant opposition movement, the union of lawful politics and movement politics, and the initiative of the latter in the struggle against the

authoritarian regime' are meant (Cho, Hee-Yeon, 2000, 'Democratic Transition and Social Movement Change in South Korea', *Sungkonghoe Daehak Nonchong* No. 15). For example, the women's movement partook in anti-dictatorial struggles and became an important part and driving force behind the pro-democracy movement (Nam, Jeong-Lim, 2000, 'Gender Politics in the Korean Transition to Democracy', *Korean Studies*, Vol. 24, pp. 94–112).

3 Refer to Hipsher, P.L., 1996, 'Democratization and the Decline of Urban Social Movements in Chile and Spain', *Comparative Politics*, Vol. 28, No. 3, pp. 273–297.

4 Ryan, Jeffrey J., 1994, 'The Impact of Democratization on Revolutionary Movements', *Comparative Politics*, Vol. 27, No. 1, pp. 27–44.

5 For Habermas, the system means highly rationalized political-bureaucratic and economic ones and it results in a new opposition against the colonization of the lifeworld by such systems (Habermas, J., 1989, *The Theory of Communicative Action. Lifeworld and System: A Critique of Functionalist Reason*, Vol. 2, trans. T. McCarthy, Cambridge: Polity; Steven Seidman ed., 1989, *Jurgen Habermas on Society and Politics: A Reader*, Boston: Beacon Press. Ch. 9, 'The Uncoupling of System and Lifeworld'). I am applying his concepts in this chapter. However, I put two limitations on it. First, the lifeworld cannot be defined as only a symbolic area but as a complex structure of symbolic and material relations, even though he defines the system as a material area and the lifeworld as a symbolic one (Ray, Larry, 1993, *Rethinking Critical Theory: Emancipation in the Age of Global Social Movements*, London: Sage, p. 73). Second, in South Korea, the system at issue is not a highly rationalized area but is one in the process of rationalization and democratization. The system for Habermas and that in the Korean context are qualitatively different. However, supposing such differences, I want to use these concepts to emphasize the differentiation of system and lifeworld and a new opposition against the problems arising within the latter.

6 In a broader sense, the social movement is the 'movement "politics"'. However, here in this chapter, politics is used to designate institutional politics in the narrow sense. In the democratic transition context, politics is alluded to as something corrupt and distrusted. However, here the concept 'politics' is used in the neutral sense to indicate activities in the institutionalized area of politics.

7 Concerning the modern history of industrialization and opposition together, see Cummings, Bruce, 1997, *Korea's Place in the Sun: A Modern History*, New York: W.W. Norton and Company; Cho, Hee-Yeon, 2000.

8 Here I use the concept, the civil society. The civil society is the modern form of society in Western Europe, implying the situation in which civil and political rights are guaranteed to general citizens and that they have a certain level of human rights consciousness and are determined to defend them. However, these kinds of rights have been formally given after the legislation of the Constitution in the Constituent Assembly in 1948. In this sense, the formal sense of the civil society began to exist after 1948 in South Korea (see Professor Jang-Jip Choi's paper about the surge of civil society in the political space after Liberation in 1945: 'Political Cleavages in South Korea', Hagen Koo ed., *The State and Society in Contemporary Korea*, Ithaca: Cornell University Press, pp. 13–50). However, in my opinion, the substantive sense of the civil society began to exist after the Great Democratic Struggle in 1987, after which civil and political rights could be guaranteed to general citizens, who are born as modern individuals who are very determined to defend them. In addition, before 1987, it was possible that Korean society did not follow the trajectory of the Western modern civil society, turning instead to a socialist one via people's revolution, and thus followed another trajectory.

9 The 'Simin Undong' can be called in South Korea, diversely: citizen's movement, civil movement, civil society movement, NGOs and so on. It is identified as the South Korean type of 'the new social movement' in the Western context, while the people's

movement is defined as 'the old movement'. 'Simin Undong' implies many characteristics of the new social movement, but cannot be defined as completely identical. Here I use the concept of civil movement for it. In the Asian context, the civil movement and NGOs are perceived as specialized movements on specific issues, sometimes funded by foreign donor countries. However, the civil movement in South Korea has quite a popular base and its budget comes from domestic sources. In addition, the grassroots people's movement (*Minjung Undong*) is not a movement of the general public, but that of the lower classes, including the working class, peasants, urban poor and others. Therefore, it is identified as the 'lower [*Keecheung*] grassroots people's movement'. (For further understanding, see Koo, Hagen, 1993, 'The State, Minjung, and the Working Class in South Korea', Hagen Koo ed., *The State and Society in Contemporary Korea*, Ithaca: Cornell University Press.) In addition, the concept of civil society is used here to cover the civil movement and the grassroots people's movement as well, based on interpreting the civil society in a broader sense.

10 Concerning the development and diversifications of the civil movement, see Cho, Hee-Yeon, 2011, 'Changes in Social Movements in the Process of Democratization in South Korean', Hee-Yeon Cho, Andrew Aeria and Songwoo Hur eds, *From Unity to Multiplicities: Social Movement and Transformation and Democratization in Asia*, Selangor, Malaysia: Gerakbudaya/SIRD; Cho, Hee-Yeon, 2003, 'Civil Society and Social Movements in the Political Change of South Korea', *Asia-Pacific Forum* No. 21, September; Koo, Hagen, 2002, 'Civil Society and Democracy in South Korea', *Good Society* Vol. 11, No. 2.

11 Cho, Hee-Yeon, 2004, *Change in Opposition Against from Abnormality to Normality*, Seoul: Arche Publishing Co., pp. 114–118.

12 In June 1987, the number of trade unions was 2,700, and that of its members was 1,050,000. However, in the wake of Great Labour Struggle, the former increased to 7,900 in 1989 and the latter to 1,930,000.

13 Concerning the political lag and proxy representation, refer to Cho, Hee-Yeon, 2004, Ch. 2.

14 Concerning the economic reform campaigns, refer to Wi, Pyeong-rayang, 2004, 'The Response of the Civil Society to Economic Issues in Democratization', *Korea Civil Society and NGOs, 1987–2002*, Seoul: Korean NGO Times. Concerning the agendas of economic reform of CCEJ, refer to CCEJ Policy Committee, 2000, *Let's Change Our Society by These Policies*, Seoul: Beebong Publishing Co.

15 Before the start of the small stockholders' movement by PSPD, they had been guaranteed rights by the Commercial Code. However, after April 1997, with the revision of the Stock Transaction Law, their rights began to be guaranteed more widely, including the right to raise questions, to wield the right of decision making, to read the account book, to summon a general meeting of stock holders, to have an outside member as a board of director and so on. Here, PSPD began a small stockholders' campaign to drive the reform of Chaebol and other economic reform, not only protecting their own interests, but also taking advantage of this change (concerning the details, see Hee-Yeon Cho, Ilpyo Hong and Jeonghun Kim, 2003, *The Role of the NGO in the Decision Making of the Government and Business: Focused on the Economic Reform Campaign of PSPD*, Seoul: Korea Institute of Public Administration).

16 Concerning the PSPD's economic reform activities, see Cho, Hee-Yeon and Park Won-soon, 2002, 'Democratic Reform and Civic Movements in South Korea', *Joint U.S.-Korea Academic Studies*, Vol. 12, pp. 93–96.

17 Refer to Cho, Hee-Yeon, 2004, Ch. 2, concerning this process.

18 This co-optation process can be viewed as 'transformational' effort for existing parties to absorb new figures with moral respect in order to increase their legitimacy. This is what 'transformation' means here. In a certain conjuncture the dominant parties co-opt individuals or groups in an opposition camp to re-legitimize themselves.

This occurs in diverse forms such as accepting agendas of opposition, and recruiting new figures from opposition (Gramsci, A., 1971, *Selections from the Prison Notebooks*, trans. by Quintin Hoare and Geoffrey Smith, London: Lawrence and Wishart, p. 58).

19 In the general election of April 2004, the liberal party (the pro-government Open Uri Party) with 152 out of 299 seats, dominated the parliament, getting rid of the first major party status from the conservative party (the Grand National Party), The labour party entered as the third major party. In the national election in 2008, the Democratic Labour Party got five seats, while another progressive party, New Progressive Party, couldn't have a seat, having one in the by-election thereafter.

7 Growth and crisis of the Korean citizens' movement

Dong-Choon Kim

Introduction

Following the collapse of military regimes in 1987, Korean society witnessed the popularization of the concept of "civil society," and the vocabularies of "civic movements" or nongovernmental organizations (NGOs) have since gained familiarity. In addition, civil society, during the time, found itself to sprout alongside capitalist industrialization, the formation of urban middle class, and growth of media in Korea. However, it is widely recognized that it was democratization that caused the flowering of civil society in Korea, not vice versa.

The collapse of the military regimes activated the Gramscian concept of "political society," the arena of political parties or political activity, and further consolidated civil society. During this time, labor unions were organized, many kinds of civic organizations were established, alternative media emerged, and diverse forms of interest groups were also founded. In particular, during the mid-1990s, civic organizations related to women, the environment, and human rights got off to a start, and many grassroots organizations formed alongside the launch of local self-governing systems.

According to the *Hanguk min-gan danche chongnam* (Directory of Korean NGOs, 2000), the number of NGOs almost doubled within the three years of 1996 to 1999. By specific field, the majority fell under the category of "civil society," which far exceeded the number of groups categorized under the title of "social service" and "culture-related" groups (*Hankyoreh*, October 20, 2000). It can be determined from this that the increase in the number of national and local civic groups was the main contributor to the numerical increase of NGOs. Interest groups and labor unions can be excluded, though some of them can be included in the broader term of NGOs. Hereby NGOs can be broadly divided into two categories: one is "groups for social service," the other "citizens' movement organizations." This chapter is primarily concerned with the latter type. For types of NGO, see Cho (2000, 129). Even more noteworthy than this quantitative growth is the increase in the influence of civic groups or citizens' movements. It is widely accepted that civic groups are no less important than government or businesses in contemporary society. In Korea, in particular, these civic organizations have exerted great influence on various matters, including the formation of public opinion, policy planning, elections, and social reforms. A survey conducted in 2001 found that citizens' groups were ranked as the fourth most influential group (*Sisa Press*, October 25, 2001), and one survey (2004) reported that citizens' groups were the most influential in Korea, surpassing the popular sway of political parties. According to the survey, the rate of respondents who thought civil groups to be the most influential was 28.9 percent, which was followed by the ruling Uri Party 23.7 percent, and the press, 18.1 percent.

However, over recent several years, Korea's citizens' movement suffered various internal hardships. The globalization of capitalist accumulation as well as neoliberal economic policy in Korea since 1997's economic crisis, have required repositioning on the substance, objectives, strategy, and method of the citizens' movement. In addition, external factors – political parties, government, and businesses – that influence the substance and scope of the citizens' movement have changed greatly. Thus, it can be said that the Korean citizens' movement has entered the stage of repositioning its societal role, while already passing the rapid expansion found in its early stage. Activists have felt that the current situation is one of crisis.

With this in mind, this chapter examines general characteristics of the Korean citizens' movement that was active following the 1990s, along with the movement's contribution to democratization of Korean society. The chapter then investigates the current status of the citizens' movement and the challenges it faces.

Characteristics of the Korean citizens' movement

Growth of the Korean citizens' movement

The Korean citizens' movement became a full-fledged one with the appearance of several citizens' movement organizations, including the Citizens' Coalition for Economic Justice (CCEJ) on July 8, 1989. The Korean citizens' movement has played a distinct role, a parallel for which cannot be found in other countries. In order to clearly understand the characteristics of the citizens' movement, it is necessary to trace the following elements: the historical trajectory of Korean society, the politico-social structure of Korea after the demise of the military regime, and the changes to social movements at the global level following the end of the Cold War and globalization.

As far as the "Korean citizens' movement" is concerned, the term of "citizen" in the Korean case is not only related to the "subjects" who are engaged in the movement as the main actors, but epitomizes its "objectives or orientation." The term "citizen" has, above all, been used in contrast to the *minjung*, a concept appropriated by Korean social movement activists since the 1970s. "Citizen" thus articulates the ideological orientation and objectives of the movement, which differs not only from those of the revolutionary political movement but also from radical political activism in the 1980s of South Korea. The "citizen" also marks an attempt to consolidate the democracy movements by institutional reforms, and to expand democracy to the social and economic realms. It can be found in the CCEJ's inaugural declaration:

> Under our organization, not only the isolated and the oppressed gather together. Those who bear good will can also be important actors in our movement. If they have good intentions, whether they be businessmen or belong to the middle class, they can be members of the movement.

Some scholars point out that the citizens' movement in Korea shares an affinity with middle-class interests – instead of advocating for the interests of socially underprivileged groups.

But it is also true that it has grown within a global context, in which similar NGOs in other regions, including the West, have been found to fill the gap made by the retreat of the state. From the historical perspective of Korean democratization, the Korean citizens' movement began to take its full shape when Korean political democratization had already progressed somewhat; when South Korea secured the advantage in "regime competition" with North Korea (due to the North–South economic exchange and South Korean enterprise's active role in that exchange); when the need was felt to expand democracy to other sectors of society, including parliament, court, administration, and enterprises. Although they represent a broad ideological spectrum, it can still be said that the citizens' movement shared a starting point with each other. Insofar as the activists who engaged in the democracy movement of the 1970s and 1980s played a leading role in the citizens' movement, which, they thought, would be an extension of the past democracy movement on the changed political context.

But while distancing themselves from the previous radical activism, the leaders of citizens' movement inherited the style or viewpoint that had existed during the military dictatorship, focusing on the Seoul-based central politics. From the 1990s, although the main organized citizens' groups used the liberal rhetoric, their main interest was in changing the socio-political system at a macro-level like the old democracy movements. As such, the Korean citizens' movement reflects the history and ongoing state of Korean civil society. Historically, students and intellectuals were the main agents in the Korean democracy. It was rare to see grassroots people who were directly engaged in national politics and the local community, which greatly defined the nature and line of Korean citizens' movement, which have been primarily managed by a few notable personalities. Accordingly, these groups suffered difficulties in terms of financial and human resources. The Third Sector Institute at Hanyang University conducted a survey as to the current status of financial and human resources for citizens' groups. According to the survey, citizen participation ranked only 1.3 points out of 3 points, citizens' and resources were more vulnerable at 1.1 points. Nonetheless, the policy influence of the groups was rated as high, at 2.5 points (*Dong-a Ilbo*, June 17, 2005). The Korean citizens' movement has yet to succeed in taking root on the grassroots level because civil society continues to be deeply conditioned by central politics on the one hand and people's lack of public participation (*JoongAng Ilbo*, February 2, 200) on the other. The participation rate for adult citizens was 10–20 percent, far lower than that of the British and American cases (50–69 percent).

From this, it can be deduced that the most important variable influencing the nature and direction of the Korean citizens' movement are historical and political conditions.

Two currents of the Korean citizens' movement

Among Korean the citizens' movement, however, while some groups bear a strong continuity with the past democracy movements, political or "general" (*jonghap*) citizens' movement, others are similar to those of the new social movements (NSMs) in terms of their objectives and philosophy.

These "general" citizens' movement organizations implicitly set as their goal macro-structural changes in Korean society, believing that their mission was the criticism of Seoul-based centralized politics. Given that party politics was corrupt and incompetent, and failed several times to reflect the needs and demands of citizens through party integration among conservatives, it is likely that the citizens' movement played the role of representative bodies, which the institutional political parties failed to do. Two examples of this are the CCEJ and People's Solidarity for Participatory Democracy (PSPD). The Citizens' Alliance for the 2000 General Election, which was led by these general citizens' movement groups including the PSPD, was originally initiated by the campaign for the National Assembly watch in the PSPD. Although the CCEJ and PSPD have habitually stressed the importance of ordinary citizens' participation in governmental decision-making processes and local politics, they actually set policy-making as their primary goal, which distances themselves from the grassroots movement.

Unlike the previous movement that pursued regime change, these "general" citizens' movement organizations have adopted as their strategies the filing of lawsuits, petitioning for legislation, presenting policy alternatives, and dealing with various civil affairs. They do not strive to reorganize state power or government anymore. They recognize the existence of political circles and the government, but criticize their arbitrary, illegal operations. These organizations have played a role in monitoring and checking the power monopoly found in the branches of parliament, court, and administration. However, they also clearly demonstrate a liberal stance in that they emphasize the restoration of individual rights and filing lawsuits. Judiciary reform, a National Assembly watch, and an anti-corruption and minority rights campaign are all enlarged parts of this politically oriented movement.

The NSM prioritizes the penetration of democracy into everyday life, rather than securing state power, and pursues the values of post-materialism by employing an identity-based mobilization strategy – that is, rather than catering to the interests of the masses, the movement emphasizes voluntary participation and networks rather than a centralized, concentrated organization (Offe 1985, 52–54). Green Korea United (GKU) and Korea Women's Associations United

(KWAU) may be seen as typical organizations that formed their basis on these values and strategies (www.greenkorea.org/www.women21.or.kr).

However, other leading citizens' movements bear a stronger similarity to old democratization movements than to Western-type NSM, as they are heavily preoccupied with national politics.

The second current of the citizens' groups includes these Korean variants of NSMs, a grassroots groups, and a community movement besides the abovementioned environmental movement and women's organization. Korean society has seen these kinds of new social movements and local residents' participatory movements become active since the mid-1990s. The latter presented new concepts of politics and rights in the field of everyday life and sexuality. The most prominent cases to appear during the 1990s were the women's and environmental groups. These two movements paved the way for creating new discursive spaces and opened new horizon for democracy and social development. These movements tried to some degree to distance themselves from the intellectual-led, centralized politics movements. While transcending the strategies of putting pressure on the state and governmental bodies, they showed a deep interest in resolving problems through the mobilization of grassroots civil society.

In short, the Korean citizens' movement, which has been often represented by several "general" citizens' movement organizations, has very diverse goals, orientations, and methods that also reveal some traits in common with other movements. Contrary to the citizens' movements of other advanced countries, especially those of Japan, the Korean citizens' movement has tended to put heavier emphasis on political transformation than transforming the everyday life of the people. The Korean citizens' movement began to appear at the same historical time that class politics and interest group politics became full-fledged in the Korean context. There are some scholars who identify the Korean citizens' movement with the new social movement. For this, see D. Cho (1996).

The role of the citizens' movement in the deepening of democracy in Korea

Democratization of the state

Korea has been often referred to as one of the countries that succeeded in democratization among the countries that implemented nation-building and industrialization following World War II. This success was made possible mainly due to the perseverance of anti-dictatorship struggles waged by students and intellectuals, but it cannot be denied that the citizens' movement since 1987 also greatly contributed to the consolidating political democracy. To reiterate what has been mentioned above, the citizens' movement played a large role in gradually reforming the state and consolidating democracy following the era of military dictatorships and the anti-dictatorship democratization movement.

It was only before the 1990s that the Korean democratization movement was able to make progress in the pro-democracy struggle by changing ruling elites while relying on the former type. However, the civic groups since 1987 tried to call for state reform and took control of the political arena and government while utilizing policy planning, filing lawsuits, and petitioning for the passage of legislation, rather than relying on resistance methods alone. Exploiting the underdevelopment of party politics and representative democracy, the citizens' movement has engaged in many activities, including the administration watches, election watches, anti-corruption campaign, and legislative petitions. It went further to pursue its agendas in local politics and a grassroots citizens' movement on a local basis, the goal of which was to democratize "the politics of everyday life." The Korean citizens' movement has contributed to the reinforcement and deepening of democracy with succeeding the previous democracy movement.

The reason the Korean citizens' movement stressed the strengthening and deepening of democracy by that means was not only because they thought the old power elites still stood intransigently against resigning, but because the parliamentary system and political parties were not consolidated yet. Also, the leaders of the movement saw the fairness in legal procedures was not guaranteed, and the administration was failing to serve the needs of the citizenry. In particular, citizens' sufferings after experiencing the economic crisis of 1997 were aggravated by the lack of democracy and equalized tax distribution under the IMF bailout system and neoliberal economic policy. In other words, the market system forced upon Korea by the IMF in exchange for a bailout package could not automatically weaken state power, bureaucratism, and political corruption; corruption did not end with the close of the military regimes and the weakening of oppressive state apparatus. The organizers of the Korean citizens' movement believed that local politics, grassroots democracy, and economic and social democracy could be guaranteed simply with the realization of parliamentary, judicial, and administrative democratization.

Democratization of the market

Civil society during the post-democratization period can be dubbed as one framed by the struggle of "civil society vs. civil society," as postulated by Professor Choi Jang Jip (Choi 2005a). The key issue here is how civic groups can check the power of capitalists that has gained tremendous power, and how to act in favor of grassroots campaigns in a time marked by capital liberalization, and the emergence of an influential press.

The citizens' movement has been often referred to generically as a "third sector," independent of political power and capital. In Korea, while it was assumed to be a politically oppressed sector under military dictatorship, after the advent of civilian government, it has been considered capable of curbing the power of capital. Under the IMF regime and the Kim Dae-jung administration, large conglomerates and the *jaebeol* grew more powerful. Large conglomerates became so influential that the Roh Moo-hyun administration has been conceived of as underpinning the *jaebeol*-state alliance (Choi, 2005b). It is in such ways that the power of private businesses has overwhelmed the public sector in all fields. The Samsung Economic Research Institute, for example, exerts a significant influence on the governmental policy agenda-setting process. According to a survey conducted by the *JoongAng Ilbo*, Samsung ranked first among 23 power groups in the categories of influence and credibility, with the PSPD being ranked twelfth and eight, respectively (May 25, 2005).

In this regard, economic democratization and business watch campaigns can be interpreted as efforts to enable the state and civil society to take control of capital accumulation, and to level the playing field for economic agents. These efforts included CCEJ's "real name system" and the idea of "public land," as well as PSPD's minority shareholder campaign. As labor's involvement in management has also not been officially allowed, the minority shareholders' campaign that aims for democratization of the corporate governance is in an initial stage. Although the minority shareholders' campaign was limited by its dependence on the interest of the shareholders, it promoted public awareness and contributed to enhancing businesses' management transparency by showing that even the *jaebeols*' governance, which had been thereto considered sanctified, could also be placed under the scrutiny of shareholders.

The Korean citizens' movement, therefore, should also strive to be independent from not only political but business power. Whether the movement can obtain its independence from business became a key issue that is closely connected to the question of whether the movement can survive after the development of market capitalism in Korea.

Crisis of the citizens' movement and a new effort at self-transformation

Institutionalization

Civilian governments such as both the Kim Young-sam and Kim Dae-jung administrations provided favorable conditions for the citizens' movement but also, in some respect, made it difficult for it to criticize them openly. The two administrations assumed themselves to be successors to democratization while believing they deserved the support of all reform-minded forces, including citizens' movement activists, and further tried to appoint activists to governmental posts. As part of showing a positive response, some activists actually joined the governments. Here, some of the groups were engaged in political parties, and other specialists who had been engaged in the citizens' movement participated in various committees under the Kim Dae-jung administration. At the local level, some heads of local government tried to share policy responsibility with civic organizations.

In the process, the neutrality and independence pursued by the citizens' movement came to be threatened when the capability of the movement and its performances were institutionalized and the movement's leaders began to play an advisory or directing role in governmental policy-making. Thus, debate over the independence or "moral purity" of the movement appeared, fuelled by criticism that viewed the citizens' movement as one partner of the government or as organizations that supported the government. This debate offered a space for conservatives to launch a total attack on the citizens' movement. Some point to the low rate of participation of citizens' movement activists in governmental posts. In 2001, for example, 474 committees were operating under 40 governmental ministries, and among former activists, those who participated in the committees totaled only six.

Though keeping "purity" for civic groups would be detrimental in sustaining the social legitimacy and integrity of citizens' movement, the argument that it should not involve itself in real politics might be regarded as a kind of myth raised by conservatives who viewed the citizens' movement negatively in the Korean context. The discourse of "purity" of the agency of social movements has had a very peculiar meaning in the Korean context, where "purity" was equal to being disinterested in politics or material gain. Thus praising the "purity" of the protestors may reflect the oppressive ruling system that does not permit the people (workers, peasants, and other interest groups) to intervene in politics. This is why the argument has come out from the conservatives as an ill-intentioned criticism against the citizens' movement. Many former activists who had occupied governmental posts or entered the political arena could not evade the criticism that they had owned the achievement of the movement rather than systematically conveying their original ideas or vision into the policy-making process in the government and political parties in emphasizing its rationale. Consequently, they could only partly succeed in institutionalizing its original slogans or demands, and allowed the citizens' movement activists to be blamed for their individual behaviors. In short, the former activists' participation in governmental bodies and politics operated as a burden on the citizens' movement, thereby causing the foundation upon which the movement stood to shrink.

In order to realize the needs or demands of citizens, it is natural for the movement to align itself with institutional politics. However, based on the Korean experience, if the leaders couldn't endure the enticement of politicization or institutionalization, the movement would face a backlash. In particular, financially vulnerable groups tend to rely heavily on governmental funding, and activists find themselves becoming project planners and rapporteurs instead. Since 1999, the Ministry of Government Administration and Home Affairs and local governments subsidized NGOs on project base. The conservatives and mainstream media, then, blamed the policy as a kind of collusion between government and the citizens' movement. Small, financially weak NGOs have no choice but to depend on the subsidy.

Some people criticized that the main actors in the movement, elites, and specialists, made it difficult for ordinary citizens to facilitate their participation. Many academics have theorized that these problems were due to the Korean citizens' movement's deep preoccupation in national macro-politics, which was the most serious problem felt by activists working in local areas (*Simin-ui sinmun*, January 3, 2005).

Recently, some rightists criticized the citizens' movement groups in Seoul by calling them a new power group that is exerting a negative impact on local citizens' participation and the expansion of grassroots democracy. Leftists also criticize the citizens' movement for acting in partnership with liberal market capitalism and neoliberalism, which contributes to the exclusion of working people and deprives them of their rights (Jeong 2000).

Such criticism from both the left and right carry their own validity, and therefore remain problems that the citizens' movement organizations need to resolve.

Neoliberalism and market fundamentalism

Globalization, corporate restructuring, large-scale lay-offs, and aggravated economic disparities threaten the existence of the middle class. The growth-oriented policy and developmentalism are being more widely accepted as priorities, making it difficult for the citizens' movement to pursue social solidarity. Neoliberal polarization is weakening the public foundation on which the citizens' movement stands, as it has increasingly failed to offer an expectation and concrete alternatives to the middle class. As has been widely recognized, market fundamentalism tends to eliminate the *raison d'être* behind the citizens' movement or civil society. Thus, the citizens' movement, which prioritizes the improvement of the corporate governance system, is likely to de-emphasize welfare, human rights, and the environment in favor of the theory that equates businesses' competitiveness with national competitiveness.

An expanded civil society and a neoliberal economic order fueled the vitality of interest groups, some of which were more influential than the citizens' movement or voluntary associations. Interest groups displayed their influence most vividly when hospitals and pharmacies were planned for separation in 2000. Civic organizations were calling for this change, and the government tried to accept the proposal. Medical doctors' groups, however, feared this development and exerted their power to block the separation. In response, they were met with intense confrontation by the citizens' movement. Even before this time, interest groups such as the Federation of Korean Industries, the Korea Employers Federation, and the Korea Chamber of Commerce and Industry made their demands via lobbying. When a mass agenda, such as political democratization, prevails nationwide, interest groups tend to be influenced by these political and economic trends. However, with the decreased influence of a singular agenda, the specific agendas of interest groups that are more difficult to consolidate are brought to the fore. Having taken this into consideration, the leaders of the citizens' movement felt they could not merely be satisfied with their moral superiority and presented concrete policy alternatives for the issues over which many interest groups were entangled.

One of the most difficult problems facing Korean society may be the social instability caused by social dissolution and isolation, both factors that have been believed to stem from neoliberal economic policy. Job insecurity and concern about the future make it difficult for citizens to voluntarily participate in social issues. It cannot be denied that destruction of social solidarity is tragic but, even so, one cannot rely on the traditional community to restore solidarity. As citizens do not have a keen awareness of their social obligations as much as they eagerly want to gain political rights, it is all the more important that Korean civil society restores social trust by overcoming insincerity and moral hazards to others (Jeong 2000).

Since the period of modernization, Korean people have increasingly found themselves to be socially unstable, and Korean society has become witness to the loss of a social trust system and the resultant collapse of social stability. As there has been a deep-rooted tradition of the state addressing all issues in Korea, citizens do not think they can solve social problems by themselves, and distrust of people in power runs very high. Thus, more than anything else, it is important for citizens to participate in social issues with integrity and maintain social integration.

The Korean citizens' movement, in such a period of market fundamentalism, is facing the tasks of correcting market failures and maintaining moral integration in Korean society. Therefore, it is increasingly important for citizens' organizations to make efforts to curb market fundamentalism, such as through business watches, consumer campaigns, the eradication of poverty, establishment of a regional welfare system, and protection of non-standard workers.

As the role of nation-states become limited with the advent of globalization, the question of whether the state or the market can meet human needs and desires has often been raised. Against this background, some people have taken an interest in the communitarian movement. Communitarian activists carefully present the building of new local communities as an alternative to the current situation, where there is a great disinterest in political parties, labor unions, elections, and the press, as well as a low rate of social participation.

Internal problems

Since the economic crisis of the late 1990s, the context of the citizens' movement has undergone many changes: a shrinkage of the middle class that was facilitated by social polarization, interest groups' active engagement in decision-making regarding many political and social issues, the consequent weakened intervening power of the citizens' movement, emergence of the progressive DLP that is capable of easily politicizing the citizens' movement agenda, and the reduction of the resource pool of citizen activists due to the depoliticization of young people in their 20s. Of course, the identity confusion that the citizens' movement has undergone, stemming from the ideological diversification of the movement activists, cannot be denied either. Besides, it can also not be ignored that the limited potential pool of activists or so-called "crisis of reproducing citizens' movement activists" was brought about when the more notable activists began to participate in the institutionalized political arena and government. This difficulty, however, was mainly produced when centralized and state-centered issues began to disappear (Yoon 2005, 67).

As mentioned above, the political and social impact of the citizens' movement on Korean society has shrunk, coupled with the entry of the *minjung* movement activists into the institutionalized political arena and the increased role played by interest groups.

Epilogue

The most significant issue that the Korean citizens' movement should resolve is that of fostering itself as an independent social force that distances itself from the state and market. Rather than expanding its political impact via institutionalized politics, it is most desirable for the movement to fuel societal change from within institutions by expanding their influence outside them. The citizens' movement should try to represent the voice of citizens who are against political groups or a government that caters to pro-capitalist forces. The citizens' movement should go beyond a role of merely being independent from the state or market to one of pioneering the pursuit of an alternative order or community.

In particular, the Korean citizens' movement should overcome its Seoul-centrism and reinforce its combination of localization, specialization, and transnationality. The largest advantage that the Korean citizens' movement can have is its influence on "central politics." In the long term, however, the advantage can hamper the development of the citizens' movement since it might lack practicality. In other words, the citizens' movement will be able to maintain its vitality only when the movement combines itself with everyday politics, a foundation of grassroot people.

References

Cho, Hee-Yeon. 2000. "Hanguk simin danche-ui yeoksa, hyeonhwang-gwa jeonmang" [The History, Current Status, and Prospects of Nongovernmental Organizations in Korea]. *Enjio-ran mueosin-ga* [What are NGOs?], edited by Kim Dong-Choon, Kim Su Hyun, Jeong Tae Suk, Cho Hee-Yeon, Chu Sung Su, and Cha Myung Jae. Seoul: Arche.

Choi, Jang Jip. 2005a. *Minjuhwa ihu-ui minjujuui: hanguk minjujuui-ui bosjujeok giwon* [Democracy during the Post-Democratization Period: Conservative Origins of Korean Democracy and its Crisis]. Seoul: Humanitas.

Choi, Jang Jip. 2005b. "Minjujuui-wa hanguk-ui nodong" [Democracy and Korean Labor]. Paper presented at a symposium commemorating the tenth anniversary of the Korea Labor and Society Institute.

Jeong, Jong-gwon. 2000. "Hanguk simin undong-eul bipanhanda" [A Criticism of the Korean Citizens' Movement]. In *Enjio-ui sidae: jigu simin sahoe-reul hyanghayeo* [The Era of NGOs: Towards a Global Civil Society], edited by Cho

Offe, Claus. 1985. "New Social Movements: Challenging the Boundaries of Institutional Politics." *Social Research* 52.4: 817–868.

Yoon, Sangchul. 2005. "1990 nyeondae hanguk sahoe undong" [Korean Social Movements during the 1990s]. *Gyeongje-wa sahoe* [Economy and Society] (summer).

8 Two concepts of human rights in contemporary Korea

Hyo-Je Cho

Introduction

By the time the former authoritarian regime gave way to more pluralist democratic politics in Korea after the late 1980s the concept of human rights was almost synonymous with the typical notion of human rights as the individual's last resort against the state's repression. To the extent that the 'mainstream' or 'traditional' view of human rights was clearly defined, however, there were very few, if any, coherent counter-arguments against the prevailing concept. While the former was abundantly documented and reported (cf. Amnesty International, 1986; Asia Watch Committee, 1987; Ranard, 1980), the latter existed only as a rather defensive argument based on the 'necessary evil' logic under the circumstances of political exigency. This meant that although there were severe restrictions on citizens' freedom in all their guises in the past there existed a largely undisputed ideal of 'universal' human rights. This is an interesting point of departure from a more articulated, albeit flawed, form of counter-concept of human rights such as the one illustrated by the so-called 'Asian value' debate. In short, the conceptual landscape of human rights in Korea in the 1980s consisted of a rather clear-cut, standard formulation of human rights as liberty-equality-fraternity on the one hand, and of a merely reactive and somewhat temperamental inclination against the rights discourse on the other, hence the vastly asymmetrical picture.

The contemporary landscape of human rights in Korea, however, is an altogether different story; it has greatly departed from the earlier picture. Nowadays two different concepts of human rights compete and clash with each other. A hasty answer to why this kind of change has occurred might be easily framed as the pro-human rights versus anti-human rights antagonism. But one needs to go beyond this simplistic interpretation and search for a more nuanced, socio-historically informed clue, since there are multi-faceted collaborating factors which have eventually led to the present state. In what follows I shall argue that the combination of policy changes, political contingencies and socio-economic conditions has acted as an important filter through which the different discourses of human rights have been tested, advocated and facilitated, resulting in the emergence of the two different human rights concepts. These socio-historical catalysts include the institutionalization of human rights discourse; changes in perceived relationship between human rights and democracy, and the proliferation of rights discourse; the penetration of neoliberal economic doctrine in many spheres of society; and the internationalization of the North Korean human rights issue.

Institutionalization of human rights

It has long been accepted that human rights discourse in Korea in its modern manifestation was borne out of the situation since the early 1970s when clashes between the authoritarian state repression and the civil society's resistance began to escalate. It might be stated that the road to official recognition of human rights fully gathered momentum during the presidencies of Kim Dae-Jung (1998–2003) and Roh Moo-Hyun (2003–2008), respectively. A number of institutionalized human rights can be identified. Among them was the creation of the National Human Rights Commission in 2001, perhaps the most symbolic, visible and tangible result of the institutionalization of human rights. The 'policy recommendation', the organization's primary means of enforcing its decision, is found to have had some notable, quantifiable effect on the criminal justice system, though not without limitations due to its non-binding nature (Lee, 2007b). Another example of the institutionalization of human rights includes attempts to look into the human rights abuses committed in the past. For the first time some of the past atrocities which had been virtually a taboo subject were openly revisited and discussed in public, with historical incidents of sensitive nature increasingly becoming subject of heated debate in academia as well as in the media. After the long political controversies the state apparatus including the judiciary began reviewing past human rights violation cases which culminated in the establishment of the Truth and Reconciliation Commission in 2005. Alongside this, separate investigative bodies were set up along the lines of specific issues such as unaccounted death cases or the Jeju island massacres of the late 1940s. Also created were some particular truth committees under the auspices of various government bodies including the police, the defense ministry and the security agency. In addition, a move to disseminate the idea of human rights through the formal educational curriculum became another manifestation of the institutionalization of human rights. There were attempts to make human rights education mandatory for the military, the police and immigration officials. Although the policy changes were haphazard and slow the very fact that such an education was ever attempted at all would have been inconceivable just a few years ago.

The traditional human rights movement has engaged with the above changes enthusiastically. The human rights movement, as well as pro-democracy civic activities in general, not only have been influenced by the institutionalization drive of human rights, but they have also become an important driver of the institutionalization process itself. It is often pointed out that Korean politics has a distinctive feature of 'movement politics' with heavy inputs from civil society, ideationally as well as in terms of personnel (Cho, 2000). Through this process the traditional discourse managed to become one of the important pillars of the governing ideology the successive governments of Kim Dae-Jung and Roh Moo-Hyun relied upon. This change in official language and policy, although far from flawless, had a profound impact on the bureaucracy in general; the discourse of human rights was allowed to penetrate into the hitherto forbidden core of the old establishment. This in turn had transforming effect on the human rights, since the institutionalization inevitably required human rights advocacy and discourse to be subject to bureaucratic rule, regulations and organizational constraints. The human rights community had to learn the 'art of governing' and, in many cases, had to allow institutionalized human rights policies to be held accountable to the normal organizational process, including a call for more public scrutiny on matters concerning budgetary control.

On the one hand, the institutionalization of human rights predictably further undercut the counter-discourse's room for maneuver. For at that time it was more difficult, if not impossible, for the counter-argument of human rights to make its case in the changed environment. But on the other hand the situation produced a rather paradoxical effect that the counter-discourse was able to acquire some policy leverage to scrutinize the traditional human rights movement with the very bureaucratic criteria the institutionalization was supposed to be subject to. This was most evidently demonstrated after the conservative Lee Myung-Bak government in 2008. Indeed the national human rights institution was forced to capitulate over the government's demand to trim down the personnel and activity level in line with the governmental overall drive to make a 'small government'. The onslaught on the institutionalized human rights using the bureaucratic organizational means proved to be an effective tactic on the part of the counter-discourse because the attack allowed the counter-discourse to criticize hegemony of the traditional human rights movement without having to oppose the human rights value in itself (Ju, 2007). It is worth noting that some segment of the press and media has been at the forefront of this attack with the intellectual input from the conservative constituency.

Proliferation of human rights and its implication on democracy

With an increasing tendency toward institutionalization came proliferation of human rights discourse and movement. For the past two decades there developed two contradictory but somehow related trends: a dramatic expansion of various human rights movements; and the proliferation of interest-based rights discourse and its associated collective action. All sorts of different issue areas of human rights ('horizontal dimension') have been brought into light with the corresponding formation of groups working for their respective causes. The speed with which this expansion has come about and the relative ease with which the public has accepted the basic tenets of these issues are remarkable. The most prominent among this trend were issues related to discrimination or, more precisely, to the struggle for 'recognition equality' (Fraser and Honneth, 2003). The disability issue was the first in a long list of 'recognition inequality', which was able to find a legislative solution (Nam, 2007). An interesting development is the 'discovery' of such sub-category within the disabled as the disabled women, an important insight into the double hardship of women with disabilities in a traditionally male-centered society (Cha, 2005; Hong and Sung, 2003). Also to be taken into account is the reality of the mentally disabled persons whose existence had been virtually hidden away from the public eye (Lee, 2007a). The plight of former patients of Hansen's Disease is another example of this resurfacing of long suppressed human rights issues (Jung, 2006). Discrimination based on one's sexual orientation has also been subject to heated public debate. As the lid on the taboo subject was lifted the protection of human rights for, and the endowment of full 'social' citizenship upon, those who are discriminated against on the basis of their sexuality began to be addressed in academia as well as in civil society (Kwon, 2009; Seo, 2005). The protection of the elderly in a rapidly aging society has also been on the agenda of human rights movement (Yoo and Kang, 2008). In addition to issues related to 'recognition equality' there emerged new human rights issues based on the re-interpretation and radicalization of freedom. These include, among others, human rights of students and children (Cho, 2007), basic rights of the enlisted service personnel (Lee, 2005), and the deprivation of education rights and persistent mental-physical abuse of the elite student-athletes (Kim, 2009b). The long-forgotten subject of those who are incarcerated on account of their conscientious objection to military conscription has been accepted as a public agenda on citizens' liberty in the last decade (Ahn and Jang, 2002; Lee, 2004b). Furthermore, new human rights issues reflecting the changed socio-economic circumstances under globalization such as rights of migrant workers have become important components of human rights movement (Gray, 2004; Seol, 2005).

The expansion of human rights agenda was accompanied by the proliferation of interest-oriented rights discourse and its related collective action. According to Lee (2004c) just as the democratization process proceeded and deepened so came into being intense social conflicts in every aspect of public policy. This was exacerbated by the some public attitude that interpreted democracy as mere interest-group advocacy (Jang *et al.*, 2002). A recently published paper vividly chronicles the prolonged and fierce opposition by certain community members to a proposed sports facility for the disabled on grounds of concern over the possible drop in property price in the neighborhood. The author of the study castigated the phenomenon as 'collective selfishness' disguised as 'rights advocacy' (Kim, 2009a). An exasperated human rights activist even suggested that 'Human rights movement no longer deserves its name sake; it is now indistinguishable from material-interest movement' (Oh *et al.*, 2007: 18).

The concurrent expansion of the human rights movement and the proliferation of rights claims of all sorts have left significant impacts on the direction of post-democratization democracy in Korea. On the one hand, the closely intertwined discourse of democracy and human rights in the past was gradually and progressively separated. The hyphenated collocation of 'democracy-human rights' became increasingly less used as the governments of Kim Dae-Jung and Roh Moo-Hyun broadened the democratic constituencies. While debate on democracy was increasingly replaced by talks about 'post-democracy', human rights discourse was increasingly fragmented into myriad 'issue fightings' without much interconnecting common fabric linking the whole human rights community (weakening of 'vertical dimension' of human rights). The trend was somewhat slowed down only after the advent of Lee Myung-Bak government when some sections of the population came to perceive that the retreat of democratic practices went hand in hand with gradual but inexorable chipping away of human rights. On the other hand, the grossly amplified rights claims and the public's general assertiveness may have helped steer the country's democracy away from a more inclusive, deliberative model toward something of a 'direct action democracy' model (cf. Carter, 2005). The raised visibility and normalization of interest-group politics had far more affinity with the counter-discourse of human rights than with the traditional discourse. The proliferation also allowed an opening of a political window through which the counter-discourse was able to argue forcefully for more possessive rights and for the inherent right to pursue one's material gain under the banner of 'rugged individualism' and 'rational' self-seeking.

Domination of the neoliberal economic trend

The radical shift toward the neoliberal economic paradigm in the last two decades in Korea was perhaps the most important structural factor for the differing evolution of human rights concepts after democratization. The response of the traditional human rights movement to this economic shift was by and large critical and resistant. One common theme which ran through the whole debate was the effect of globalization on poverty and widening inequality. In this regard Lim's (2006) assertion that human rights movement must be first and foremost a fight against poverty in a rapidly globalizing era was testament to a paradigm shift from the pre-democratization era when the human rights struggle was exclusively an antithesis of authoritarian rule in a political sense. This shift in emphasis is clearly observable from the human rights community. A survey of human rights NGOs in Korea revealed that the primary focus of their activity at the time of investigation was to expose the extent to which people suffered in the wake of economic crisis, that human rights NGOs engaged in efforts to bring international pressure to bear on the government to solve problems related to poverty, and that the NGOs called for necessary measures to establish social welfare safety net for those who are most at risk (Kim, 2004). Irregular workers usually comprised the largest portion of those who were legally sanctioned against the backdrop of flexible labor policy, strict adherence to law-and-order policy and alleged bias of prosecutorial power (Lee, 2006). It is noteworthy that women in particular are found to have been subject to multiple suffering under globalization condition, which is more gender-specific and more discriminatory (Shim, 2006). Moreover, South Korea is no exception in terms of exploitation of women through human trafficking in a more globalized world. This was compounded by a geo-political situation of the country where large-scale US troops are stationed. The influx of women into these military bases from places like the Philippines and former Soviet republics made the already unbearable condition of women more internationalized and more difficult to contain (Lee, 2004a). Related to this there has also been a surge in interest within human rights community on the rights-based corporate social accountability (Cho, 2008a).

One of the most interesting aspects of neoliberal globalization in relation to human rights is that it has actively been engaged in formulating a more proactive, coherent counter-discourse of human rights. The new counter-discourse claimed that free market alone could deliver true fulfillment of human rights through encouragement of the individual's competitive instinct and the unprecedented material improvement. This kind of 'possessive human rights' concept had as its central tenet the principle of property rights from which flows the notion of other rights. Another notable development was the specific application of legal logic to support the neoliberal concept of human rights. This was one of those classical examples where neoliberal predominance was given intellectual justification (Cho, 2008b, Park, 2008; and for a more critical understanding see Park, 2007). The impetus for a vigorous counter-conceptualization of human rights mainly came from the business-related associations such as the Federation of Korean Industries and economists of neoliberal leaning. It should be made clear that this 'minimalist' understanding of human rights not only is not conducive to the accepted consensus on the inclusive 'indivisibility' principle of human rights, but also refuses to acknowledge the norms and standards of the International Covenant on Economic and Social Rights that South Korea had ratified in the early 1990s.

The North Korean human rights issue

Interest in and publicity about the human rights situation in North Korea started to take a clearer shape in the 1990s when a series of famines struck the country with devastating results including deaths, starvation, chronic malnutrition, diseases like tuberculosis, displaced people and 'economic refugees'. The plight of North Koreans seeking food and shelter in Northeast China was put on the international agenda, and North Korean refugees coming to and settling in South Korea have become a normal part of social life here. Alongside this phenomenon of humanitarian nature emerged sketches of human rights atrocities inside North Korea that echoed familiar repertoire of totalitarian repression such as surveillance and control of population, labor camps for political prisoners and a very low level of citizens' liberty. The North Korean human rights situation has become one of the most fiercely debated subjects in South Korea in the last several years. The stark polarity in opinion on the issue means that even the very basic aspect of the debate has not been agreed upon, let alone solved. The North Korean human rights issue has become an important horizontal element – an indispensable issue area within the whole gamut of human rights issues – for the counter-discourse. Indeed the counter-discourse took a firm shape as a visible alternative challenger to the traditional human rights movement through the North Korean human rights issue.

Based on normative arguments Kim (2005c, 2006b) usefully classified the main controversies surrounding the issue in three parts: first, a debate over primacy between human rights and sovereignty; second, a debate over priority of civil rights versus priority of the right to life; and, third, a debate over the relevance of individual human rights versus the significance of the right to peace. In each category there are disagreements between the traditional human rights movement and the new conservative human rights movement. In contrast to the case of neoliberal economic trend it was the new movement that took the active initiative on the North Korean case.

The new movement's proactive approach is well reflected in the sheer amount of literature it has generated. For example, Youn (2005) justifies an active outside intervention on North Korea with an analysis on forced labor camps for political prisoners. In the same vein Han (2006) describes human rights violation in all its forms in North Korea including abuses in civil and political rights as well as arbitrary deprivation of people's right to feed themselves. Huh (2005) is scathing about the lack of sufficient public concern over the North Korean human rights situation and suggests that the more attention it receives the more likely it could be improved. For those who are taking a hard-line stance and who are supportive of North Korea's democratization, a regime change approach appears to be virtually the only solution for improving the human rights situation in the country. Another characteristic of the new movement is that it often describes itself as an internationalist in that it regards international intervention (American assistance and involvement in particular) as an integral part of any solution (Kim, 2005a, 2005b) and that it seems to believe in the ultimate effectiveness of external coercion and pressure (Kim, 2008). The new human rights movement's stance may have been bolstered by the George W. Bush administration's equally hard-line policy toward North Korea (Kim, 2006a). Those who are major actors in raising North Korean human rights issues comprise a small number of long-standing human rights groups, the so-called New Right Movement, some church-supported NGOs, some right-wing media and intellectuals with neoconservative views.

The response of the traditional human rights movement to the North Korean human rights issue was by and large the opposite to that of the new movement. The former considers sovereignty of North Korea as an important starting point of the debate, thereby rejecting external intervention as dangerous and ineffective, emphasizes the right to survival and right to peace, believes that reports of human rights situation in North Korea tends to be exaggerated or inaccurate, regards the United States as the problem-giver in the first place rather than the problem-solver (Kang, 2005), and finds solution in the form of humanitarian assistance, more cooperation between the two Koreas and reconciliation. It must be noted, however, that the traditional human rights movement has been criticized as having acted with a double standard that it did not take as universal and principled stand toward North Korea as it had done toward authoritarian rule in South Korea in the past. This does not necessarily mean that there is no interest or concern from its side; the reverse may be true (cf. Suh, 2007). But critics of the traditional human rights movement point out that its problem lies in its general reluctance to face up to the reality, let alone confront the problem, with its usual vigor and moral fortitude.

Two concepts of human rights

As has been explained, by the time the military dictatorship came to an end the concept of human rights in Korea was almost always associated with democracy and pro-democracy movement at the time; human rights were indeed seen to have a collocated relationship with democracy both as a qualifier of and as a catalyst for democracy (Cho, 2002, 2006). This line of interpretation was within the firm grasp of traditional pro-democracy human rights movement. The experience of last 20 years, however, has changed the rather monistic approach of the traditional human rights discourse. But at the same time an alternative discourse of human rights, which had originally started as a justificatory rhetoric of conservative ideology, has risen to some prominence, after having reinvented itself as a distinctive, if idiosyncratic, voice of human rights from a right-wing perspective. Therefore, it may be possible to claim that there now exist two rather diametrically placed conceptions of human rights in contemporary Korea.

It has been argued that the reason for and process of the emergence of two different concepts of human rights can be attributed to the four contingent developments in the intervening years. The parameters have helped redefine conceptual contours of the traditional human rights movement and have also allowed room for a new concept of human rights to emerge. Owing to the institutionalization of human rights the traditional discourse has had to formalize and rationalize its concept of human rights according to rules and regulations of the official governing structure. The institutionalization has also enabled the counter-discourse to attack the traditional discourse not on the basis of human rights principles per se but of political accountability, thereby securing some foothold for its own existence. The expansion of human rights issue areas and the concurrent proliferation of rights claims steered the traditional discourse away from the correlative twin concept of 'rights-duty' toward the concept of de-monopolizing vested interests at all levels, creating a whole new set of human rights movements which are civil society-led and 'maximalist' in character. Interest groups of all kinds quickly took advantage of the situation the proliferation of rights claim created, adding additional voice to the self-seeking rights concept of the counter-discourse. The neoliberal economic paradigm triggered the traditional discourse's deeper and broader commitment to economic rights and social justice, while the paradigm provided the counter-discourse with a stimulus to formulate a 'minimalist' human rights concept along the lines of a 'free market plus law-and-order' model, thereby furnishing a vertical dimension of human rights of its own. The North Korean human rights issue has left the traditional discourse with an obvious lacuna in terms of an important issue area within the 'horizontal' dimension of human rights movements. The deficit has also left a distorting impact on the hitherto 'universal' human rights concept of the traditional discourse. The counter-discourse has vigorously pushed the North Korean issue into the international as well as domestic human rights agenda, justifying it as one of the most urgent human rights issues of our time.

The corollary of this differing evolution of human rights discourse is a clear bifurcation between the two seemingly irreconcilable concepts, i.e. the maximalist, civil society-oriented concept versus the minimalist, illiberal, internationalist human rights concept. Therefore it may well be that the future of human rights in Korea will be dependent, at least partly, on the interaction and rivalry of the two alternative human rights concepts, and on their future evolutionary trajectory.

References

Ahn, Kyong-hwan and Bok-Hee Jang, eds. 2002. *Conscientious Objection*. Seoul: Saram-saenggak.

Amnesty International. 1986. *South Korea: Violations of Human Rights*. London: AI.

Asia Watch Committee. 1987. *A Stern, Steady Crackdown: Legal Process and Human Rights in South Korea*. Washington, DC: Asia Watch Committee.

Carter, April. 2005. *Direct Action and Democracy Today*. Cambridge: Polity.

Cha, Seon-Ja. 2005. 'Discrimination and human rights protection of women with disabilities'. *Journal of Civil Law* 13(2): 133–166.

Cho, Hee-Yeon. 2000. 'Democratic transition and institutional politics, people politics and citizen politics'. *Economy and Society* 46: 170–198.

Cho, Hyo-Je. 2002. 'Human rights in Korea at the crossroads: A critical overview'. *Korea Journal* 42(1): 204–227.

Cho, Hyo-Je. 2006. 'Human rights as a qualifier and a catalyst for Korea's democracy'. H.M. Hsiao, ed., *Asian New Democracies: The Philippines, South Korea and Taiwan Compared*, pp. 179–204. Taipei: Taiwan Foundation for Democracy Foundation.

Cho, Hyo-Je. 2008a. 'A preliminary study on human rights-based corporate social accountability'. *Journal of Asiatic Studies* 51(3): 128–160.

Cho, Jae Hyun. 2008b. 'The comment on function and role of National Human Rights Commission of Korea'. *Korean Constitutional Law* 14(2): 67–97.

Cho, Kum-Ju. 2007. 'Outcome of surveys on human rights of middle and high school students in 2006'. *Korean Journal of Youth Studies* 14(3): 189–216.

Fraser, Nancy and Axel Honneth. 2003. *Redistribution or Recognition? A Political-Philosophical Exchange*. London: Verso.

Gray, Kevin. 2004. 'The "underclass" of migrant workers in Korea'. *Journal of Asiatic Studies* 116: 97–128.

Han, Ki-Hong. 2006. 'Human rights situation in North Korea'. *Philosophy and Reality* 68: 80–91.

Hong, Seok-Joon and Jung-Hyeun Sung. 2003. 'A study on the self-identity and human rights of women with disabilities: focused on construction of group identity as community and human rights'. *Asian Women* 42: 47–83.

Huh, Man-Ho. 2005. 'Should we keep silent about human rights issues in North Korea'. *North Korea* 407: 67–74.

Jang, Sang-chul, Hyo-Je Cho, Sang-Pil Park, and Won-Oh Chung. 2002. 'Democratization and interest groups: State, non-profit organization, and social capital'. *Trends and Perspectives* 54: 156–185.

Ju, Seong-Young. 2007. 'No justification of existence for the National Human Rights Commission'. *Korean Unification* 1: 76.

Jung, Keun-Sik. 2006. 'Dissolution of settlement village and network of migration in Hansen's Disease ex-patient communities'. *Society and History* 69: 43–81.

Kang, Jeong-koo. 2005. 'Responsibility of the U.S.A. for the human rights problems in North Korea'. *Reunification of Korea* 259: 68–71.

Kim, Jong-il. 2005a. 'Human rights situation in North Korea and international society 1'. *North Korea* 400: 152–157.

Kim, Jong-il. 2005b. 'Human rights situation in North Korea and international society 2'. *North Korea* 401: 122–127.

Kim, Jong-il. 2008. 'Human rights situation in North Korea cannot be achieved without its regime change'. *North Korea* 434: 94–103.

Kim, Ki-Sup. 2009a. 'Collective selfishness shown to the construction of a sports facility for the disabled'. *Korea Journal of Sports Science* 18(3): 359–369.

Kim, Nyung. 2004. 'Neo-liberalism, poverty, and the role of human rights NGOs in Korea'. *Korean Journal of Humanities and the Social Sciences* 93: 67–99.

Kim, Sang Kyum. 2009b. 'A study on human rights of student athletes and on the protection of educational right'. *Sports and Law* 12(1): 11–34.

Kim, Su-am. 2006a. 'Bush administration's human rights policy on North Korea'. *Korean Journal of Political and Diplomatic History* 27(2): 345–372.

Kim, Woen Sick. 2005c. 'The situation and prospect of discourse on North Korean human rights'. *Society and Philosophy* 9: 99–129.

Kim, Woen Sick. 2006b. 'The examination of normative arguments in the discourse on North Korean human rights'. *North Korean Studies Review* 10(1): 75–95.

Kwon, In-Sook. 2009. 'Analysis of sexuality within the army, focusing on sexual desire, masculinity and homosexuality'. *Economy and Society* 82: 38–65.

Lee Cheol-ho. 2007a. 'The Mental Health Law and the human rights of persons with medical disorders'. *Korean Constitutional Law* 13(4): 229–258.

Lee, Gwang-Ryol. 2006. 'Human rights of imprisoned workers and democracy in Korea'. *Situation and Labor* 17: 97–105.

Lee, Ho Jung. 2007b. 'Five years of Korean national human rightscommission: evaluation and prospect; effects and limits of policy recommendations of NHRCK-focused on the effects to the criminal justice system'. *Democracy and Law* 33: 59–91.

Lee, Jung Ok. 2004a. 'The globalization of human rights and the human security of women in sex industry'. *Korean Journal of Women's Studies* 20(1): 195–227.

Lee, Kye-su. 2005. 'Premodern military culture and human rights of the soldier'. *Democratic Law Studies* 28: 160–180.

Lee, Nam-seok. 2004b. *Conscientious Objection and Civil Disobedience*. Seoul: Greenbee.

Lee, Young-Hee. 2004c. 'Democratization and social conflicts: focusing on social conflicts and public policies'. *Trend and Prospect* 61: 36–67.

Lim, Chae-Hong. 2006. 'Poverty and human rights'. *Yeungnam Law Journal* 12(1): 45–58.

Nam, Chan-sop. 2007. 'The meaning and main contents of the act to prohibit discriminating against people with disabilities'. *Health and Welfare Forum* 127: 23–33.

Oh, Wan-Ho, Min-shik Choi, Yong-mok Kim, Sang-woo Park and Chang-soo Lee. 2007. 'Human rights movements at local level'. *Human Rights* 1: 17–20.

Park, Rae-Goon. 2007. 'Neoliberalism, collapse of the state of rule of law and human rights movement'. *Radical Review* 34: 10–25.

Park, Cheoll. 2008. 'Rule of law and economic development'. *Justice* 106: 39–79.

Ranard, Donald L. 1980. 'Korea, human rights and United States foreign policy'. Tom J. Farer, ed., *Toward a Humanitarian Diplomacy: A Primer for Policy*, pp. 177–226. New York: New York University Press.

Seo, Dong-Jin. 2005. 'Human rights, citizenship and sexuality'. *Economy and Society* 67: 66–87.

Seol, Dong-Hoon. 2005. 'Migrant workers and human rights'. *Democracy and Human Rights* 5(2): 39–77.

Shim, Young-Hee. 2006. 'Globalization and women's security in Korea'. *Gender and Society* 5: 11–52.

Suh, Bo-Hyuk. 2007. *North Korean Human Rights: Theory, Practice and Policy*. Seoul: Hanul.

Yoo, Seong Ho and Sun A. Kang. 2008. 'Nursing home staff's knowledge on the 2004 revised Older Koreans Act for elder abuse, reports of elder abuse and attitudes about sanctioning mandatory reporters'. *Social Welfare Policy* 33: 311–333.

Youn, Hwang. 2005. 'An analysis on the realities of human rights policy and prison camps of the political criminals in North Korea'. *Reunification Strategy* 5(2): 172–228.

9 A frame analysis of women's policies of Korean government and women's movements in the 1980s and 1990s

Kyounghee Kim

Introduction

Since the early 1990s, gender equality has become a major social policy issue in Korea as well as in the international society. In Korea, a number of unprecedented developments have since been made by gender policies, including the establishment of the Ministry of Gender Equality and positions of officers in charge of women's policies in other ministries. At the same time, the women's movement, which started as part of the democratization movement in the 1980s, has shifted the focus of its agenda to such women-specific goals as equal opportunity for employment, maternity protection, and women's human rights, among other issues. It has also begun to participate in institutional politics, abandoning its previously antagonistic attitude toward the state.

Until the early 1990s, the government had little concern with women's policies. Women's issues that were dealt with in the National Assembly were mostly related to the mobilization of female manpower for economic development, birth control as part of the population policy, and using housewives as volunteers in society. The women's movement did not look to the state for any substantial solution to women's problems. Instead, it tended to criticize the idea of formal equality before the law. However, since the beginning of the 1990s, the state has been recognized as an arena in which to find a solution to women's problems. The government and the women's movement are both working to achieve equality de facto.

Gender equality, the proclaimed goal of women's policies in Korea, is clearly expressed in the government's policies on women and it is the major agenda of the women's movement. However, even though the government and the women's movement employ the same terminology, an analysis has yet to be undertaken to examine how each group uses the language in formulating women's policies. Existing studies on the relationship between women's policies and the women's movement focus on the extent of legitimacy the state and the women's movement have in politics and their impact on forming women's policies (Kim 2000a; Kim 2000b; Jeong 1993; Ji and Gang 1988). Especially when it comes to women's policies which deal with issues specific to women, most research has concentrated on the form in which such policies are legislated.

Consequently, it has been difficult to identify the gap and tensions that exists between the formal political discourse of the state and the policy discourse of women's movements.

In this context, by undertaking a frame analysis of the paradigm change in women's policies of both the government and women's movements in the 1980s and 1990s, the present study will examine the formulation and characteristics of the women's agendas in Korea. A frame, as a central idea or "plot" that gives meaning to an event or an issue which is still unfolding, provides a position from which to suggest policy responses and direction in dealing with that issue. A collective action frame in social movements accounts for the causes of injustices which engender collective sufferings and the alternatives to them while interconnecting various experiences into a coherent point of view. It is formed within political, social, and cultural contexts through the strategies, tactics, and organizational methods of social movement organizations (Snow and Benford 1988, 1992; Snow *et al.* 1986).

In general, the frames of policies and social issues are not different from those of social movements in their concepts and characteristics. Existing methods of policy analysis have largely been concerned with the examination of legal bills or statutes. These methods are limited in that they have no choice but to deal with a few legal bills and their provisions at face value. In contrast, by organizing and clustering into packages ideas which are associated with a particular issue, the frame analysis can reveal the key ideas which give meanings to a series of events or speeches (Gamson and Modigliani 1989).

The present study attempts to analyze frames of the government and the women's movement revolving around women's policy issues by comparing the 1980s and the 1990s.

Data

In examining frames of women's policy issues of the women's movement, this study focuses on activities of the Korea Women's Associations United (KWAU) and analyzes the proceedings of its regular general meetings and its periodical *Minju Yeoseong* [Democratic Women]. The progressive women's organizations in Korea formed the KWAU as a national association of 21 women's organizations in 1987, contributed to the June democratization movement, and led women's movements in the 1990s with the issues of women's right to lifelong work, maternity protection, the elimination of sexual violence, national unification, comfort women, and politics of everyday life.

For the frame of the government's official policies on women, I analyzed the records of the National Assembly. The analysis uses speeches delivered on women at the regular plenary sessions from 1981 to 1999 National Assembly. Since the National Assembly is Korea's most important legislative institution, it is indispensable to the study of the policy-making process and the formation of discourse. The data for this study were obtained by searching the database of the National Assembly Library for all the records which include the word "women."

A total of 235 cases have been established by classifying the contents of speeches according to the themes they deal with and counting each theme as a case. Here the records of women's affairs are roughly classified into family, labor, sexuality, welfare, and politics, for each of which specific issues are further identified. A frame can then be constructed by picking out the key ideas which underlie the specific issues. In addition, by quantifying how often a particular issue is brought up, I perform a content analysis to determine the tendency of increase or decrease of support for a particular package of ideas in each period.

Women's policy frame of the government

Development approach to women's agenda in 1980s

The results of the content analysis of policy agendas on women at the National Assembly are provided in Table 9.1. It shows that in the 1980s the government had no positive perception of women's policies, and women's agendas in the National Assembly were very few in number when compared to the 1990s.[1] Among the total of 235 cases, 50 speeches were delivered in the 1980s, which amounts to about one-fourth of the 185 speeches that were delivered in the 1990s (see Table 9.1 and Figure 9.1). Among the specific issues discussed in the National Assembly: tele-work and maternity leave in the area of labor, the family law and the amendment of tax laws in the area of family, unemployed female heads of households and pensions in the area of welfare, femininity in the area of sexuality, and women drafted by Japanese military for sexual slavery, are new issues that have emerged in the 1990s (see Figure 9.2).

In the 1980s, women-related policies of the government were dominated by the population policy centered around birth control and the labor policy about utilization of female labor. Because there were no institutions to take full charge of women's affairs, the government was not able to carry out consistent policies for women. Nevertheless, the United Nations' (UN) policy orientation and

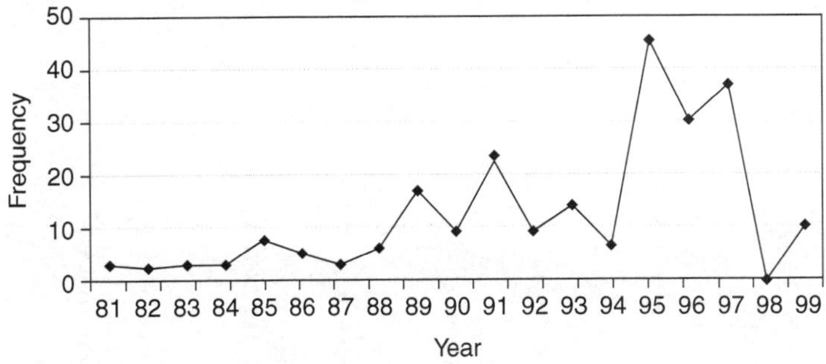

Figure 9.1 The trend of women-related issues discussed at the regular plenary sessions of the National Assembly by year.

Table 9.1 Women-related issues discussed at the regular plenary sessions of the National Assembly, by year and by issue

Issues	*1981*	*1982*	*1983*	*1984*	*1985*	*1986*	*1987*	*1988*	*1989*	*1990*	*1991*	*1992*	*1993*	*1994*	*1995*	*1996*	*1997*	*1998*	*1999*	*Total*
Labor																				
Utilization of female manpower	1	–	1	1	1	1	–	–	2	1	7	2	1		5	1	4	–	1	29
Discrimination in employment	–	–	–	–	2	1	2	2	9	2	4	2	7	5	3	3	–	–	1	43
Expansion of nursing facilities	–	–	–	–	–	–	1	–	3	3	6	1	3	2	5	2	4	–	1	32
Maternity protection	–	–	–	–	–	–	–	–	–	–	–	–	–	–	2	1	1	–	–	4
Public work, volunteering service	–	–	–	–	–	–	–	–	1	1	1	–	1	–	–	–	–	1	1	6
Value of domestic labor	–	–	–	–	–	–	–	2	–	–	–	–	–	–	–	–	1	–	–	3
Tele-work	–	–	–	–	–	–	–	–	–	–	–	–	–	–	–	1	1	–	–	2
Maternity leave	–	–	–	–	–	–	–	–	–	–	–	–	–	–	–	1	–	–	1	2
Family																				
The Family Law, Amendment of Tax Laws	–	–	–	–	–	–	–	–	–	1	1	–	–	–	1	1	–	–	–	4
Population control	1	–	1	–	–	1	–	–	–	–	–	–	–	–	–	–	–	–	–	3
Disproportion of two sexes	–	–	–	–	1	–	–	–	–	–	–	–	–	–	1	1	2	–	–	5
Welfare																				
Unemployed heads of households	–	–	–	–	–	–	–	–	–	–	–	–	–	–	1	1	1	–	1	4
Pension for women	–	–	–	–	–	–	–	–	–	–	–	–	–	–	–	–	2	–	–	2
Women's quality of life	–	–	–	–	–	–	–	–	1	–	–	1	–	–		1	–	–	–	3

Politics																				
Low political participation	–	–	–	–	4	–	–	–	1	–	1	1	–	–	2	2	4	–	1	16
Quota system	–	–	–	–	–	–	–	–	–	–	–	–	–	–	1	3	1	–	–	5
Ratification by the UN	–	–	–	1	–	2	–	–	–	–	–	–	–	–	2	–	–	–	–	5
Establishment of women's institutions	–	2	–	–	–	–	–	1	–	1	1	–	–	–	3	–	–	–	–	8
Ten major tasks	–	–	–	–	–	–	–	–	–	–	–	–	–	–	4	–	2	–	–	6
Abasement of women by National Assembly Members	–	–	–	–	–	–	–	–	–	–	–	–	–	–	–	1	2	–	2	5
Sexuality																				
Unmarried mother, prostitutions	–	–	–	1	–	–	–	1	–	–	2	1	–	–	1	1	–	–	1	8
Prevention of sexual violence	–	–	–	–	–	–	–	–	–	–	–	–	1	–	1	–	–	–	–	2
Sexual morals	–	–	–	–	–	–	–	–	–	–	–	–	–	–	–	3	4	–	–	7
Views on women																				
Feminity	–	–	–	–	–	–	–	–	–	–	–	–	–	–	8	4	1	–		13
Socially vulnerable women	–	–	1	–	–	–	–	–	–	–	–	–	1	–	3	–	4	–	1	11
Thoughtless women	–	–	–	–	–	–	–	–	–	–	–	–	–	–	–	1	1	–	–	2
Comfort women	–	–	–	–	–	–	–	–	–	–	–	–	–	–	2	2	1	–	–	5
Total	3	2	3	3	8	5	3	6	17	9	23	9	14	7	45	31	37	–	10	235
	50									185										

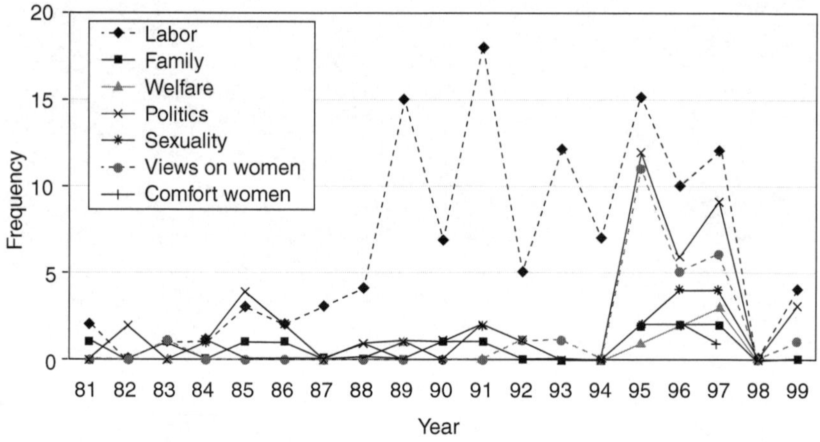

Figure 9.2 The trend of specific issues on women discussed at the regular plenary sessions of the National Assembly by year.

programs for women greatly affected the endeavors to make the problem of women a policy issue in Korea in the 1980s. As is shown in the analysis of the records of the National Assembly, the UN project of women's development and the ratification of international treaties were the two major sources of external pressure which the Korean government could not avoid. Proclaiming the year of 1975 as World Women's Year, the UN adopted the Women in Development (WID) approach to help solve women's problems by undertaking various projects for women's development throughout the 1980s. WID paid attention to the role of women alienated during the course of economic development in developing countries and recognized them as a resource that can be used for economic growth (Moser 1993; Miller and Razavi 1998). In this context, certain progress – such as the establishment of the Korean Women's Development Institute in 1983, the setting up of the Basic Plan on Women's Development in 1985, and the amendment of the Mother and Child Health Act in 1986 – was made which brought women's issues to the level of policy discourse under the agenda of women's development. However, such women-related organizations were isolated from the center of policymaking and implementation and their budgets occupied less than 1 percent of the total budget.

In particular, the demands women made during the course of the constitutional amendment and the struggle for democratization in 1987 compelled the government to stress the prohibition of discrimination against women in the economic sphere, the pursuit of women's welfare and the protection of maternity in its policymaking. During this period, the government set the goal of women's policies at the abstract level of "Co-participation of Men and Women, Co-responsibility for Society" (Second Minister of Political Affairs 1998). However, with the increase of women's participation in economic activities and the expansion of the women's movement, the Office of the Second Minister of State for Political Affairs was launched as the administrative organization to deal with the affairs of women. Major women's policies formulated in this period include the enactment of the Gender Equality Employment Act in 1987 and its amendment in 1989 and the enactment of the Mother and Fatherless Child Welfare Act in 1989 (Kim 2000b).

All-inclusive but not enough for realizing gender equality in the 1990s

In the 1990s, women's policies eventually became all-inclusive and comprehensive for the realization of gender equality.

Among the specific issues discussed in the National Assembly, tele-work and maternity leave in the area of labor, the family law and the amendment of tax laws in the area of family, unemployed heads of households and pensions in the area of welfare, femininity in the area of sexuality and comfort women are new issues that have emerged in the 1990s (see Table 9.1).

The Kim Young-sam government (1993–1997) appointed three female ministers and a female vice-minister, set up the office of a secretary of political affairs in charge of women under the secretariat of the President, and established the Special Committee on Women's Affairs in the National Assembly for the legislation of women's policies. It also launched the Globalization Promotion Committee and included women's issues in its ten priority tasks. It amended the Gender Equality Employment Act in 1995 and thereby prohibited the recruitment or employment of women on the basis of physical features, and enacted the Act on the Punishment of Sexual Crimes and Protection of Victims in 1994 (Namnyeo pyeongdeung-eul wihan gyosu mo-im 1994). By adopting the idea of gender mainstreaming in 1995, the major international strategy for women's policies, the government enacted the Framework Act on Women's Development which has been the basis for carrying out systematic women's policies above and beyond those of the 1980s. In the Framework Act, the basic objectives of women's policies are the realization of gender equality, the promotion of women's participation in society, and the enhancement of women's welfare. Based on the Framework Act, the government set up the First Basic Plan for 1998–2002 and selected 20 major tasks (Second Minister of Political Affairs 1998; Kim 1996).

While the women's policies of the 1990s reached a considerable level of formality, we can find certain tendencies in the ways in which women-related problems are understood.

First, with respect to the area of labor, women's economic activities tend to be seen in terms of using human resources to increase national competitiveness. This policy frame has been consistently sustained from the 1980s through to the 1990s. The following speech supports this point: "By expanding opportunities for employment for women including housewives, it can facilitate women's employment and help solve the problem of high wage, such that it will relieve corporations of the wage burden" (October 30, 1996, Korean National Assembly Record). In the records of the National Assembly of the 1990s, the end of discrimination in employment and the expansion of childcare facilities are seen as important for increasing female participation in the workplace. Beginning from the 1990s, maternity protection (maternity leave), public work and volunteering services, tele-work, and flexible work have been proposed as ways to increase female participation in the labor market. The methods proposed to use the female workforce tend to draw a line between employed and unemployed women (or housewives). They suggest that unemployed women should be used in unpaid volunteer services or group activities. Also, the use of the female workforce in the 1990s is compared to the aged and the disabled who have been alienated from the labor market, as well as to immigrant workers. The analysis of the records of the National Assembly shows that discussion expanding women's employment only in terms of using female workforce are not necessarily conducive to solving the fundamental obstacles to women's economic participation – the age-old practice of discriminating against women.

Second, an analysis of the records indicates that from the end of the 1980s the National Assembly has intermittently raised the issue of women's welfare, particularly in relation to those who need protection from the government. In the 1990s, the issue begins to be brought up in terms of globalization and quality of life – the government's basic policy orientation. The welfare issue related to women is still monopolized by speeches about women who need social protection, such as prostitutes and low-income women, whereas the welfare of women in general is mentioned mainly in speeches which concern social insurance. What is to be noted in this regard is that women's mental health is being raised as an issue. With no doubt it is a new issue when we consider that the issue of welfare has up to now focused on the material side of social life. The welfare of rural women who have been marginalized in women's policies is also being raised.

Third, the political issues related to women are dominated by speeches about improving women's low political representation and status that are little more than mere rhetoric. As a means of rectifying the low political representation of women, the establishment of an institution in charge of women's policies and the adoption of the quota system are most frequently mentioned in the National Assembly. There are virtually no remarks that try to describe the significance of the low political representation of women's matters and why it should be rectified.

Fourth, the policy frame of family stresses family as a unit of social reproduction and support: "The basic unit for community is family. It is in the framework of a warm family that the happiness of youth, housewives and the elderly people should be fostered" (October 22, 1996, Korean National Assembly Record); "The problem of the elderly suffering dementia is aggravated by the spread of nuclear and small-size families, the employment of women, the weakening of the traditional filial piety toward parents and the elderly, etc." (July 7, 1999, Korean National Assembly Record). Besides, the population policy which gave priority to birth control in the 1970s and 1980s has now begun to shift because of the disproportionate gender ratio resulting from the preference of sons and the decline of the childbirth rate.

Finally, speeches on sexuality delivered at the National Assembly have concerned the following issues: unmarried mothers and prostitutes, sexual violence, and the corruption of sexual morals. Among the three, the first two are considered the consequences of the degradation of sexual morals. The following speech shows the frame of the sexuality-related agenda: "Since prevention goes first before anything else, it is necessary to cure our social ills and establish a morally healthy society" (July 12, 1995, Korean National Assembly Record). The images of women at the National Assembly are discriminating against mothers, sound working women, women as a socially vulnerable group who need protection, those who are blamed for familism and overconsumption, and others.

When women's agendas are clustered according to policy frames, women's policies of the 1980s and those of the 1990s exhibit differences in content but are almost identical in terms of policy frames (see Table 9.2).

Table 9.2 Frames of women's policies observed in the National Assembly plenary sessions

Areas	*The 1980s to 1990s*
Labor and economy	Policy frame: utilization of female labor for national competitiveness • Diagnosis: inequality and discrimination in employment • Prescription: tele-work and part-time work, volunteering services of unemployed housewives, public work
Sexuality	Policy frame: recovery of sexual ethics • Diagnosis: rapid increase of human traffic, sexual violence, unmarried mother, prostitutes, etc. • Prescription: strict regulations through women's policies for the recovery of sexual ethics
Family	Policy frame: reproduction and unit of support • Diagnosis: population growth as an obstacle to economic growth (1970s–1980s), preference of sons, disproportion of two sexes, decline of the childbirth rate (1990s) • Prescription: population control (1970s–1980s), enhancement of quality of population, amendment of tax laws (1990s)
Welfare	Policy frame: protection of socially vulnerable strata • Diagnosis: low-income single-mother family, prostituting and vagrant women • Prescription: public aid and social services for women who need protection
Politics	Policy frame: tokenism • Diagnosis: women's low political participation according to international standards • Prescription: establishment of institutions in charge of women's policies and adoption of the quota system

The only difference lies in the area of family: whereas policy in the 1980s concentrated on birth control since population growth was thought to be an obstacle to economic growth, its focus had shifted in the 1990s to the problem regarding the disproportion between the two sexes and the decline in the childbirth rate.

Although women's agendas proposed by the National Assembly have changed both in terms of quantity and diversity, they are not enough to achieve gender equality. The establishment of such institutional apparatuses as the Framework Act on Women's Development and the Gender Equality Employment Act has encouraged women's organizations to play the role of pressure groups to monitor the implementation of the laws since the early 1990s. Consequently, this has prevented women's policies from becoming perfunctory or ending up as nothing more than political slogans. Furthermore, the difference between the women's movement and the institutions in how they see the issue of women have always created tension or a conflict in the process of formulating women's policies.

Women's policy frame of the women's movement

Women's movements for democratization and working class in the 1980s

Given that the major social issues in the 1980s in Korea were the exclusionary and authoritarian rule of the military regimes, the grim reality of the divided nation, and the problem of working classes, issues concerning women were not primary. Under this circumstance, the women's movement was no exception in making social democratization, national autonomy, and people's acquisition of power as its own frame.

The Gwangju Uprising in 1980, the transfer of power to the Chun Doo-Whan regime, and strong anti-governmental struggles constituted the political background against which the working class-oriented women's movements came into existence. In particular, the appeasement policy of the Chun regime in 1983 provided more expanded political space for social movements than ever before (Jo 1990; Wells 1995). It is in this phase of appeasement that many women's movement organizations – such as the Alternative Culture, the Korea Women's Hot Line, the division of Women's Affairs of the United Front of Youths for the Democratization Movement, and the Women for Equality and Peace – were established. These organizations sought to distinguish themselves from the liberal women's movement centered around the Korean National Council of Women (Yi 1998; Yi 1994; Yi *et al.* 1989). Participants in those organizations were mainly women activists who had been engaged in the students' movement, women scholars who graduated from Ewha Womans University, social education trainees of the Christian Academy, and women worker activists of the 1970s.[2]

As the survival right of the urban poor and women workers became a social issue after 1984, the problem of working women emerged as an important agenda for the progressive women's movement and became a focal point around which different women's organizations began to consolidate (Jeong 1993). In pursuing women workers' rights, progressive women's organizations held the first Women's Conference in 1985 under the slogan of "women's movements along with nation, democracy and people" (Yi *et al.* 1998).

In the course of transition to democracy in 1987, the experience women had in participating in the social democratization movement brought into sharp relief the need for an independent and national association that could organize around various needs of women. In the political phase represented by the constitutional amendment, the political consciousness of the people in general was raised and a variety of issues that had never been raised before were brought to the attention of the public, including those related to female manufacturing and clerical women workers, housewives, sexual violence, religion, environment, and childcare. Taking advantage of the relatively open political atmosphere, 21 progressive women's groups formed a nationwide organization called the KWAU while a number of large and small organizations such as the Korea Womenlink came into existence (Yi *et al.* 1998).

However, the transition to democracy and the upsurge of the problem of women did not automatically bring a favorable situation to women. It was the old political forces that won most of the elections held in the process of transition to democracy. During this period, the KWAU still concentrated its efforts on the task of how to have many women participate in the democratization movement. Ever since its inception, it continued to join the national alliance for the democratization movement and to participate in demonstrations demanding Constitutional amendment in support of the direct election of the President.

The establishment of the military government elected by popular vote and the embarkment of the National Assembly in which the opposition commanded the majority, resulted in the enactment and reformation of women's policies, though in a way that was incomplete and distorted. In the late 1980s, the political activities of the KWAU were double-sided. Not only was it involved in the anti-governmental movement, but also at the same time that it strived for institutional changes and the legislation of women's demands (Yi *et al.* 1998).

Besides, the collapse of the Eastern Bloc began to undermine the legitimacy which Marxism and *Minjung* [people] ideology had enjoyed in Korea and, consequently, called into question socialist and Marxist feminism which constituted the theoretical basis of women's movements in Korea (Louie 1995; Sahoe-wa Sasang 1989).

This was because the women's movement, as part of the general political culture centered around democratization and anti-governmental movement at that time, revealed its limitations in gaining the trust of a larger segment of women, those beyond women workers and poor women. In this respect, the institutional politics and public policies were not regarded as a space for solving women's problems but rather as a target of criticism, while the government's policies for women were also largely perfunctory.

Transforming the frame of the women's movement and making women's agenda into policy in the 1990s

Women's rights were the frame of the progressive women's movement in the early 1990s. The frame was critically questioning the imperfect democracy, and the argument that equal citizenship was in fact based on the exclusion of and discrimination against women formed the core of the frame. This frame was intended to correspond to the interests of women in general through such issues as lifelong equal work, the protection of maternity, sexual violence as the violation of human rights, and pacifism of women.

Equal employment was raised as the issue of "women's right to lifelong work and the protection of maternity." Recognizing that childbirth and rearing were the main obstacles to women's social participation, which eventually led to gender inequality, the KWAU demanded the reevaluation of the protection of maternity, urged the public to consider the protection of maternity as a problem of labor, and took it as a means of securing the right to lifelong employment.[3] Protection and equality, which have always been the foci of debate in feminism, co-existed without a conflict in the discourse of women's rights of the KWAU. The concrete activities of the KWAU included the amendment of the Gender Equality Employment Act, the enactment of the Infant Care Act, the defense against the abolition of menstruation leave, and resistance to the enactment of the Act on Worker Dispatch System among others, most of which were intended to cope with the government's labor policies that were unfavorable to women.[4]

This discourse of women's rights corresponded to the needs and interests of women which became diversified after 1987 and, at the same time, fell within the contexts of international organizations like the UN and global feminism. With respect to the issues of protection and equality, the standards of international organizations played a role in justifying the discourse of women's rights.

The agenda of sexual violence, which was the priority project of the KWAU during 1992 through 1993, aimed at a social campaign for the elimination of sexual violence and the enactment of laws for its prevention. More specifically, this project aimed at the conversion of the existing conception of sexual violence, the loss of chastity and morality on the part of the victim, to the violation of human rights (Korean Women's Hot Line 1991). In order to achieve the enactment of laws concerning sexual violence, the KWAU organized an alliance among women. Taking advantage of the presidential election which was scheduled for this time, the enactment of the sexual violence prevention law was adopted as a campaign pledge by the presidential candidates. Although the issue of sexual violence had been raised ever since the establishment of the Korea Women's Hotline in 1983, the focus of concern shifted greatly in the 1980s. That is, the issue of sexual violence was extended to cover the experiences of women in general, going beyond the efforts to politicize it as a control mechanism used by the non-democratic government against women activists and workers or to utilize it as part of the anti-US cause for national autonomy.

After the establishment of the civilian government in 1993, the women's movement was dominated by the frame which adopted a "women's perspective" as a way of seeing society. This discourse marked a turning point from the frame of women's rights which had until then played a leading part, not only in changing social consciousness and government policies, but also in forming the identity of women in general in line with the broader popular trend toward feminism. In 1994, the KWAU redefined its own objectives as follows to promote cooperation and exchange between women's organizations and to bring about gender equality, women's welfare, democratization, and national unification. The programs which were designed to achieve these objectives, including lobbying for the enactment and improvement of laws and institutions for the promotion of women's rights and interests, programs for women's welfare and for women workers, and programs related to national unification, etc.[5] Breaking from the previous view of women as "those who are oppressed," the women's movement turned the focus of its concern to the role of women as "those who transform and create a new society".[6] The frame was well in accord with the social discourse on the quality of life and globalization as well as the women's policies of international institutions and global feminism. It was in the same context as the slogan for the Beijing World Conference on Women, "See the World with Women's Eyes."

Issues concerning the nation and national unification, which the progressive women's movement continued to raise, were also interpreted within the discourse of a woman's perspective. The programs for the national unification carried out by the women's movement organizations in the 1990s can be seen as the combination of the issues of gender and nation, through which the KWAU tried to demonstrate that the pacifism of women can contribute to the unification movement. They also further stressed the need for women to continue to participate in the movements for the nation and democratization.

The frame of women's perspective could expand itself socially and culturally by raising the issue of "everyday life politics." In 1994, the KWAU created a catch phrase, "Open Politics, Everyday Life Politics." Specifically targeting four local council elections held in 1995, it aimed at the political empowerment of women through politics in everyday life. Given that the political process in Korea was dominated by men, controlled by particular parties or groups, and that party politics was also based on a certain person or region, it was not easy for women to participate in politics. Under these circumstances, the KWAU saw participation in local councils as a relatively easier way to advance into the arena of politics.[7] "Everyday Life" politics was based on the view that all the problems which arose in the private sphere of women's everyday life could be politicized into social issues.

Frames of the women's movement were realized as the "politics of engagement" at the level of practical activities. The demands that had been since the early 1990s for the right to lifelong work, the elimination of sexual violence as the violation of human rights, and unification and democratization, materialized into specific policies through engagement in the institutional politics. These features show that the women's movement in the 1990s no longer saw the state as an antagonist, but as an arena where women's problems could be tackled. This change of perception facilitated the process of turning organizations of the women's movement into legal entities.

Whereas the women's movement until 1987 could be characterized as activists centered, it was transformed in the 1990s into diversified and professionalized movements that reflected various strata, concerns, and interests of women.

Conclusions

Women's policies in Korea up to the 1980s were largely determined from above. Since there have been few opportunities for realizing women's agenda via official channels, the women's movement itself has assumed the role of quasi-party and has thus contributed considerably to the development of women's policies in the 1990s. Women's policies, which have continued to be improved on since the mid-1990s, and the creation of institutions in charge of them in central and local governments, are valuable resources for the development of Korean women. In 1998, the Kim Dae-jung government established the Presidential Commission on Women's Affairs as the government institution in charge of coordinating women's policies. To strengthen the enforcement power of the Commission, it also appointed the officer in charge of women's policies within the six Ministries of Labor, Health and Welfare, Justice, Government Administration and Home Affairs, Agriculture and Forestry, and Education and Human Resources Development. In 2001, the Commission was transformed into an independent state institution, the Ministry of Gender Equality.

Under the Kim Dae-jung government, one of the most remarkable phenomena was the emergence of feminist bureaucrats and politicians who majored in women's studies and had activist experience in women's movements. However, they have been facing the task of a feminist way to engage in politics within the government (Kim 2000). In addition, as the women's movement led by the KWAU has begun to work under the banners of political engagement and gender mainstreaming since the 1990s, the relationship between the politics of engagement and alternative politics has become a point of issue (KWAU 2000).

Seen from the vantage point of the early 2000s, Korean society possesses such valuable resources as government organizations and feminist officials in charge of women's policies, laws and institutions for the implementation of women's policies, and the spread of women's movements. The future of gender politics surrounding women's policies in Korea depends on appropriately using these resources to achieve gender equality.

Notes

1 The data on 1998 and 1999 are missing or incomplete due to some difficulties involved in searching them. This can be attributed to the fact that the two consecutive years were the period of economic crisis during which it was difficult even to put women's issues on the agenda in the National Assembly. Therefore, the two years are not included in

the discussion of the results of analysis, but only their characteristics are briefly mentioned in the conclusion of this study.

2 Materials from the Christian Academy Study Group on Women and Society and *Yeoseong pyeong-u-hoe* [Women's Organization for Equality and Peace].

3 KWAU, *Minju Yeoseong* 9, 1990: 37.

4 KWAU, *Jeonggi chonghoe*, 1991.

5 KWAU, *Jeonggi chonghoe*, 1995.

6 *Minju Yeoseong* 18, 1995.

7 KWAU, *Minju Yeoseong* 17, 1994.

References

Christian Academy Study Group on Women and Society. *Yeoseong-gwa sahoe* [Women and Society]. Seoul, November 1978, December 1978, January 1979, February 1979, March to May 1979.

Gamson, William A. and Andre Modigliani. 1989. "Media Discourse and Public Opinion in Nuclear Power." *American Journal of Sociology* 95: 1–38.

Jeong, Hyeon-baek. 1993. "Peonhwahaneun segye-wa yeoseong haebang undongron-ui mosaek: seong-gwa gyegeup munje-reul jungsim-euro" [The Search for Feminist Theories in the Changing World: Focusing on the Issues of Gender and Class]. *Yeoseong-gwa sahoe* [Women and Society] 4: 138–165.

Ji, Eun-hi and I-su Gang. 1988. "Han'guk yeoseong yeon-gu-ui jaseongjeok pyeongga" [A Reflective Evaluation of Women's Studies in Korea]. In *80nyenodae inmunsahoegwahak-ui hyeondan-gye-wa jeonmang* [The Present State of the Human and Social Sciences in the 1980s and their Prospect]. Seoul: Yeoksa bipyeong-sa.

Jo, Hi-yeon. ed. 1990. *Han'guk sahoe undongsa* [The History of Korean Social Movements]. Seoul: Juksan.

Kim, Bok-gyu. 2000. "Urinara yeoseong jeongchaek-ui byeonhwa-wa baljeon gwaje" [Changes in Women's Policies of Korea and Tasks for Their Development]. Proceedings of the International Forum on the Government and Women's Participation, the Korean Association of Public Administration, Seoul.

Kim, Elim. 1996. *Yeoseong baljeon gibonbeop-ui naeyong-gwa gwaje* [The Contents and Tasks of the Framework Act on Women's Development]. Seoul: Korean Women's Development Institute.

Kim, Mi-gyeong. 2000. "Yeoseong jeongchaek-gwa jeongbu yeokhal-ui byeonhwa" [Women's Policies and the Changing Role of the Government]. Proceedings of the International Forum on the Government and Women's Participation, the Association of Korean Public Administration.

Korean Women's Associations United (KWAU) Special Committee for the Enactment of Laws on Sexual Violence. 1992. *Hyeonhaeng seongpokryeok gwanryeon beop mu-eot-i munjein-ga* [What are the Problems of the Current Laws on Sexual Violence]. Seoul: KWAU.

Korean Women's Associations United (KWAU). 2000. *Jeonggi chonghoe, 1990–2000* [Proceedings of the General Meetings, 1990–2000]. Seoul: KWAU.

Korean Women's Hot Line. 1991. *Seongpokryeok gwanryeon beop ipbeop-eul wihan gongcheonghoe jaryeojip* [Collected Materials of the Public Hearings for the Legislation of the Laws on Sexual Violence].

Louie, Miriam Ching Yoon. 1995. "Minjung Feminism: Korean Women's Movement for Gender and Class Liberation." *Women's Studies International Forum* 18: 417–430.

Miller, Carol and Shahra Razavi. 1998. "Gender Analysis: Alternative Paradigms." Gender in Development Monograph Series #6. Geneva: UNDP.

Moser, Caroline O. 1993. *Gender Planning and Development: Theory, Practice and Training*, Routledge: London and New York.

Namnyeo pyeongdeung-eul wihan gyosu mo-im [The Group of Professors for the Sexual Equality Employment]. 1994. *Jikjang nae seonghirong-eul eotteoke bol geot-in-ga? Seouldae seonghirong sageon-eul gyegi-ro* [How to Perceive the Sexual Harassment in Workplace? With the Case of Seoul National University as a Momentum]. Proceedings of the Forum on Sexual Equality Employment, Seoul.

Sahoe-wa sasang [Society and Thought]. 1989. *80 nyeondae sahoe undong nonjaeng* [The Controversies on Social Movement in the 1980s]. Seoul: Han-gil-sa.

Second Bureau of Political Affairs. 1998. *Yeoseong jeongchaek gibon gyehoek* [The Basic Plan on Women's Policies]. Seoul: Second Bureau of Political Affairs.

Snow, David A. and Robert D. Benford. 1988. "Ideology, Frame Resonance, and Participation Mobilization." *International Movement Research* 1: 197–217.

Snow, David A. and Robert D. Benford. 1992. "Master Frames and Cycles of Protests." In Aldon Morris and Carol M. Muller. eds. *Frontiers in Social Movement Theory*. New Haven, CT: Yale University Press.

Snow, David A., Burke Rochford Jr., Steven K. Worden, and Robert D. Benford. 1986. "Frame Alignment Processes, Micro Mobilization, and Movement Participation." *American Sociological Review* 51: 464–481.

Yi, Hyojae. 1989. *Han'guk-ui yeoseong undong* [Women's Movements in Korea: Yesterday and Today]. Seoul: Jeong-u-sa.

Yi, Mi-gyeong. 1998. "Yeosung undong –gwa minjuwha undong" [Women's Movement and Democratization Movement] in Yeosungdanche yeonhap. *Yeosungdanche sipnyunsa* [The History of the Korean Women's Association United 10 Years]. Seoul: Dongduk Women's University.

Yi, Seung-hi. 1994. *Yeoseong undong-gwa jeongchi iron* [Women's Movement and Political Theory]. Seoul: Nokdu.

Wells, Kenneth M. ed. 1995. *South Korea's Minjung Movement: The Culture and Politics of Dissidence*. Manoa, Center for Korean Studies: University of Hawaii Press.

10 The netizen movement

A new wave in the social movements of Korea

Jinsun Lee

Introduction

South Korea now leads the world in terms of Internet use, with 77.8 percent of the population identified as Internet users (KISA and KCC, 2010). Based on highly developed technological infrastructures, the Internet has been broadly used for progressive and oppositional civic actions and political campaigns in Korea since the 1990s. While a number of previous studies have analyzed the political uses of the Internet, most tend to focus more on the Internet as a "tool" of mobilization mainly adopted by "established institutions," including social movement organizations (SMOs) and political parties. But this tendency will likely to fail to explain new, significant phenomena arising in Internet-based activism fields.

Recent years have witnessed individual Internet users who, neither mediated nor mobilized by any specific political organizations, are increasingly involved in social movements. As Earl and Schussman (2003) assert, new media technologies have reduced the incentives of established activist groups, such as social movement organizations, allowing "movement entrepreneurs" to emerge as new agencies who act outside the framework of institutions. Movement entrepreneurs are defined as non-professional individuals "who are motivated by individual grievances to undertake social movement activity and who rely on their own skills to conduct their actions" (Garrett, 2006, p. 211). As individual actors emerge, new technologies affect the internal structures of social movements, particularly structures relating to decision making and leadership. In lieu of organizational membership and hierarchical leadership, ad hoc and discretionary decision making and horizontal leadership become paramount in this new mode of activism. These changes, in turn, inspire citizen participants to foster alternative political ideals influenced by the logic of peer-to-peer networking and decentralized nomadism (Juris, 2005).

This study approaches current social movements in Korea through the framework of the netizen movement. Netizens – most of whom maintain independence from institutionalized political groups, such as social movement organizations, labor unions, and political parties – have broken new ground of civic activism in Korea. This chapter delineates the historical context in which the Internet and new media have been adapted to progressive and oppositional civic actions, and furthermore examines the ways in which these new forms of civic action have reshaped the political and social landscape of Korea.

Korean netizens

Defining netizens

The neologism "netizen," a compound word of "Internet" and "citizen," broadly refers to "people who use the Internet for a certain purpose" (Lee Byoungkwan *et al.*, 2005). The definition of netizen, however, should be reconsidered in and tailored to specific cultural contexts. Hauben and Hauben (1997), who coined the term in their study on the impact of Usenet in the US, identified netizens as net users who are empowered by collecting, creating, and sharing information and knowledge with others, and who, at a grassroots level, help make the world a better place. In their view, the net – including Usenet, Free-Net, email, electronic newsletter, and the World Wide Web – is a "grand intellectual and social commune," which anybody on the globe can access "to improve the quality of human life" (p. 3). Their view, however, tends to overemphasize the technological advantages of the net, neglecting what helps to situate, create, and develop the *online citizenship* of Internet users in specific historical and political context. To understand the varying meanings of the netizen, which may differ under relativistic conditions, one should examine the political and historical background where online citizenship is constructed.

In Korea, the netizen has diverse connotations. By netizens, some people refer to Internet-based protesters that are radical, "irresponsible, and inadvertent" (Lee Y., 2005). For others, netizens represent "reform-minded and participatory Internet users who have reshaped journalism and politics for the better" (Oh, 2004). This study defines netizens as *amorphous and hybrid groups of Internet users who are aware of citizenship, participating in a variety of collective action in horizontally networked forms*. In particular, this research focuses on Korean netizens who autonomously participate in collective action, independently from institutionalized activist groups like SMOs and labor unions, and who have introduced innovative forms of movement repertoires in Korean social movements.

Demographic characteristics of Korean netizens

As of May 2010, 77.8 percent (approximately 37 million people) of the Korean population aged three or over are using the Internet (KISA and KCC, 2010). According to the demographic data measuring the age of Internet users, the largest age segment that uses the Internet comprises citizens in their 30s, followed by those in their 40s (Table 10.1).

While almost all of those in their teens and 20s (99.7 percent) and most of those in their 30s and 40s (90.2 percent) use the Internet, Internet usage rate in the

Table 10.1 Korean Internet users by age group

Age	*3–9*	*10–19*	*20–29*	*30–39*	*40–49*	*50–59*	*60+*	*70+*
Number of population (thousand)	3,410	6,570	6,830	8,100	8,380	6,710	3,740	3,550
Number of Internet users	2,920	6,570	6,820	8,040	7,310	3,700	1,350	230
Internet use rate (percent)	85.5	99.9	99.9	99.3	87.3	55.2	33.8	8.3
Age composition of Internet users (100%)	8.0	17.7	18.4	21.4	19.8	10.4	4.4	

Source data: KISA and KCC, 2010.

older generations (50 and over) abruptly declines: 44.8 percent in the ages 50–64, and 13.6 percent in the ages 65 and over. The 30–39 age segment accounts for 21.4 percent of Internet users, and the 40–49 segment accounts for 19.8 percent. Though in most countries the younger generation more actively uses the Internet, the age gap is more remarkable in Korea.[1] For instance, a comparative study of Korean and American Internet users (NIDA, 2009) reveals that more young Koreans use the Internet than do young Americans (Figure 10.1). This finding implies that Koreans in the 30–49 age group play a more predominant role in shaping public opinion on the Internet than do the 50-and-over demographic.

On average, Korean Internet users stay online 14.7 hours weekly (KISA and KCC, 2010). With respect to the purpose of their Internet use, over 90 percent of users go online for gathering information or data (91.6 percent), for leisure

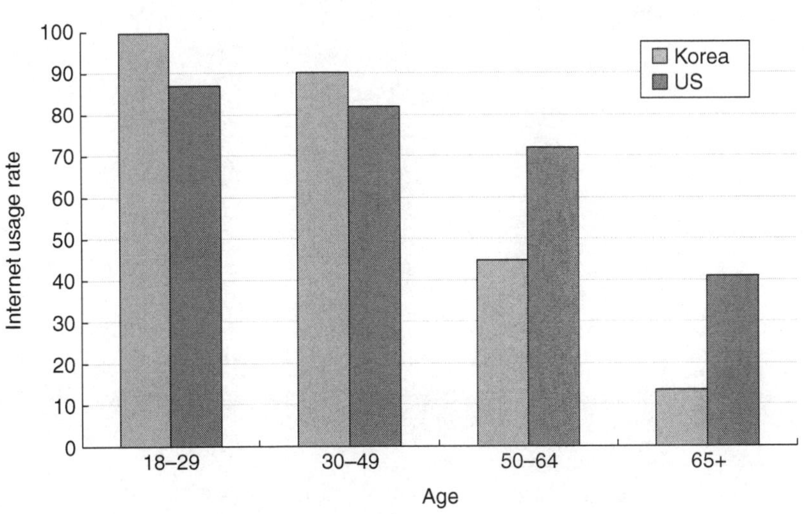

Figure 10.1 Koreans' and Americans' Internet usage by age (source: NIDA, 2009).

activities (89.1 percent), such as the consumption of music, games, and videos, and for emails and instant messengers (88.4 percent). Compared to US users, Koreans use the net less actively for online shopping and banking[2] and more actively for reading online news (NIDA, 2009). An average of 86.7 percent of Korean users aged 18 and over read news online, which is higher than 70 percent of US users (Figure 10.2). In understanding the netizens' actions in Korea, it is

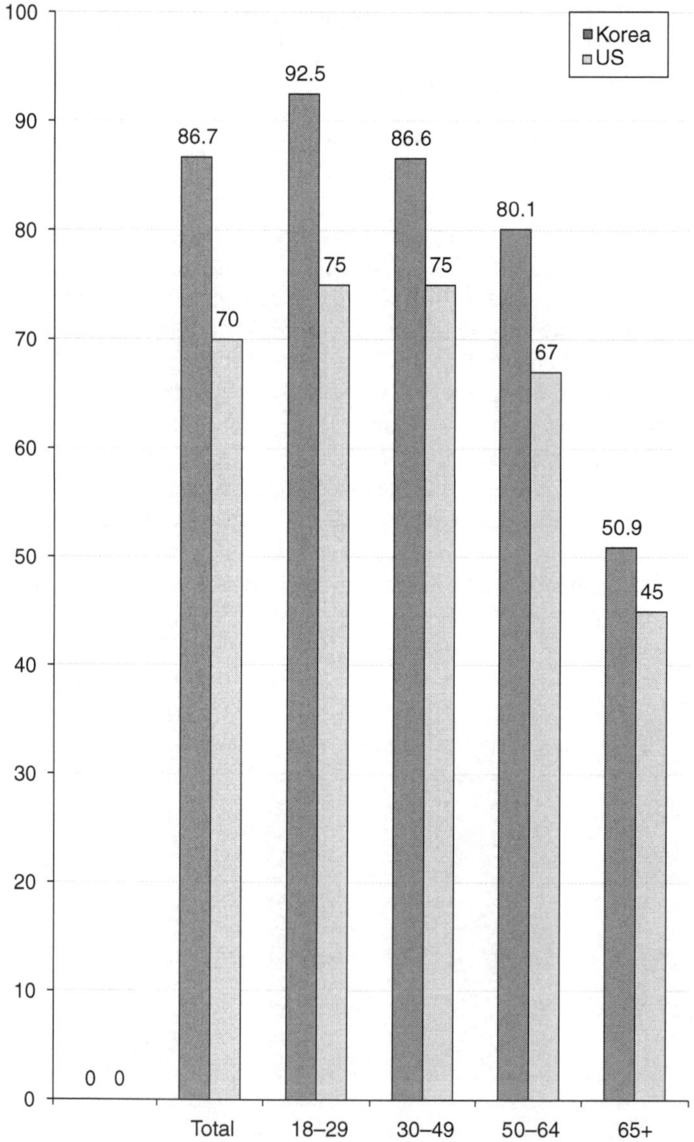

Figure 10.2 Internet use for reading online news (source: NIDA, 2009).

noteworthy that: (1) those in their 30s and 40s constitute two major netizen groups; (2) those aged 50 and over are far less likely to be netizens; and, (3) Koreans actively use the net for information seeking and news reading.

The netizen movement in Korea

By the *netizen movement*,[3] this study refers to social movements mobilized and coordinated online or offline mainly by netizens. Since the pioneering use of the Internet in the Zapatista movement in the mid-1990s and the Seattle anti-WTO protest in 1999, social scientists have been paying increasing attention to the Internet's impact on civic action at the global, national, and local level (Bennett, 2004; Bimber *et al.*, 2005; Carroll and Hackett, 2006; Kahn and Kellner, 2004). While some scholars focus on the effectiveness of the Internet from the theoretical perspective of resource mobilization (Kahn and Kellner, 2004, 2005; Vegh, 2003), others identify the Internet, from the framework of new social movements, as a postmodern field of action where spontaneous participants seek to subvert dominant meaning and knowledge and rearticulate their identities (Froehling, 1997; Lievrouw, 2011; Poster, 1995; Van Aelst and Walgrave, 2004). Despite different theoretical approaches, many scholars agree that traditional theories do not fully take into account the main aspects of contemporary social movements, as Internet-based movements have fundamentally distinct features in agency, movement repertoires,[4] and organizational forms of action (Bimber *et al.*, 2005; Chadwick, 2005, 2007; Flanagin *et al.*, 2006; Froehling, 1997).

Borrowing McLuhan's famous the "medium is the message" thesis, Chadwick (2007) asserts that Internet-mediated communication substantially restructures not only movement repertoires but organizational values and ideological goals. Focusing on emerging forms of Internet-based communications, Chadwick characterizes digital network repertoires according to four principles: (1) creating convergent forms of online–offline action; (2) fostering "distributed trust," or people's tendency to trust the outcomes of collective decisions made on horizontal and leaderless networks more than claims produced by single, authoritative information sources; (3) fusing sub-cultural and political discourses; and (4) constructing "sedimentary online networks," by which Internet-enabled protests can exist in the long term through loose but integrated communication infrastructures that reconfigure civic action in response to new demands.

Drawing on Chadwick's framework, this study discusses the emergence of Korean netizens as newly rising movement actors who have pioneered changes in movement repertoires. Unlike Chadwick's model, which addresses how SMOs innovate movement repertoires in the "national context of the contemporary US" (2005, p. 3), the Korean case demonstrates netizens' predominant role in leading a new wave of collective action independent from conventional social movements. Providing an overview of a series of Internet-fueled civic campaigns since the 1990s, this section describes three historical stages in the netizen movement: (1) the formation of the netizen movement (1990–2000); (2) the evolution of the netizen movement (2000–2007), and (3) netizen-dominated social movements (2008 to present).

The formation of the netizen movement

In the initial phase of the netizen movement, online networks began to emerge as alternative spaces in which radical and progressive users publicized social issues and organized their collective actions. As "PC tongsin" [Personal Computer Communication], computer-mediated networks that existed prior to the Internet, first emerged in the late 1980s,[5] progressive college students and white-collar workers first adopted new technologies (Kim Gibo, 2006). The first indication of the netizen movement is found in the organization of "Bar-Tong-Mo"[6] [The meetings for good communications] in November 1990.[7] About 200 netizens declared the democratic mission of Bar-Tong-Mo:

> Bar-Tong-Mo is an association of independent online users gathered to solve the problems in cyberspace ... Based on a culture of right-thinking communication, we, the members of Bar-Tong-Mo, aim to develop our knowledge and information about society and technology. We will also strive to solve the problems of cyberspace by proposing democratic alternatives and solutions. We will construct spaces open to everybody to expand the democratic power of online communicators.
>
> (Min, 2002, p. 102)

Before long, Bar-Tong-Mo became a hub of progressive activists online. On the one hand, it embarked on the "consumer movement" to improve online service of IT companies and to extend freedom of expression. It successfully directed, for instance, the protest against an unexpected suspension of network services for the "Hitel [enamed from *Ketel*] User Association," opposing Ketel's arbitrary deletion of users' postings and online censorship (Choi Se-jin, 2006; Min, 2002). On the other hand, Bar-Tong-Mo promoted "progressive social movements," mobilizing support for political campaigns and petitions online and offline. In the presidential election of 1992, it dispatched its members to ballot-counting offices to monitor the counting processes and prevent the rigged election some had anticipated. The ballot-counting processes were reported online in real time and were compared with government reports by election management officials. From the beginning of the netizen movement, online–offline convergence of action was routine.

Among the most notable changes introduced by Bar-Tong-Mo was the adoption of non-hierarchical styles of communication. Bar-Tong-Mo recommended that netizens keep "netiquette" (net etiquette), which includes the usage of "Nim," an honorific suffix, in addressing the online parties with whom one is communicating. In a Korean society where honorific expressions had been traditionally reserved for respected elders, the designation of online acquaintances with Nim – regardless of age, gender, and social status – was a pioneering action that promoted non-hierarchical and horizontal relationships among all online users. It is also notable that PC tongsin members were asked to avoid the specialist, elitist, leftist, and/or Marxist jargon that had been frequently used among activist groups. In the previous generation, when Marxist jargon was customary, radical or progressive activists were collectively called "Un-dong-kwon [an activist circle]," which might give the impression of exclusivity and self-centeredness. Some terms common in critical social science – such as mass, hegemony, propaganda, and anti-these – as well as some abbreviated words – like PD (people's democracy) or NL (national liberation)[8] – became signifiers of whether the speaker was Un-dong-kwon, and even of what ideological faction he or she belonged to (Kim Gibo, 2006). Aiming to share open discussions with anybody who might have different opinions – whether Un-dong-kwon or a layperson, PD or NL – the online community members agreed to restrict the use of factionalist language.

Following Bar-Tong-Mo on the *Ketel* (*Hitel*) site, many communities, such as Hyn-Chul-Yeon (*Hyndai-Chulhak-Donghohwe* [Modern Philosophy Forum]) on *Chollian* and Chan-Woo-Mul [Cold Springs] on *Naunuri*, were established, pursuing progressive social reform and online freedom of speech (Table 10.2). Although the number of online participants was fewer than one million until 1995, these incipient online communities pioneered the netizen movement in Korea.

As the Internet's popularity soared in late 1990s, preexisting SMOs – including college student associations, labor unions, and civic activist organizations – rushed to adopt new media technologies for more effective resource mobilization. Many SMOs began to create "Closed User Groups" (CUGs) to share information among their members and launched homepages to promote

Table 10.2 Online activist communities in the 1990s

Network server	*Online communities*	*Political orientations*
Hitel (formerly Ketel)	Bar-Tong-Mo [Meetings for good communications]	Social reform, speech freedom
	Daejoong-Maeche-Monitoring-Donghohwe [Media Monitoring Club]	Media reform
	Tonghap-Kwahak [Integrated Science]	Progressive usage of IT science
Chollian	Hyun-Chul-Yeon [Modern Philosophy Forum]	Radical social reform
	Hee-Mang-Ter [Places of Hope]	Moderate social change
Naunuri	Chan-Woo-Mul [Cold Springs]	Moderate social change
	Jinbo-Chungnyun-Donghohwe [Progressive Youths]	Radical social reform
	Mae-Ah-Ri [Echo]	Moderate social reform

citizens' participation.[9] Three months before the General Election of 2000, approximately 500 Korean SMOs inaugurated a civic alliance named "Citizens' Solidarity for the General Election" (CSGE).[10] Pleading with voters and political parties to neither nominate nor support corrupt or unethical candidates, CSGE announced a blacklist of 86 candidates, regardless of their political party or affiliation. These CSGE Election Defeat Campaigns were greatly successful: 68.6 percent of the candidates on the blacklist were defeated in the election (Min, 2002). Surprised by citizens' fervor for and active involvement in the campaigns, some commentators called the success of the Election Defeat Campaigns an "electoral revolution" or "the second June Civil Uprising" (Choi Jang-jip, 2000). The decisive factors of this success include effective utilization of the Internet and the flexible combination of online and offline campaigns (Choi Jang-jip, 2000; Min, 2002). Throughout the 2000 Election Campaigns, the SMOs played a leading role, while a relatively small number of online community activists supported them. Despite great differences in their forms of communication and leadership, SMOs and netizen groups collaborated tremendously during this formative period of the netizen movement. After expanding their movement after 2000, however, netizens began to reveal their own voices distinct from those of the SMOs.

Evolution of the netizen movement

The Korean netizen movement entered a new phase in 2002, when serial collective action, including the World Cup Cheering, the Candlelight Vigils, and the 16th Presidential election, occurred within a year.[11] Even if the World Cup Cheering is not a political action in itself, it provided a significant opportunity to engage people in a large-scale collective action online and offline. The "Red Devils,"[12] an Internet-based fan club for the Korean national soccer team, successfully mobilized 22 million people, directing street cheers across the nation. The Red Devils mainly appeal to those in their teens and 20s, a generational demographic which had been presumed to be politically apathetic. With no authoritarian leadership or hierarchical structure, the Red Devils carefully planned their massive cheers through online discussion and voting (Kim Young-chul, 2004). They discretionarily determined cheering slogans, dress codes, and mass events for each match, such as card sections in the stadium and street cheering in major cities (Cho-Han, 2004; Han, 2007). As many scholars assert, the World Cup experience strongly encouraged people to participate in online and offline actions in the 2002 Candlelight Demonstrations and the subsequent presidential election (Cho-Han, 2004; Han, 2007; Lee Hyun-Woo, 2005; Song, 2003).

In the midst of the World Cup Cheering in the summer 2002, a tragic accident occurred in Euijungbu, just north of Seoul, where the 2nd Infantry Division of the US Forces Korea (USFK) was stationed. On June 13, two middle-school girls, Mi-sun Shim and Hyo-soon Shin, were crushed to death by a US armored vehicle driven by two US soldiers. In November 2002, a US military tribunal in

Korea acquitted the two soldiers of negligent homicide, and the accused left Korea soon after the judicial ruling. This case was adjudicated under the "Status of Forces Agreement"[13] (SOFA) signed in 1966 between the US and South Korea, which allows the 37,000 US service members (and their dependants) stationed in South Korea to be tried in a US court. Though some oppositional social movement organizations[14] had consistently highlighted the law's unfairness and sought to expose the absurdity of the SOFA, most Koreans were reluctant to openly air complaints and grievances, as anti-Americanism had been long equated with pro-communism since the Korean War. The deaths of Hyo-soon and Mi-sun, however, provided a "tipping point"[15] (Kim and Kim, 2005) that spawned anti-American sentiments in a mostly pro-American country (Han, 2007).

While mainstream media paid little attention to this incident, an anonymous citizen reporter of *OhmyNews*, a progressive online news site, triggered the start of nationwide demonstrations against the US juridical decision. On November 30, 2002, an *OhmyNews* citizen reporter with a virtual ID "Angma" [devils][16] first suggested holding candlelight vigils as a memorial to the two girls:

> It is said that dead men's souls become fireflies. Let's fill downtown with our souls. With the souls of Mi-Sun and Hyo-Soon, let's become thousands of fireflies ... Holding a candle and wearing black suits, let's have a memorial ceremony for them ... We are not Americans who avenge violence with violence ... Let's fill downtown with our candle-lights. Let's put out American violence with our dream of peace.

Supporting Angma's suggestion, a number of citizens began to gather each weekend at the Kwanghwa-moon square, demanding that: (1) President George W. Bush issue a public apology for the deaths of Mi-sun and Hyo-soon; (2) the SOFA be amended to eliminate immunity from prosecution for US soldiers; and (3) equal relations between Korea and the US be established. Approximately 422 candlelight demonstrations were held for at least 20 months, from November 2002 to June 2004.

Fueled by the unexpected success of the candlelight vigils, a number of SMOs decided to join the struggle, reorganizing an allied SMO committee, "Bum-Dae-Wee"[17] (Kim Gisik, 2006). While Bum-Dae-Wee formally asserted that it would support citizens' spontaneous involvement, some doubted that it successfully embraced the increasing autonomy of the netizens. While many netizens demanded free discussion equally open to all participants, the SMOs remained entrenched in hierarchical leadership when directing the vigils. Angma argued that the SMOs' stubbornness resulted from their conventional leadership, which was predicated on vanguardism and authoritarian, top-down decision making:

> Many people on the net said that they would go to the vigil because they truly wanted to do anything for the dead girls, even though they didn't like the "Undong-kwon [activist circle]" ... They wanted to talk about their own

> stories as they did online. They wanted free and open discussion ... But for Bum-dae-wee, those people were still "ignorant masses" – that is to say, the masses that had to be informed and educated by SMO leaders.
>
> (Kim Gibo, 2006)

In the midst of the vigils, a well-known online commentator "Ulcar-man" posted his observation on the progressive news carrier *Daejabo*:

> A lot of their [SMOs'] flags blocking all the sights, [people were sitting in] a radial pattern around a podium, stunning speeches sounded through electric amplifiers, and VIPS engaged in routine agitationism ... all of their conventional movement repertoires were so tiresome and irritating.

The symbolic contrast between flags (representing SMOs) and candlelights (representing netizens) is noteworthy. Flags symbolize conventional social movements that tend to homogenize citizens under the banner of an organization, while candlelights here symbolize individuality and the equal status of the participants, who hold candles regardless of gender, age, political affiliation, and socioeconomic status. Later, Bum-Dae-Wee recommend that its affiliated SMOs not hold flags and factional pickets. However, the conflict between Bum-Dae-Wee and some netizen groups was never fully resolved. The two contentious parties were ultimately protesting in different directions.

Bum-Dae-Wee aimed to develop and transform the candlelight vigils into anti-American mass struggles. Spurred by widespread anti-Americanism mounting nationwide, it directed a march toward the US Embassy to visualize the hostile relationship between Koreans and US Power. As a demonstration around the US Embassy was legally prohibited, demonstrators could not avoid violent confrontations with the police, who had been ordered to keep the US Embassy from the protesters and subdue them if necessary. Dissenting from the Bum-Dae-Wee's direction, Angma and some netizen groups shifted their focus more toward antiwar and pacifist issues:

> Our candlelight vigils should be directed toward anti-war protest and peace rallies ... Current candlelight vigils (led by Bum-Dae-Wee) fail to effectively deliver the message of anti-war world peace, clinging to the discourse of national independence ... I object to marching toward the U.S. Embassy. It unnecessarily causes violent struggles. Peacefully holding a candle is enough to convey our will to oppose the Bush administration. Now it is time to move to the anti-Iraqi war protest, cooperating with the international society beyond the boundaries of nation-states.
>
> ("Interview with Angma," *OhmyNews*, January 3, 2003)

The candlelight demonstrations gradually declined after the separation of the netizen groups. However, the 2002 vigils offered a significant opportunity for the netizen movement to diverge from institutionalized social movements, representing a new wave of civic activism by non-institutionalized, networked individuals. Their differences were revealed in the movement repertoires and organizational forms, as well as by netizens' political directions (Table 10.3).

A month after the 2002 Candlelight Vigils, in December 2002, the 16th Presidential Election newly demonstrated the critical power of netizens in shaping Korean politics. The support of progressive, Internet-savvy young voters carried to victory a new face in the New Millennium Democratic Party (NMDP),[18] Roh Moo-hyun, who defeated dramatically conservative Grand National Party (GNP)[19] candidate Lee Hoi-chang (who was backed by several major newspapers). The victory was stunning in light of the fact that Roh Moo-hyun steadily fell behind Lee Hoi-chang for most of the presidential campaign. There is little doubt that this surprising outcome was initiated by the foundation of "Nosamo" (a Korean acronym for "People who love Roh Moo-hyun"), an online-based supporter community for Rho (Lee Keehyung, 2005; Rhee, 2003). Conservative newspapers labeled this election "the victory of 2030 [those in their 20s and 30s] over 5060 [those in their 50s and 60s]" (*Chosun*, 2002). Many analysts spoke of a "revolution by netizens" (Kim Seong-Sun, 2003) and a "victory of new media" over old media, such as major right-wing newspapers (Kim and Johnson, 2006; Rhee, 2003). In the second stage, the netizen movement started to reveal its own voices independent from SMOs, as it collaborated and competed with existing SMOs, and successfully orchestrated the 2002 protests and the election campaigns.

Netizen-dominated social movements

In the third phase after 2002, the netizen movment continued to mature, reshaping the whole of Korea's social movement landscape while the leadership of preexisting SMOs seriously declined. Unlike the 2002 Election, the Presidential Election of 2007 saw GNP candidate Lee Myung-bak elected by a great margin, representing a conservative victory.[20] Observing a rapid upsurge of right-wing power on the web, some have expressed skepticism regarding the sustainability

Table 10.3 Netizens and SMOs in 2002 Korea

	Netizens	*SMOs*
Movement repertoires	Candlelight vigil Open forum	Street march with flags Podium-led rally
Organizational forms	Horizontal networks Amorphous multitude	Hierarchical structure Federation at the national level
Decision-making processes	Bottom-up Diversity	Top-down Unanimous approval
Political goals	SOFA revision Anti-War, World Peace	SOFA revision National sovereignty

of the progressive netizen movement (Daejabo, 2006; Lee Keehyung, 2005; Sisa Seoul, 2006; Yu Sukjin, 2006). Emphasizing contrastive outcomes between 2002 and 2007, they asserted that civic power on the net is only "temporary and ephemeral" (Dong, 2007). Within a half year, however, when the 2008 anti-US beef protests plunged President Lee into crisis, the netizen movement appeared not fleeting but rather reconfigured and reinvented, much as Chadwick (2007) refers to the resurgent potential of "sedimentary networks."[21]

On April 18, 2008, a day before the summit conference of Lee Myung-bak and George W. Bush, the Lee administration announced that both parties had reached an agreement to resume the importation of US beef, which had been banned after a 2003 case of mad cow disease had been discovered in the US. This resolution sparked harsh criticism, for no other countries had agreed upon such a concessive, even humiliating, settlement, which included revoking the ban on beef older than 30 months and prone to mad cow disease. Subsequently, on April 29, the Korean television network MBC aired a segment of its documentary program *PD Diary* entitled "Is US Beef Really Safe?" The documentary accused the Lee administration of compromising public health standards in order to push a Free Trade Agreement between the US and Korea (BBC News, 2008). Following the program, a variety of online communities started online actions demanding the withdrawal of the settlement and the impeachment of the president, who gave up "national food sovereignty" (Cho H. 2010; *Kyunghyang Daily*, 2008; *Sisa-In*, 2009). On May 2, 2008, "Nationwide Movement to Impeach the President" (NMIP: http://café.daum.net/antimb) held the first anti-US beef candlelight vigil, which activated subsequent protests. Advancing upon the movement repertoires started in the 2002 candlelight vigils, the 2008 candlelight vigils exhibited evolutionary advancements in both size and scope.

First, a diverse range of people, including teenage groups and young female communities, appeared as new leaders throughout the 2008 vigils. Major leading groups were online communities that had been considered non-political and non-partisan. At the initial stage, junior and senior high school students, who accounted for 60 percent of the participants (*Joongang Daily*, 2008), stimulated adult groups to join the protests.[22] As time went by, age groups became more divergent and the number of participants increased. In particular, it is striking that young female netizens played a critical role online and offline. Namely, the "top three female communities," which led online signature collection, conducted anti-Cho-Joong-Dong campaigns and mobilized unexpected groups of people for street protests, including members of non-political, consumerist online groups such as "Sangko" (café.daum.net/ssanguryo), which shares information about plastic surgery, Soul-Dresser (café.daum.net/SoulDresser), which discusses fashion trends, and Hwajangbal (café.daum.net/makingup), which reviews cosmetic products.

Second, the 2008 vigils proposed a new way of civic action that simultaneously raised a variety of national issues without centralized leadership. Though the vigils began with discontent fueled by the resumption of US beef imports, the protests went far beyond economic issues of international trade. As American beef was rather a symbol of the US superpower dominating a global economy, President Lee lifting the ban on US beef imports was interpreted as his slavish eagerness to gain the political support of Washington by "selling out the nation" (*Kyunghyang Daily*, 2008; *Sisa-In*, 2009). Censuring Lee's dogmatism, protesters shouted a wide range of slogans against high unemployment, over-competitive education policies, the privatization of public companies, pro-business economic policies, and budget cuts in welfare. Different people proposed different agendas in different ways. Unlike the 2002 candlelight vigils, however, there was little conflict creating by dissonant sloganeering. The slogans here, despite their diversity, converged into "anti-Lee Myungbak."

Third, the movement repertoires became unprecedentedly satiric and entertaining. While the police used water cannons to disperse people, young protesters sang and danced under the water. Families with children camped out on the downtown square during the vigils, enjoying impromptu concerts by voluntary citizens, as if they had come for a picnic (*Christian Science Monitor*, 2008; Lee S., 2008). When the police built a container barricade to stop demonstrators from advancing toward the President's House, protestors put the signboard "Myungbak's Fortress" on the containers to deride President Lee as a clumsy coward struggling against his people. Observing the autonomous festival-like protests, one reporter described the 2008 vigil as the "protest 2.0" or "postmodern demonstrations" (Lee S., 2008):

> This is strange. Even as anti-government demonstrations in South Korea go, this is an odd, odd scene ... "It's like a festival. They are even using a laser projector to write their protest words in the air. It's effective because it's fun" ... With no leaders leading, the protest might be considered "ineffective." People are protesting individually, shouting different slogans, marching in different directions; different people with different agendas.
>
> ("Party Time at South Korea's Protest 2.0," *Asia Times*, June 13, 2008)

Most importantly, the netizens took a predominant position, supplanting institutionalized activist groups, including SMOs and labor unions. While some netizens in the 2002 vigils challenged the authority and leadership of the SMOs, netizens in 2008 played a decisive role in leading the protests. As the SMOs had organized Bum-Dae-Wee as a control tower in the 2002 demonstrations, approximately 1,000 SMOs established the "Dachak-Wee"[23] to lead the 2008 vigils. Unlike the Bum-Dae-Wee, however, Dachak-Wee hardly played a leading role throughout the protests (Kim Munjoo, 2008; Lee S., 2008; *Weekly Kyunghyang*, May 7, 2009).[24] The 2008 vigils exhibit a new rise in the leadership of netizens in Korean social movements:

> It is a revolutionarily distinct phenomenon that the (2008) vigils were led by online groups. This is rather dramatic as it was never expected. While the first candlelight protest in 2002 was suggest by a single netizen Angma, the 2008 vigils were suggested and projected by online communities, not a

> single person, such as "Alliance for MB Impeachment" and "Citizens' Solidarity for Anti-MB Policies," both of which have 180 thousand members in total . . . Currently, the online groups has moved to the center of Korea's social movements from the periphery. This is a just starting stage of their movement and their influence will be far more expanded in the future.
>
> (Kim M., 2008)

The 2008 protests became a historic milestone that represents a paradigm shift in Korean social movements. Since the 2008 vigils, Korean netizens have represented the most pivotal agency of civic activism, replacing SMOs' centralized and hierarchical leadership with the netizens' decentralized and nomadic autonomy. While Korean social movements until 2008 had been advanced by advocacy groups of professional activists, civic action after 2008 represents a new rise of "citizens that aspire to become an independent subject of talking, acting, and deciding, not satisfied with being mediated by institutionalized activists" (Kim Gisik, 2011).

The impact of the netizen movement

The emergence of the netizen movement has exerted a dramatic impact on social movements in Korea. First, the political and cultural influence of traditional mainstream media has suffered a relative decline. Korean netizens have challenged the exclusive authority of mainstream media and conservative intellectuals by producing and distributing their own discourse and deconstructing texts produced by mainstreams. Netizens led, in opposition to mainstream media, collective action in the 2002 Candlelight Demonstrations, the 16th Presidential Elections, and the 2008 Protest. In addition, the netizen movement has blurred the distinctions between political and subcultural discourses, struggles and entertainments, and struggles and festivals. As netizens openly expressed their anti-authoritarianism by producing and using satirical image-graphics, black-humored songs, and parodic music videos, they constructed a sense of solidarity and collective identity in opposition to dominant hegemony. As political and subcultural discourses have converged, the traditional boundaries between struggle and entertainment have also become destabilized. In the netizen movement, protests were kinds of exciting adventures, even field-trips, rather than grave struggles. Political struggles were no longer defined – as they had been in previous generations – by street protests concomitant with violent clashes with the police. While this new form of "entertaining" civil action may at first seem frivolous, it has actually provided more secure social platforms on which citizens become empowered.

Further, the netizen movement has prompted novel forms of leadership. Horizontal communication forms, spontaneous involvement, and non-hierarchical and decentralized forms of leadership have challenged the conventions of institutionalized social movements. While it may be true that, as Chadwick (2007) has asserted, SMOs in Western countries have introduced some innovatively "non-hierarchical" forms of organization, in Korea it has been netizens who have offered alternatives to SMOs beholden to hierarchical, pseudo-political-party forms. Unlike European countries, where representative democracy and party politics had been introduced long ago, Korean society is still recovering from a decades-long authoritarianism, and Korean political parties and radical SMOs are still relying on the centralized leaderships that arose during the authoritarian regime. Although the SMOs and political parties in Korea have been adopting the Internet as a tactical tool, they have failed to adopt the deeper values of direct democracy embedded in the netizens' movement repertoires. The Korean case suggests a distinct model in the evolution of social movements in the digital age, demonstrating that netizens can play a critical role in restructuring political environments in which political parties and SMOs lag far behind in innovativeness and progressiveness.

Notes

1 In particular, it is noteworthy that Koreans' Internet usage rate in the 30–49 age segments (90.2 percent) is higher than Americans' rate in that segment (82.0 percent), while American Internet usage in the 50–64 age segments (72.0 percent) is much higher than Koreans' (44.8 percent).

2 Koreans use the Internet for online shopping (57.7 percent) or Internet banking (38.4 percent), while 71 percent of American users access the Internet for online shopping and 55 percent for online banking.

3 The netizen movement has also been referred to as Internet activism (Kahn and Kellner, 2004; Lee Jinsun, 2009), online activism (McCaughey and Ayres, 2003; Vegh, 2003), cyberactivism (McCaughey and Ayres, 2003), cyberprotest (Van de Donk *et al.*, 2004), online movement (Kang, 1998), E-movement (Earl and Schussman, 2003), and computer-supported social movement (Juris, 2005). Despite its significance in the contemporary age, these definitions have not been clarified. At the most general level, many scholars broadly point to "political activism using the Internet" (Kahn and Kellner, 2004; Vegh, 2003).

4 According to Charles Tilly (1995), a movement repertoire is defined as "a limited set of routines that are learned, shared and acted out through a relatively deliberate process of choice" (p. 26).

5 *Chollian*, owned by *Dacum*, launched its bulletin board service in 1985, followed by *Ketel* (predecessor of *Hitel* and now *Paran*) in 1986 and *Naunuri* in 1994. Though the number of PC tongsin users as of 1990 was no more than 100,000, most online participants, composed mainly of student activists and progressive white-collar workers, enthusiastically discussed pressing issues and shared information to bring about media reform and social change (Kim Gibo, 2006).

6 Its full title is "Barun-Tongsing-ul-wihan-Moim".

7 In the PC tongsin era, one of the online network service providers, Ketel, was repackaging news data from only two news outlets: *Nae-Ue-Tongin*, an extremely right-wing news carrier supported by the Korean Intelligence Service, and *Maeil-Kyungjae*, an economic news outlet. Some progressive Ketel users demanded that it extend news services to include *Hankyoreh-Sinmun*, by which they could access more politically progressive news and information. When their demand was refused by Ketel administrators, the Ketel users initiated an autonomous campaign to copy and post *Hankyoreh* news reports on the Ketel site by themselves (Min, 2002). Some activist participants involved in this campaign soon agreed to found their own network for progressive reform of cyberspace.

8 PD and NL represented two different activist groups: the PD group emphasized class liberation based on a Leninist revolutionary model, while the NL group stressed national liberation inspired by North Korea's model.

9 According to a survey conducted by an SMO, Civic Action All Together (www.action.or.kr), 81.0 percent of Korean SMOs had their own homepages as of 2000; the major purposes of the homepages include PR (63.8 percent), information sharing (14.9 percent), and communication among members (10.6 percent). To support these SMOs and promote civic engagement in the new media age, Jinbonet was launched in 1998, with the voluntary participation of highly computer-literate activist technicians.

10 Its original Korean name is "Chongsun-Simin-Yeondae."

11 The catalyzing event was the nationwide World Cup Soccer Cheering in May and June 2002, followed by the 2002 Candlelight Demonstrations beginning in November and the 16th Presidential Election in December of the same year.

12 The Red Devils fan club started with 200 members in 1997. By the time of the World Cup, it boasted 200,000 members. It has open membership: "Anyone who loves soccer can be a member of the Red Devils" (Red Devil's Code of Conduct).

13 The full title is the "Agreement Under Article IV of the Mutual Defense Treaty Between the United States of America and the Republic of Korea, Regarding Facilities and Areas and the Status of United States Armed Forces in the Republic of Korea." This agreement was signed in 1966 as a supplementary pact of the Mutual Defense Treaty between the US and South Korea devised at the end of the Korean War in 1953.

14 SMOs such as "No Crimes by US Troops" and "Peace Korea" reported that approximately 52,000 crimes, including rape, murder, and kidnapping, were committed by 59,000 US service members stationed in Korea from 1967 to 2002.

15 According to sociologist Morton Grodzins, a tipping point is defined as a previously rare phenomenon becoming rapidly and dramatically more common.

16 As he drew the attention of the media, he disclosed his real name and identity: Kim Gibo, a white-collar salaryman in his 30s.

17 Abbreviation of Bum-Gukmin-Dachak-Wee.

18 In Korean, the New Millenium Democratic Party is *Sae Chonnyeon Minjudang*. It was a moderate liberal party, founded by President Kim Dae-jung, which served as a ruling party and a minority in the Korean National Assembly from 1997 to 2004.

19 In Korean, the Grand National Party is *Hannara Dang*. It was the conservative opposition party, which had 150 seats of a total of 273 seats as of December 2002.

20 In the 2007 Election, Lee Myung-bak garnered 48.7 percent of the vote, beating United New Democratic Party (the successor of New Millennium Democratic Party) rival Chung Dong-young, who had 26.1 percent of the vote. The electoral gap between Lee Myung-bak and his rival Chung Dong-young was the largest since the direct presidential election system was revived by the June Civil Uprising in 1987 (*Chosun*, December 20, 2007).

21 Chadwick (2007) has argued that online network-based social movements can reconfigure old networks over time in response to new demands or a perceived desire. For instance, MoveOn has switched its campaign issues in response to new demands, remobilizing supporters, and reorganizing its network power. While some scholars have questioned the permanence of Internet-enabled forms of political mobilization, Chadwick contends that Internet-based activism persists over time despite a lack of fixed membership or centralized control.

22 Teenagers are referred to as a new movement generation, following the 386 (those in their 40s) and the post-386 (those in their 30s) generation, the so-called "candlelight generation." The teenage generation is characterized by proficient utilization of the Internet and mobile phones as major information sources and mobilization networks and identifies itself as informed net-based citizens (Kim Munjoo, 2008).

23 This is an abbreviated title of Kwangwoo-Byung-Dachak-wee [The Committee for the Solution of Mad Cow Disease].

24 For instance, when Dachak-Wee announced a meeting at the Chung-gye square on May 6, 2008, some leading online communities suggested a gathering in a different place, in front of the National Assembly on the same day. While merely 5,000 – most of whom were organization members – followed Dachak-Wee's order, more than 20,000 citizens autonomously gathered in front of the National Assembly (Kim Munjoo, 2008).

References

BBC News. June 25, 2008. Q&A: S Korea beef protests. Retrieved on May 10, 2011 from http://news.bbc.co.uk/2/hi/asia-pacific/7457087.stm.

Bennett, W.L. 2004. Communicating global activism: Strengths and vulnerabilities of networked politics. In W.V.D. Donk, B.D. Loader, P.G. Nixon, and D. Rucht (Eds.), *Cyberprotest: New media, citizens and social movement* (pp. 123–146). New York: Routledge.

Bimber, B., Flanagin, A.J., and Stohl, C. 2005. Reconceptualizing collective action in the contemporary media environment. *Communication Theory*, 15(4), 389–413.

Carroll, W.K. and Hackett, R.A. 2006. Democratic media activism through the lens of social movement theory. *Media, Culture and Society*, 28(1), 83–104.

Chadwick, A. 2005. The Internet, political mobilization and organizational hybridity: "Deanspace", MoveOn.org and the 2004 US Presidential campaign. Retrieved on October 16, 2007 from www.rhul.ac.uk/politics-and-ir/About-Us/Chadwick/pdf/A_Chadwick_Internet_Mobilization_and_Organizational_Hybridity_PSA_2005.pdf.

Chadwick, A. 2007. Digital network repertoires and organizational hybridity. *Political Communication*, 24(3), 283–301.

Cho, H. 2010. The fourth estate's influence on deliberative democracies: Media framing of the 2008 US–South Korea beef imports controversy. *GNOVIS*, 10(3), Summer. Retrieved on May 20, 2011 from http://gnovisjournal.org/journal/fourth-estates-influence-deliberative-democracies-media-framing-2008-us-south-korea-beef-imp.

Cho-Han, Haejoang. 2004. Beyond the FIFA World Cup: An ethnography of the local in South Korea around the 2002 World Cup. *Inter-Asian Cultural Studies*, 5(1), 8–25.

Choi, Jang-jip. 2000. Korean democratization, civil society, and civil social movement in Korea: The significance of the Citizens' Alliance for the 2000 general elections. *Korea Journal*, 40, 26–57.

Choi, Se-jin. 2006. *If I can't dance, it's not my revolution.* Seoul, South Korea: May Day Publication.

Chosun Ilbo. December 26, 2002. Young antiques and old treasures. Jin-sungho Column.

Christian Science Monitor. June 11, 2008. South Korea's beef protests: Lee's woes deepen. Retrieved on June 28, 2011 from www.csmonitor.com/layout/set/print/content/view/print/22999173.

Daejabo. 2006. Degradation of the Internet: Ideological struggles on the net. Retrieved on November 21, 2008 from www.jabo.co.kr/sub_read.html?uid=16003%A1%D7ion=section5.

Dong, A. December 18, 2007. The lack of passion in Internet election campaigns … why? Retrieved on February 7, 2008 from http://blog.joins.com/media/folderlistslide.asp?uid=cjh59&folder=1&list_id=8871357.

Earl, J. and Schussman, A. 2003. The new site of activism: Online organizations, movement entrepreneurs, and the changing location of social movement decision making. *Consensus Decision Making: Northern Ireland and Indigenous Movements*, 24, 155–187.

Flanagin, A.J., Stohl, C., and Bimber, B. 2006. Modeling the structure of collective action. *Communication Monographs*, 73(1), 29–54.

Froehling, O. 1997. The cyberspace "War of Ink and Internet" in Chiapas, Mexico. *Geographical Review*, 87(2), 291–308. Retrieved February 3, 2006 from www.jstor.org/journals/00167428.html.

Garrett, R.K. 2006. Protest in an information society: A review of literature on social movements and new ICTs. *Information, Communication and Society*, 9(2), 202–224.

Han, Jongwoo. 2007. From indifference to making a difference: New networked information technologies (NNITs) and patterns of political participation among Korea's younger generations. *Journal of Information Technology and Politics*, 4(1), 57–76.

Hauben, M. and Hauben, R. 1997. *Netizens: On the history and impact of Usenet and the Internet.* Los Alamitos, CA: Wiley-IEEE Computer Society Press.

Joongang Daily. May 3, 2008. Three mad cows spark rebellion against Lee. Retrieved on May 22, 2011 from http://joongangdaily.joins.com/article/view.asp?aid=2889347.

Juris, J.S. 2005. The new digital media and activist networking within anti-corporate globalization movements. *Annals of the American Academy*, 597(1), 189–208.

Kahn, R. and Kellner, D. 2004. New media and Internet activism: from the "Battle of Seattle" to blogging. *New Media and Society*, 6(1), 87–95.

Kahn, R. and Kellner, D. 2005. Oppositional politics and the Internet: A critical/reconstructive approach. In M.G. Durham and D.M. Kellner (Eds.), *Media and cultural studies: Revisited* (2nd ed.) (pp. 703–725). Malden, MA: Blackwell Publishing Ltd.

Kang, Myung Koo. 1998. The grassroots online movement and changes in Korean civil society. *Review of Media, Information and Society*, 3, 109–128.

Kim, Daekyung and Johnson, T.J. 2006. A victory of the Internet over mass media? Examining the effects of online media on political attitudes in South Korea. *Asian Journal of Communication*, 16(1), 1–18.

Kim, Dongwhan and Kim, Hunsik. 2005. *The mechanism of candlelight@ public squares.* Seoul: Book Korea.

Kim, Gibo. 2006. *Interview with Jinsun Lee.* June 2006, Daeku, South Korea.

Kim, Gisik. 2006. *Interview with Jinsun Lee*. July 2006, Seoul, South Korea.

Kim, Gisik. 2011. *Interview with Jinsun Lee*. July 2011, Seoul, South Korea.

Kim, Munjoo. 2008. The beautiful new power: The birth of candlelights. Sae-Sa-Yeon [Research Institute for New Society] Column. Retrieved on June 10, 2011 from www.saesayon.org/journal/view.do?pcd=EC01&page=1&paper=20081212214122451.

Kim, Seong-Sun. 2003. *Online journalism.* Seoul: Dori.

Kim, Young-chul. 2004. *Let's meet in Kwang-hwa-moon.* Seoul: Sangkak-kwa-Nukim publication.

KISA (Korean Internet Security Agency) and KCC (Korean Communications Commission). 2010. *2010 survey on the internet usage*. Seoul: KISA. Retrieved on June 10, 2012 from http://isis.kisa.or.kr/eng/board/?pageId=040100&bbsId=10&itemId=315.

Kyunghyang Daily. July 8, 2008. Amazoness that lead the candlelight vigils at every crisis: Why we have held the candles? Retrieved on June 22, 2011 from http://news.khan.co.kr/kh_news/khan_art_view.html?artid=200807082309535&code=940707.

Lee, Byoungkwan, Lancendorfer, K.M., and Lee, Ki Jung. 2005. Agenda-setting and the Internet: The intermedia influence of Internet bulletin boards on newspaper coverage of the 2000 general election in South Korea. *Asian Journal of Communication*, 15(1), 57–71.

Lee, Hyun-Woo. 2005. *The 2030 generation and governance by participatory politics.* Seoul: Korea Information Strategy Development Institute (KISDI).

Lee, Jinsun. 2009. Net power in action: Internet activism in the contentious politics of South Korea. Doctoral dissertation, Rutgers University, New Brunswick, NJ.

Lee, Keehyung. 2005. Mediated politics in the information age: The emergence of the 'net power" and the politics of the Internet media in contemporary South Korea. *Korean Journal of Communication Studies*, 12(5), 5–30.

Lee, S. June 23, 2008. Party time at South Korea's protest 2.0. *Asia Times*. Retrieved on June 20, 2011 from www.atimes.com/atimes/korea/JF13Dg01.html.

Lee, Y. 2005. New social movements in South Korea: Netizens, electronic democracy, social protest and democratization. Paper presented at the annual meeting of the International Studies Association, Hilton Hawaiian Village, Honolulu, Hawaii. Retrieved on January 13, 2009 from www.allacademic.com/meta/p_mla_apa_research_citation/0/7/2/1/6/p72163_index.html.

Lievrouw, L.A. 2011. *Alternative and activist new media: Digital media and society series*. Malden, MA: Polity Press.

McCaughy, M. and Ayers, M.D. 2003. Introduction. In M. McCaughy and M.D. Ayers (Eds.), *Cyberactivism: Online activism in theory and practice*. New York and London: Routledge.

Min, Keongbae. 2002. *Study on online social movement in the information age: The Korean case study*. Seoul: Korea University Press.

NIDA (National Internet Development Agency of Korea). 2009. *A comparative study of Internet usage between Korea and the U.S.* Seoul: KISA. Retrieved on June 10, 2012 from http://www.nida.or.kr/notice/view.jsp?brdId=06031516292800l000&aSeq=090706111900002001.

Oh, Yeon-ho. 2004. *OhmyNews: a special product of South Korea*. Seoul: Humanist publication.

Poster, M. 1995. CyberDemocracy: Internet and the public sphere. Retrieved on September 20, 2005 from www.hnet.uci.edu/mposter/writings/democ.html.

Rhee, In-Yong. 2003. The Korean election shows a shift in media power: Young voters create a "cyber Acropolis" and help to elect the president. *Nieman Reports: International Journalism*, Spring, 95–96.

Sisa-in. April 28, 2009. The candlelights have changed my life: Interviews with 100 people. Retrieved on May 25, 2011 from www.sisainlive.com/news/articleView.html?idxno=4323.

Sisa Seoul. June 30, 2006. It is because of Roh Mu-hyun. Retrieved on November 21, 2008 from www.sisaseoul.com/news/articleView.html?idxno=2160.

Song, Ho Keun. 2003. Politics, generation, and the making of new leadership in South Korea. *Development and Society*, 32(1), 103–123.

Tilly, C. 1995. Contentious repertoires in Great Britain, 1758–1834. In M. Traugott (Ed.), *Repertoires and cycles of contention* (pp. 15–42). Durham, NC: Duke University Press.

Van Aelst, P. and Walgrave, S. 2004. New media, new movements? The role of the internet in shaping the "anti-globalization" movement. In W.V.D. Donk, B.D. Loader, P.G. Nixon, and D. Rucht (Eds.), *Cyberprotest: New media, citizens and social movement* (pp. 97–122). New York and London: Routledge.

Van de Donk, W., Loader, B.D., Nixon, P.G., and Rucht, D. 2004. Introduction: Social movement and ICTs. In W.V.D. Donk, B.D. Loader, P.G. Nixon, and D. Rucht (Eds.), *Cyberprotest: New media, citizens and social movement* (pp. 1–25). New York and London: Routledge.

Vegh, S. 2003. Classifying forms of online activism: The case of cyberprotests against the World Bank. In M. McCaughy and M.D. Ayers (Eds.), *Cyberactivism: Online activism in theory and practice* (pp. 71–96). New York and London: Routledge.

Weekly Kyunghyang. May 12, 2009. A year after the candlelight vigils: What remains to us? Retrieved on June 20, 2011 from http://newsmaker.khan.co.kr/khnm.html?mode=view&code=115&artid=19840&pt=nv.

Yu, Sukjin. 2006. The changes in elections and Internet media. Presented at the Forum for Open Media and Open Society, June. Retrieved on January 1, 2011 from www.openmedia.or.kr/bbs/view.asp?dbn=BBS_seminar&sm=pds&code=60.

11 Corruption in government–business relations in Republic of Korea

Rajiv Narayan

Corruption is seen as an essential aspect of government and business (especially big business or *chaebols*) relations in the Republic of Korea (Korea, hereafter). In part, this is, as this chapter points out, because corruption in government–business relations is not new. Since Korea's independence in 1948, it has taken various forms including bribery, cronyism, patronage, extortion, nepotism. While successive governments in Korea sought to remove corruption between government and business, no leader or ruling party since 1948 to date has escaped being tarnished by corruption.

In this chapter, there is an attempt to show how the corruption in government–business relations reveal a Korean state that is not as autonomous as previously understood, even under the Bureaucratic Authoritarian Industrialising Regimes of Park Chung-hee and Chun Doo-Whan. This chapter attempts to argue that corrupt ties have contributed to the decreasing autonomy of the state and its institutions.

With the onset of democratically elected governments since 1987, and the subsequent need for political funding, business appears to have used its financial clout to make increasing inroads into the polity, the state and its institutions. The 1997 economic crisis and the election of a president from the opposition ranks did prompt the Kim Dae-jung government to create mechanisms, pass and implement anti-corruption measures, and while that did show an impact in reducing corruption, the subsequent deregulation of the economy appears to have reduced the capacity of the state to control corruption.

Definitions

Corruption has been defined here to refer to personalised secret financial transactions for the purpose of private gain or concessions; in short, as "abuse of power for private gain" (You, 2008). According to the Office of the Prime Minister of RoK, there are three categorical causes of corruption in RoK: (1) organisational and administrative causes; (2) social and cultural causes; (3) psychological and attitudinal causes (Office of the Prime Minister's overview of corruption, cited by Lho and Cabuay, 2005) The causes, as cited by the Office of the Prime Minister, are elaborated as below:

Organizational and administrative causes:

- Unrealistic or unnecessary regulations
- Unclear definitions and operational standards in laws, rules, and regulations
- Complicated and intricate administrative procedures
- Low salaries and poor benefits for public officials.

Social and cultural causes:

- Collusive connections among politicians, government officials, and businessmen
- Social structure which supports high-handed personal administration and privileges for former government officials
- Cultural environment encouraging unreasonable and inordinate treatment, cash gifts commonly given to express gratitude, and excessive gifts (usually in the form of cash) commonly given to express congratulations and condolences.

Psychological and attitudinal causes:

- Low level of integrity and ethics in public office
- Prevalence of egotism, nepotism, regionalism, and academic cliques in society.

(Office of the Prime Minister, cited by Lho and Cabuay, 2005)

Focus of this chapter

This chapter will focus on corruption in government–business (especially *chaebol*) relations under the different governments from 1948 until the late 1990s and will make brief analysis of how it shaped under the Kim Dae-jung and Roh Moo-hyun and the present Lee Myung-bak presidencies. The study acknowledges the uniqueness of Korea that despite corruption being an integral part of the relationship between two of the important actors in its development saga since 1948, it has recorded admirable economic achievements. However, that aspect is beyond the scope of this study. It will also not focus on the rise of a civil society and a media that also have gained some veto capacity in this relationship.

Political funding under the Rhee government: facilitating cronyist capitalism

The Syngman Rhee government (1948–1960) had encouraged the emergence and consolidation of a cronyist relationship with business groups as the aid-dependent RoK economy progressed into the early stages of Import-Substitution Industrialisation. The distribution of "vested colonial properties" at exceptionally low prices favoured those business groups which supported and contributed to Rhee's electoral successes. There were similar considerations of cronyism that influenced the Rhee government's clientelist distribution of the generous US aid to business groups after the 1950–1953 Korean War.

The infant *chaebols* were products of a clientelist government that encouraged the belief amongst them that continued maintenance of cronyist ties with the ruling party was essential both for their survival, and also for their further development. Given the lack of institutionalised channels of influence between government and business, political funding at a personal level proved to be the major conduit for the maintenance of such relations between government and business. The widespread impression was that no big entrepreneur could survive without being allied with Rhee's Liberal Party. The impression was not wrongly founded. One of the most blatant instances of the state's partiality and its insensitivity to business concentration was the sale in 1956 – marking the final stages of the divestiture of vested properties – of four commercial banks. The banks were awarded to the third highest bidders, Samsung and Samho, on the rationale that the stocks would be purchased in bulk. Interestingly, the payment was later arranged to be made in instalments spread over eight years so that the successful bidders could acquire the remaining stocks. The state thus openly rigged the public auctions in order to give banks to its favoured capitalists (one of its favourites, Kaepung, was allowed the privilege of setting up a new commercial bank in 1959), and, in a sense, encouraged the establishment of monopolies in the financial sector.

State domination of business was evident in the manner in which Rhee's Liberal Party, which had little credible opposition from other political parties, exacted political contributions from the nascent *chaebols*. Moreover, for each of the presidential and general elections in 1954, 1956 and 1958, the Liberal Party had pressurised the Commerce Bank (this bank was privatised in 1956 and re-nationalised in 1961) to loan money to businessmen who in turn handed the money over to the Liberal Party for campaign funds. Later, the compliant bank presidents were rewarded and in some cases even appointed members of the cabinet (Kim, 1975). Not surprisingly, this proximity of businessmen to the government in power provided the basis for the long-standing popular notion that *chaebols* were, first and foremost, political entrepreneurs.

Corruption and the Chang government: a means to punishment reduction

The popular demand as the Rhee government came to an end was to punish these businessmen, and it was widely accepted this punishment would be meted out by the former opposition party, the Democratic Party government of Chang Myun that came to power on 14 August 1960. The Chang government's position was that the existing tax law should be applied in dealing with the case. But the Democratic Party also had links with these same businessmen. The apparent commitment of the state managers to punish the businessmen was overshadowed by a pressing need for political funds. Earlier, during the campaign for the 29 July elections under the new constitution, the Democratic Party asked for political funds from businessmen. Ten leading Democratic Party members, including Chang Myun and Yoon Bosun, who were elected as prime minister and president respectively, secretly met with six representatives of big business. In that meeting, 220 million hwan was contributed to the Democratic Party coffers and the party promised in turn to respect the policy recommendations of the business groups (FKIBH #2).

And so the Chang government announced fairly light punishment in the illicit wealth accumulation case based on the existing tax law: 24 *chaebol* or 46 firms would have to pay 8.7 billion hwan of fines and 10.9 billion hwan of additional charges for tax avoidance (*Donga Ilbo*, 2 September 1960). The bill passed in the Senate even revised the definition of illicit wealth accumulation, which now referred "to those who voluntarily contributed more than 30 million hwan to the March 15 election political fund" (FKIBH #10). The previous bill was intended to include almost all the illegal economic activities under the preceding Rhee government, under which about 60,000 bureaucrats and businessmen were to be brought to book. Under the revised bill, only nine businessmen were to be subject to punishment. Thus business escaped punishment. But this was not for long, as the Chang government was overthrown nine months after assuming office.

Political funding and the Park government: financing the gradual transformation of a corporatist relationship

The Park Chung-hee government (1961–1979) was an unknown entity as it comprised a military leadership that was complete outsiders to the Korean political sphere. The Park government strove hard to maintain its distance and took actions to punish business, especially the *chaebols*, severely. It was more successful than the preceding governments, as it had nationalised the financial sector and thereby come to possess a major instrument that combined with the onset of the plan process to influence, at times force, business on to the development path preferred by itself and its autonomous policymakers.

Initially, Park and his party were not in favour of institutionalising the distribution of political funds, as it found that the existing informal channel successfully blocked equal distribution to opposition parties. But given its bad experiences in the early 1960s when businessmen found themselves on the punishment block mainly because the channel was not institutionalised, any kind of dealings between businessmen and politicians were looked upon with the greatest of suspicion and generally regarded as illegal, business found that it was essential that there be institutionalisation and the existence of proper channels. In 1965, following the business interest group, the Federation of Korean Industries' (FKI) persistent demands, the Law of Political Funding was enacted to legalise and institutionalise the contribution of political funds by the business community (FKIBH #35).

Subsequently, businessmen regularly contributed political funds in an open manner. In 1968, FKI members demanded that one-way contributions of political funds to the state managers should be developed into a forum for dialogue between the contributors and the receivers. Put differently, the FKI, as a representative body of the sponsoring business community, demanded a channel through which it could convey its opinions to the state managers when they contributed their money. The *chaebols* thus demanded a transformation in the FKI's position as a corporatist channel. It was an indication of the increasing importance of political funding and thereby the growing strength of the *chaebols* in their relationship with the Park government. This argument was accepted and the Politico-Economic Conference (PEC), a corporatist channel, was established on 23 July 1968 with the attendance of the Prime Minister, the chairman of the National Assembly and leaders of both the dominant and the opposition parties, as well as 80 business leaders (FKIBH #36). Political funding thus contributed to the gradual emergence of the business community as an interest group. While it is difficult to establish a direct link between political funding and the dominance of *chaebols* as the major beneficiaries of the rents extended by the Park government, there is no doubt that political funding did play a substantial role in the emergence of the skewed nature of industrial development that took place in Korea at this time. There were some *chaebols* that were closer to Park than others. They attained this privileged position by a combination of political funding and achievement of ambitious targets – in the fields of exports and industrial production – that had been set by the Park government.

> The political imperative of the state to achieve the developmental project explains the privileges showered upon the *chaebols*, and the corruption that accompanied the collusive relations with business leaders. The state relied on the *chaebols* to convert economic resources into wealth-generating enterprises. This in turn necessitated pro-business policies at the expense of wiser societal interests.
>
> (Hundt, 2009)

Political funding and the Chun government: protection money to keep the predatory state away

The Chun Doo Hwan government (1980–1987) did not have the advantages of being outsiders to the power structure that the Park government had. Despite continuing a bureaucratic authoritarian government during a period of economic crisis, it could not maintain the distance that Park could from the *chaebols*. This government witnessed large-scale political funding by business. For instance, in 1985, a revitalised PEC contributed 1.11 billion won of political funds to the state managers (FKI Annual Report 1985). It was reported that from 1982 to 1988, the business community (the FKI, Korean Chamber of Commerce and the Korean Trade Association) donated $84 million, of which 98 per cent went to the ruling Democratic and Justice Party and the rest to minor parties (FKI Annual Report 1985).

Political donations have been perceived by business as a necessary quasi-tax, an insurance that businesses were expected to pay in order to ensure the preferential care of the government in the long term. This aspect of the relationship reflected the extractive nature of the RoK state. The *chaebols*, to cite an example, had to make contributions to such causes as heart-disease child relief funds, "let's help needy neighbors campaign" funds and national defence contributions. The amount of the contributions was equivalent to 0.74 per cent of total sales of private companies in 1987.

The *chaebols* openly questioned, criticised and fought the Chun government's attempts at industrial rationalisation in the early 1980s. The *chaebols*' dissidence was sought to be checked by the Chun state. Some of the doubters were punished more than the others, as revealed in the manner in which the Kukje *chaebol* collapse in the mid 1980s was conducted. Kukje, the seventh largest *chaebol*, was declared bankrupt in February 1985. It was claimed by the chairman of the bankrupt Kukje *chaebol*, Yang Chung Mo, that his *chaebol* had been "sacrificed" because: (1) Yang did not contribute enough money to the New Village (*Saemaul*) Movement fund, which was controlled by President Chun's brother (he was later indicted for embezzlement of the fund); (2) Yang did not actively participate in and finance the Ilhae Foundation, a quasi-research foundation established by President Chun, which also acted as a major depository of his political funds. While it was true that Kukje had run up a large amount of debts, when one looks at how the Kukje firms were later refinanced and doled out to the other *chaebols*, it appeared that the state had acted harshly against Kukje.

An analysis of the recipients of Kukje firms showed that the state rewarded those *chaebols* that had contributed large sums to various funds created by President Chun and the first lady. Hanil Synthetic Textiles *chaebol*, which took over five of the Kukje companies, also happened to be the second-largest contributor of political funds to Chun's party. Between 1982 and 1988 it contributed almost 13 billion won to Chun's party (Park, 1989). Thus, *chaebols* like Hanil that had developed close cronyist relations with the Chun government, thanks to their generous political funds, were rewarded by being chosen by the government to take over the insolvent companies at extremely favourable terms. Hanil, by this takeover, more than doubled its total assets from 676 million won to 1.49 billion won (based on 1985 figures) and jumped from twenty-third to fourteenth largest *chaebol*. Hanil's large political funding to the Chun government had paid off. Moreover, the government provided lucrative incentives to assist the takeover of insolvent companies. These included: (a) reduction of the interest rate for a significant share of the insolvent companies' debt; (b) infusion of new loans with a low interest rate of 10 per cent with ten year repayment and ten year grace period; (c) reduction of the loan by 50 per cent of the amount above the assets, which were simply reclassified as "bank loss" by the involved banks; and (d) tax breaks for companies that took over the insolvent companies.

The takeover of the Kukje firms seems to illustrate the influence that corrupt ties symbolised by political financing had given to a few chosen *chaebols* over the Chun government.

The Chun state's extractive nature revealed a transition in the state-dominated government–business relationship, especially when we compare it with that of the preceding Park government.

> The chaebol had to make unofficial contributions to the President, the ruling party and politicians, to recompense the state for its patronage and to maintain their economic vested rights. For them, to hold an amicable relationship with high-ranking state officials was essential to the prosperity of their business ... No chaebol, it was believed, could survive an intensive government tax probe or flourish without governmental support.
>
> (Lee, 1997)

Political funding under President Roh Tae-woo: a catalyst for greater business role in government–business relations

The demands for political funding only increased with the onset of democracy and the first elected leader since 1961, Roh Tae-woo (1988–1992) who used the connections and funds from his predecessor, former military compatriot and close friend Chun Doo-Whan. "The democratic transition had ... major implications for the pattern of money politics in Korea ... an increase in demand for political payoffs shifted the advantage to business" (Kang, 2002). With democratisation came needs on leaders to finance their political parties. In the 1988 legislative elections, it was calculated that the average candidate of Roh Tae-woo's party, the Democratic and Justice Party (DJP), spent nearly $1.5 million; some spent nearly $3.5 million; several spent over $7 million to gain a legislative seat. The *chaebols* allegedly "donated" $3 to $4 million to many candidates (*Donga Ilbo*, 30 November 1988). The lack of a proper channel of distributing funds meant that the leader had to be in charge of the funds that were collected in the name of the ruling party. Being in charge of party funds meant power. In May 1989 when it was widely reported that Chun had given Roh over $300 million to manage the presidential and legislative elections (*Donga Ilbo*, 30 November 1988), Roh claimed that the money that was in his hands was basically party funds.

A major unofficial source of political funding constituted of personal donations made by chairmen of individual *chaebols* to the President. According to a study conducted in the early 1990s, the donations of Korean, US and Japanese companies corresponded to 3.14 per cent, 1–1.5 per cent and 0.96 per cent of pure profit, respectively (*Chungang Ilbo*, 19 April 1991). Financially, Roh found that business contributions were the main source of funds towards his "costs of governing" (Park, 1995) and this in turn ensured his influence and the dominance of his faction in the DLP.

The DLP's Finance Committee, managed by Roh himself, comprised some 73 persons, including some of the wealthiest industrialists in the nation who comprised the major donors of political funds. The scale of donations made or brokered by Committee members in the process of the merger into the DLP in

January 1991 is unknown, but based on the disclosures made by Hyundai founder Chung Ju-Yung and the subsequent revelation that a committee member, the President of the now-insolvent Hanbo Corporation, Chung Tae-Soo, contributed at least 500 million won in political funds, it is not far-fetched to suppose that hundreds of millions, if not billions of won, were donated by industrialists aligned with the DLP (Park, 1995). The DLP publicly had an annual budget of 18 billion won; sources of this funding included 7.2 billion won from state subsidies, 6.5 billion won from the Finance Committee, which included most of the major *chaebols*, about 2 billion won from Assembly Members or other party operatives and 500 million won from central party support associations.

Political donations were not just restricted to the *chaebols*. POSCO, the world's second largest steel maker and one of the most profitable state-owned enterprises in RoK also contributed, but its funding was used to further the political ambitions of its long-serving chairman Park Tae-joon. Park, while remaining POSCO chairman, became a National Assembly member in the 1980s and soon rose to the important post of chair of the Finance Committee. When the DLP was created by the merger of Roh, Kim Young Sam and Kim Jong-Pihl's parties, Park became the leader of the Minjong (ex-DJP) faction in the DLP, and was to emerge as a potential presidential successor to Roh. To further his cause, he distributed about 20 billion won to 237 candidates in the National Assembly elections of March 1992 (Park, 1995).

These secretive corrupt political donations furthered the so-called *chongkyong yuchak* or "political economic adhesion" between government and business. These donations

> greatly advantaged the ruling party within an institutional framework, that already confined legal opposition to very narrow parameters. In exchange, business received a plethora of economic concessions: lax or non-enforcement of legal provisions concerning labour rights (often extending to violent physical intervention against workers) and public safety; deliberate oversight of irregularities in company accounts and holding patterns; subsidization of private investment from public funds ("policy loans"); the right to import scarce materials controlled under a restrictive trade government: and government toleration of vast real estate acquisitions.
>
> (Kong, 1996)

The influence of these political funds could be seen when under Roh's presidency, the six largest construction companies of the *chaebols* carried out 45 of 56 major government-ordered construction projects. In terms of construction cost, they accounted for 88 per cent of the amount (*Chosun Ilbo*, 26 November 1995).

Corruption under Kim Young-sam presidency: attempts to clean up but…

President Kim Young-sam, the first elected civilian leader since Chang Myun in 1960, felt the need to put a curb on the corruption aspect of government–business relations. A series of reform bills were promulgated to reduce political corruption. "A new campaign election law increased penalties for corruptive practices. The reforms also included raising the amount of government subsidies for political parties and for political candidates so as to reduce individual spending on campaigns" (Lho and Cabuay, 2005). Moreover, a measure to reduce the bias of political funding to the ruling party was sought to be established with the passage of a new accountability system for political contributions, which allowed parties and candidates to hand out anonymous receipts for political donations monitored by the election commission.

Additionally, the Kim government attempted to introduce greater transparency in political funding when it introduced the "real-name financial transaction system" (*silmyeongjae*) in 1993 (for bank accounts) and in 1995 (real estate). The 1993 measure

> aimed to end the practice of political donations being made from bank accounts held under false names. The *chaebols* opposed it because such a system would limit their capacity to make campaign donations and to transfer funds within and between affiliates through false bank accounts.
>
> (Hundt, 2009)

As Kang points out, "there was a horrific outcry from the business community. The Ministry of Finance estimated that in 1993 politicians and businessmen used over one million false names, accounting for over 30 trillion won ($40 billion) in assets" (Kang, 2002).

The *chaebols* were not entirely unsuccessful as they were able to muster enough political pressure to make the Roh government go slow on the proposed implementation of legislation leading to the *silmyeongjae*.

Ironically, the *silmyeongjae* backfired on Kim Young-sam. Investigations consequent to the enactment of this real name financial system in 1995 revealed that Roh had created a political war chest of 500 billion won (about $650 million) which had been inherited by his successor to the DLP leadership and the RoK Presidency, Kim Young-sam. Roh had even contributed $2.5 million to the electoral expenses of his rival, Kim Dae Jung, when he ran for the 1992 presidential race and $10 million to the other rival, Kim Jong Pihl. To quell public discontent,

> Kim Young-Sam … mandated investigations of "money politics" under predecessor Roh Tae Woo, inquiries that eventually included the leaders of the top 30 *chaebols*. Nine businessmen were indicted, and five convicted; Roh himself was convicted and sentenced to jail.… Chun Doo Whan …

> was brought to trial in 1996, convicted, and condemned to death (a sentence later commuted) for both corruption and his role in political violence in 1979 and 1980.
>
> (Johnston, 2009)

President Kim's attempts to lead a "clean government" suffered consequently. The Daewoo's Heavy Industries bribery scandal in late 1996 in which the company was implicated to have given money to the then Defence Minister for receiving the contract for military procurements was a further revelation of the influence-enhancing aspect of political financing in Kim's government. Worse was to follow when the fourteenth largest *chaebol*, Hanbo *chaebol*, became insolvent in January 1997. Hanbo, at that time the second largest Korean steel company, had accumulated debts amounting to nearly 5 trillion won or US$5.6 billion. It resulted in the imprisonment of its founder Chung Tae-soo for 15 years for

> bribing politicians and bankers to pressure banks to extend huge bank loans to Hanbo. Nine other persons were convicted including Chung's son, who was jailed for three years for bribery and embezzlement, and Kim Hyun-Chol, the second son of President Kim Young-Sam, who was sentenced to three years jail and fined US$1.5 million.
>
> (*New York Times*, 1997, cited by Quah, 2011)

The Hanbo scandal was to reduce Kim's capabilities of reform drastically. The Hanbo scandal "discredited his [President Kim's] promise to sever the ties between big business and politics" (*The Economist*, 1997 cited by Quah, 2011). Despite the many regulations that had been formulated, the corrupt linkages of government and *chaebols* seemed to continue almost unchecked. Acceptance of business money in the pursuit of power became an aspect of an expediency that characterised the style of the politics associated with the leading governing and opposition politicians, of personalism and office seeking above all else.

Political funding did have an important role in the *chaebols* successfully persuading the Roh administration to go slow on the effective enforcement of the anti-monopoly and fair trade regulations. It also, as noted above, gave the *chaebols* undue advantage in demanding and receiving from the government economic concessions such as a substantial allotment of policy loans and the government overlooking financial irregularities, among others. Political financing helped *chaebols* gain access to government officials and policymakers, thereby contributing to the eroding autonomy of the state apparatus.

The bureaucracy was also no longer autonomous and it had changed its ideology. According to Hundt, "in the 1980s and 1990s", the bureaucracy

> informed the state about the liberal policy that it espoused with increasing intensity. Conflict and rivalry with the bureaucracy also degraded the infrastructural capacity of the state … the government suffered from a "cognitive

> failure" when it came to *chaebol* reform: Kim Young-sam failed to appreciate what reform really meant and how to execute it. With conflicting advice being offered by various aims of the bureaucracy, the state's infrastructural power capacities were seriously impaired.
>
> (Hundt, 2009)

Corruption under Presidents Kim Dae-jung and Roh Moo-hyun – one step forward, one step back

Following the 1997 financial crisis, influences from the International Monetary Fund and the election of presidents like Kim Dae-jung (1998–2002) and Roh Moo-hyun (2003–2007) who were both seen as outsiders, it was widely accepted that anti-corruption measures had to be taken. This became expedient as corruption was identified as a significant factor leading to the 1997 economic crisis, especially after the Hanbo scandal. Under Kim Dae-jung, an "Anti-Corruption Bill, focussing on ten major areas, including tax and law enforcement reform for anti-corruption research measures, was passed, and also the Anti-Corruption Act, which addressed the administrative and legal sectors" (Lho and Cabuay, 2005). These legal measures were accompanied by mechanisms such as a Presidential Commission on Anti-Corruption, Introduction of Online Procedures Enhancement for Civil Applications (OPEN), Introduction of Integrity Pact, and Introduction of various evaluation systems (Lho and Cabuay, 2005, Table 4.1). The introduction of new mechanisms for oversight, analysis and prosecution increased the level of transparency.

Despite these efforts against corruption, Kim Dae-jung fell on the sword of corruption.

> Allegations of corruption on the part of President Kim's Prosecutor-General during the December 2002 election campaign and the subsequent accusation of bribery committed by two of President Kim's sons caused his resignation from the Millennium Democratic Party. He was forced to publicly apologize for these scandals and left office with a severely tarnished image.
>
> (Lho and Cabuay, 2005)

One of the sons, Kim Hong-up, was sentenced to 3.5 years in prison after prosecutors alleged in June 2002 that he had accepted US$820,000 from a construction firm.

Besides, the "cash for summit" corruption scandal tainted Kim Dae-jung's greatest achievement, the historic June 2000 North–South Korea summit. The Hyundai Corporation was accused of giving $200 million to North Korea to encourage it to participate in the summit.

Like most of his predecessors, President Roh Moo-hyun described corruption as the biggest challenge to democracy. He also promised to fight corruption by all means. He made these views in a closing speech in 24 May 2003 at the International Anti-Corruption Conference (IACC) in Seoul. On the same day, a former senior official, Lee Ki-ho was arrested for abusing his position, in 2000, in forcing a state-run bank to give loans to Hyundai subsidiaries.

Corruption turned lethal when it was to claim the life of ex-President Roh Moo-hyun. He committed suicide on 23 May 2009 following a probe by prosecutors on suspicion that Roh, while he was president, had solicited a total of $6 million from a shoe manufacturer, Park Yeon-cha. Roh maintained that the money received from Park was either borrowed by his wife to pay debts or was legitimately invested in a company owned by his brother's son-in-law. Roh said he did not know about the transactions until after he retired. Shortly before his suicide, several of his aides and relatives were arrested or questioned on charges of taking bribes. His elder brother also was arrested in December 2008 on bribery charges.

Corruption and President Lee Myung-bak – shadowed by corruption

The present President Lee Myung-bak (2008–2012), a former head of Hyundai Construction, was dogged by corruption, for instance the BBK scandal, even before he stood for presidential elections. Now, in the last year of his presidency, several of his close relatives and aides are under investigations by the prosecutors on other unrelated corruption charges. Besides, prosecutors are expected to summon his elder brother Lee Sang-deuk, a five-term ruling party lawmaker, for questioning over an unidentified 800 million won ($704,000) which the authorities found while tracing his secretaries' bank accounts. One secretary was arrested in December 2011 on suspicion of receiving cash payments from the SLS Group chairman. The chairman of the Korea Communications Commission (KCC), Choi Si-joong, is yet another of President Lee's presidential aides under investigation for alleged bribe taking. On 2 January 2012, President Lee Myung-bak "apologized for a recent series of corruption scandals that implicated his former aides and relatives" (Choe, 2012).

President Lee Myung-bak's corruption woes linking his brother and relatives reveal the importance of familial ties and connections in Korean politics and lends to the personalism that characterises many of the corruption scandals that have occurred under the rule of democratically elected Presidents. As this chapter shows, we could track this "relative" connection from the Hanbo scandal where Kim Young-sam's son was involved and convicted and later in the involvement and convictions of Kim Dae-jung's sons and in the case of Roh Moo-hyun's family.

Conclusions

This chapter has attempted to show that the Korean state was never autonomous; business with its corrupt ties – in the form of bribery, cronyism, rent-seeking, nepotism, political funding – with the state always had made inroads, influenced state policy and obtained crucial finance, policy loans, bank credit with little or no collateral and at low interest rates among other governmental privileges.

In this study, we find how corruption has emerged in different avatars reflecting the political-economic context. Under Syngman Rhee, we note cronyism in the early days of nascent *chaebols* within a context of a post Korean War ravaged Korea dependent on US largesse. Under the authoritarian Park Chung-hee, we witness state dominated developmentalism with hand-picked *chaebols* who had to achieve goals but despite their relative weakness, managed to institute corporatist linkages. We note corruption unravelling the extractive aspect of the Chun Doo-Whan presidency where the state dominated but had to face a fractious and consolidating business community. Political funding emerged as a crucial aspect once elections emerged as the road to Korean presidency. Roh Tae-woo struggled under his legacy and connections of a military past and close links with the authoritarian Chun and inherited close corrupt ties with business. The civilian presidents, Kim Young-sam, Kim Dae-jung and Roh Moo-hyun tried to use populist measures to eradicate corruption and close ties with big business. In Kim Dae-jung's presidency, the 1997 financial crisis made his establishment of mechanisms and measures to combat corruption expedient. But they all ended up tarnished by corruption, essentially due to their relatives. President Lee appears to epitomise the contradictory nature of a President with a strong big business past. He was dogged by corruption and at the last year of his term, remains dogged by corruption, though at this stage it appears he is as much affected by suspicions of his own past as that of his relatives and aides.

Corruption has played its part in the transition towards a new political settlement between government and business. By understanding a political settlement as "the political balance which constitutes the alignments and mobilisations behind an existing structure of economic rights" (Khan, 1989), the study accepts that the dominant classes including business, trade unions, among others undergo changes in their influence of the state. During the transition to democratisation, the increased globalisation of Korean economy and its *chaebols*, the deregulation of its economy and the increased demands for political funding, corruption has persistently eroded statist institutions.

Being in a transition towards a more contested relationship, it is inherently unstable and increasingly conflictual as both actors try to redefine their boundaries, their areas of influence. After the 1997 economic crisis, the Korean state did recover some of its control over business by the use of anti-corruption measures and the need for economic stability. The government still has the agenda-setting capability, but business has an enhanced veto-stating capability, assisted and influenced undoubtedly by the collusive corrupt ties that government and business still share in Korea.

References

Choe, Sang-Hun, 2012, *New York Times*, 2 January.

FKIBH #2, #10, #35, #36, Articles serialised in *Chugan Chun Kyung Ryun* [FKI Weekly], various issues.

Hundt, David, 2009, *Korea's Developmental Alliance: State, Capital and the Politics of Rapid Development*, London and New York: Routledge, pp. 73, 84, 91.

Johnston, Michael, 2009, "Japan, Korea, the Philippines, China: Four Syndromes of Corruption", in Ting Gong and Stephen K. Ma (eds), *Preventing Corruption in Asia: Institutional Design and Policy Capacity*, London and New York: Routledge, p. 124.

Kang, David C., 2002, "Bad Loans to Good Friends: Money Politics and the Developmental State in South Korea", *International Organization*, v.56, pp. 193, 199.

Khan, M.H., 1989, "Corruption, Clientelism and Capitalist Development", Unpublished PhD Dissertation, Faculty of Economics and Politics, University of Cambridge.

Kim, Joungwon, 1975, *Divided Korea: The Politics of Development, 1945–1972*, Cambridge, MA: Harvard University Press, p. 152.

Kong, Tat Yan, 1996, "Corruption and its Institutional Foundations: The Experience of RoK", *IDS Bulletin*, v.27, n.2, pp. 49–50.

Lee, Yeon-Ho, 1997, *The State, Society and Big Business in South Korea*, London: Routledge, pp. 84–85.

Lho, Kyongsoo and Joseph Cabuay, 2005, "Corruption in the Korean Public and Private Sectors", in Nicholas Tarling (ed.), *Corruption and Good Governance in Asia*, London and New York: Routledge, pp. 82–83, 90, 91, 94–95.

Park, Byeong-Seog, 1995, "Political Corruption in South Korea: Concentrating on the Dynamics of Party Politics", *Asian Perspective*, v.19, n.1, pp. 173–174, 178.

Park, Chong Yol, 1989, "Chipchung Haepu: Okonghwakuk Chongchi Chakum [An In-Depth Analysis: The Fifth Republic's (the Chun Government) Political Financing]," *Shindonga*, January, pp. 280–300.

Quah, Jon S.T., 2011, *Curbing Corruption in Asian Countries: An Impossible Dream?* Research in Public Policy Analysis and Management, vol. 20, Bingley: Emerald Group Publishing Limited, pp. 307, 308.

You, Jong-Sung, 2008, "Explaining Corruption in South Korea, Relative to Taiwan and the Philippines: Focusing on the Role of Land Reform and Industrial Policy", East Asia Institute Working Paper Series 15, p. 2.

12 The environmental movement in South Korea*

Sungbok Yun

Environmental problems, politics and the environmental movement in Korea

Korea is the country with the highest density population in the world, and, moreover, about 70 percent of the national land consists of mountains. The overpopulation makes Koreans sensitive and competitive to the land use and pollution. Under these conditions, civic experiences of environmental problems which capital and the state have, to a large extent, produced, have been enough to induce militant environmental movements to defend the life-world threatened. The environmental movement can be defined as a set of social reactions seeking reform or transformation of social structures and human activities producing environmental problems.

Environmental problems that people experience are regarded as injustices or as disturbances of life-support activities. The environmental injustices appear as an economic damage, a demographic change, a health problem and an aesthetic and moral concern (Goldblatt. 1996: 28). As environmental problems are embedded in global and/or domestic economic and social structures and processes, their resolutions or the goals of the movement are only by changes of such structures and processes (Dobson. 1990).

Korea has experienced compressive rapid industrialization since the early 1960s. One reason for the success of the compressive rapid industrialization was the state intervention. It was rapidly promoted by the Five-Year Plans of Economic Development under the auspices of the state. The state intervention of the market economy accelerated industrialization through its total mobilization of resources. According to the Economic Plans, labour intensive light industries had been deployed in cities since the early 1960s; capital-technology intensive heavy-chemical industries have been deployed in the newly developed coastal areas or near cities since the early 1970s. Mass production, centering on heavy-chemical industries, has been prevalent in the Korean economy: steel, nonferrous metals, petrochemicals, machinery, shipbuilding and electronics. These industries emit more pollutants, use more energy and deepen more environmental pollution than other industries do (Jungjun Lee. 1994: 321–330; Yongsun Oh. 2008: 150). As the state intervention of the market for rapid economic growth accelerated, environmental problems developed further and quicker, degrading the environmental conditions of life.

The environmental movement from the 1960s to the 1980s

There have been various tendencies of environmentalism against the degradation of the conditions of life in Korea. The collective actions are too diverse to lump together under the name of environmental resistance. It is evident that environmental movements emerge out of a complex combination between the environmental problems, conditions of life and political conditions which vary according to time and space.

Environmental movements were previously regarded as exclusive to rich Western democratic countries, that is, postmaterialism (Inglehart. 1990). However, it is now obvious that environmental movements can emerge during the early stages of industrialization in nondemocratic, poor or developing capitalist countries. In Korea, there has been environmental resistance by peasants, fishermen, the urban poor, labourers and, recently, by urban middle classes. It seems that the source of grassroots environmental resistance is a threat to the right to live. Considering this point, a grassroots environmental movement is characterized by the resistance to environmental injustice.

The grassroots anti-pollution movement[1]

> Pollution is concentrated on the Third World internationally, and it is concentrated on the farmers, fisher men and labourers nationally. The residents, as its unilateral victims, are fatally suffering from it.... As they have been deprived of a living basis of farming and fishery, and suffered from environmental diseases, they are demanding a collective emigration. The collective emigrations have already been launched in Ulsan, Onsan and Yeochun Industrial Complex.
>
> (KRIPP. 1986: 4)

Most grassroots environmental movements start with a protest demanding economic compensation. As factories began to emit black smoke, waste water and industrial wastes, a visible and persistent environmental struggle occurred near the Ulsan Industrial Complex. Farmers, cultivating rice, began to demand compensation for the loss of production incurred in 1969. Since then, they established the pollution countermeasure committee in 1971 and developed the collective actions for compensations regarding economic and health damages as well as subsidies for moving their houses elsewhere. The movement continued for almost 20 years, until 1991, when the Collective Emigration Plan had been finished (KRIPP. 1986; To-wan Ku. 1996; See-Jae Lee. 2000: 143). Until the early 1980s, grassroots organizations developed isolated struggles without outside support.

A typical movement, symbolizing an anti-pollution movement at the grassroots level, emerged from the Onsan Industrial Complex,[2] where 12 heavy chemical factories had begun to operate since 1978. The Onsan grassroots movement was similar to the one at the Ulsan Industrial Complex in its early stage; it was ignited by economic constraints, demographic change and health problems. However, the decisive difference between the two lies in a pollution disease, that is, the Onsan disease, or the Korean *itai-itai* disease. Of course, the residents in Ulsan also experienced many kinds of diseases such as skin diseases, eye diseases, respiratory diseases, the increase of tubercle and other similar afflictions caused by pollutants (KRIPP. 1986: 75–78), whereas the case of Onsan was more serious. Approximately 13,000 residents of 16 villages lived between factories or between factories and the sea, where the government or companies did not purchase land or establish an emigration plan due to the huge amount of purchasing and compensating costs before the operation of factories on the Onsan Industrial Complex district (KRIPP. 1986: 89). As a result, Onsan residents were directly and intensively exposed much more to pollutants.

The residents faced the critical situation that threatened their right to live from the rapid environmental degradation in terms of the factories' persistent emission of pollutants. They organized themselves, protested and demonstrated about 350 times against authorities and factories from 1979 to 1986 despite the political repression (Sookyoung Lee. 2001: 35). Despite their protests, they had suffered from many kinds of diseases after the establishment of the complex. Their symptoms exacerbated and developed. Their demand of the collective emigration meant that they gave up making their livelihood by farming and fishing, as it was the only method to save their lives and escape pollution. They screamed and appealed for help from the authorities, the companies and the societies, "Although we suffer death, please spare our children their lives" (KRIPP. 1986: 112). Activists of the KRIPP, who had monitored and intervened in Onsan, revealed the Onsan pollution disease in a newspaper despite the government's surveillance (*Hankook Ilbo*. January 18, 1985), and consequently, other mass media followed suit. Suddenly, Onsan disease became a national issue. The key issue of Onsan disease was whether or not it was a disease caused by pollution. The KRIPP, activists and mass media demanded the government for a proper examination of this reality. Thus, the Korean Environmental Agency carried out an epidemiological survey for a week under such pressures,[3] and announced that the Onsan disease was not a pollution disease. Despite pressures of the KRIPP and mass media, the government did not take a step further and attempted to obscure the reality. With its denial of pollution disease, instead, the government made the collective emigration plan, which the residents had constantly demanded, in a hurry.[4] The collective emigration policy was implemented to avoid being exposed to, but not to remove, pollutants. Such efforts of the government worked such that the reality of the Onsan disease increasingly became forgotten in people's memories.

Environmental movement organization (NGOs) as reflection

In the early 1980s, the Korean environmental movement saw the emergence of radical environmental activists and groups, indicating a departure for environmental politics. The first official environmental movement organization was the KRIPP, established in 1982, which focused on the emission of pollutants threatening people's subsistence. It was divided into the KRIPP and the Korea Anti-Pollution Movement Association (the KAPMA) in 1988; the collective name was then changed to the Korean Federation for Environmental Movement (the KFEM) in 1993.

Under the repressive political opportunity structures of military regimes, grassroots protests as well as the environmentalists' activities were rigidly restricted.[5] However, as environmental problems deepened in large cities and industrial complex districts, expanding nationally, the activists realized the needs for organizational and systematic responses to environmental problems. At that time, most forces of social movements and progressive academics drew attention to capitalist inequality and non-democracy, but rarely ever to the environmental destruction of industrialization. It was clear that the KRIPP was the first and only social group that paid attention to the potential and possibilities of grassroots environmental mobilization and to the environmental dangerousness of industrialization. With this reflection, its ideological configurations could not help but be radical to the existing systems as its activists saw that environmental problems and injustice would not be resolved under the social structures that gripped people's lives and the environment. Moreover, they saw the potential environmental resistance had against the environmental injustice at the level of grassroots, possibly leading to a social change. Due to the early environmentalists' dedicated efforts, the environmental issues that were excluded or alienated by the state and existing social movements formed and developed as a branch of social movements.

The dependent position of Korea on advanced countries, economically Japan and politically and militarily the USA, made it especially vulnerable to the adoption of environmentally damaging practices (Yun. 2001). Most factories attracted from advanced countries were located in industrial complexes like Ulsan, Masan and Onsan Industrial Complex. Some of them were those expelled because of environmental protests, the emission of pollutants and tighter regulations in Japan (KRIPP. 1986: 70; See-jae Lee. 2000). In fact, the governments had, positively and with a plan, attracted and fostered such factories for the rapid achievement of industrialization with loose environmental regulations. The attraction of investment led by the governments acts as the absolute element for the success of capital accumulation in the stages of industrialization in developing countries. For the governments, a tightening of environmental regulations can mean the failure of attracting investment, foreign capital and technology from advanced countries, which may make the rapid achievement of industrialization difficult and lead to their political failure. For these reasons, the governments seldom implemented environmental regulations and tacitly approved the emission of pollutants. The environmental contradiction of industrialization over time was accumulated in most of the Industrial Complexes, especially the Onsan Industrial Complex; and with the political repression of resistance, the grassroots living near them came to suffer from environmental problems. An environmentalist wrote, "Environmental destruction has been deepened as multi-national companies of advanced countries, dictatorship and *chaebol* have imprudently introduced declining industries in Korea where contradictions of world capitalism have concentrated" (Yol Choi. 1990: 5).

The 1990s environmental movement after 1987

As social movements broke down the military regime in 1987, formal democracy advanced. Relatively open political structures erupted various demands and impacted social movements, resisting the state's policy rather than the legitimacy of the state power. The threats toward the right to live caused by pollution were increasingly reduced by implementations of environmental policy through social pressures, such as the environmental movement, the 1988 Summer Olympic Games in Seoul, the phenol pollution of the reservoir and tap water in Daegu in 1991 and so on. The gradual tightening of pollution control required a strategy of accumulation different from that of the existing one, which centered on manufacturing.

Industrialization is directly connected to large scale land developments (Sungtae Hong. 2007: 63). In reality, state-led businesses facilitated the development of nature for active mass production, export and logistics. National projects were pushed ahead with little social resistance under the dictatorships, and even during the 1990s, under the necessity for civic life. In particular, the land development related to civil demand was less resistant than others. However, on the other hand, land development was another way of accumulation for capital and the state. It required massive investments through fiscal spending and thus provided opportunities for businesses; for developing related industries like civil engineering and construction, for nuclear industry, for leading economic growth and sometimes for overcoming economic crises such as the New Deal Plan. As these mechanisms sometimes increased the demands for land developments more than need be, environmental destruction was deepened.

The anti-nuclear movement

In Korea, nuclear power stations should be understood in both the contexts of infrastructure supplying electricity, and an atomic bomb and militarism for national security. With the active developments of the anti-pollution movement, massive anti-nuclear movements emerged in Yeongdeok in 1989, Yeonggwang in 1989, Anmyon Island in 1990, Goolup Island in 1994, Buan in 2003 and in Samcheok in 2011 with respect to the policies of nuclear power stations and waste disposal units. It was very difficult for movement organizations and grassroots to tackle these issues under the repressive political structures; nonetheless, most of the organized social movements paid attention to anti-nuclear, anti-war, disarmament and peace issues. Because Korea is a divided nation consisting of North and South Korea, the businesses and policies related to the national security have been exclusively monopolized by the state. The structure of this division explains the difficult nature of raising nuclear issues which have been controlled by the governments. However, paradoxically, the issues in the environmental and peace movements have been dealt with more heavily than other environmental issues, despite the strict control of the governments.

Compensation committees at the level of grassroots formed around nuclear power plants. The grassroots experienced and/or witnessed damages in fishing and tourism, a leak of heavy water, an illegal dump of nuclear wastes, births of deformed babies, cancers, deaths and so forth. The recognition of danger provided enough momentum to turn the compensation movement into an anti-nuclear movement. For example, anti-nuclear grassroots movement organizations were established in Yeodeok, Yeonggwang, Kwangju, Shinan, Jangheung, Boseong, Goheung and Yeosu after the government announced the proposed sites of nuclear power stations and/or waste disposal units in 1989 (Dongho Shin. 2007).

Most Koreans seemed to have recognized the hazards of nuclear technology. Most anti-nuclear movements have grown to massive scale and attracted national attention. This may be due to the preexisting national awareness of the fatal and/or potential dangers of radioactive materials, of experiences from damages from a nuclear power station, of the explosion of the atomic bomb in 1945 in Japan;[6] and of the accident in Chernobyl in the former Soviet Union. Another reason may be overpopulation and the possibility of an outbreak of war.

The anti-nuclear movement came to be suddenly national, beyond the local boundary. Repressed grievances with experiences of damages and the illegal dumping of nuclear wastes erupted at Gori in 1988. The Gori residents' protests and sit-ins at headquarters at the Korea Electric Power Corporation (KEPCO) in Seoul were beyond the local boundary, and marked the first protests in terms of regional solidarity in Gori and Yeonggwang at the same time. With this as momentum, events like the Citizen's Rally for Anti-Nuclear Peace (*Banhaik Pyongwha Simin Daehoi*) occurred in concert with the grassroots organizations around the areas of nuclear power stations, with health and medical organizations and with environmental organizations like the Korea Anti-Pollution Movement Association (the KAPMA) in 1988 in Seoul.

A massive grassroots movement occurred in Yeongdeok, one of the proposed sites for a nuclear waste disposal unit. It was the first anti-nuclear movement that massive participation and militant protests forced the withdrawal of the government plan in 1989. With this as impetus, national organizations, such as the National Anti-Nuclear Power Station Movement Center, were established, and public activities, such as the One Million Signature Movement Center for Anti-Nuclear Power Station and Waste Disposal Unit (http://antinuke.kfem.or. kr/history.htm/Hyejung Kim), emerged. The tendencies of national organization and the solidarities between the grassroots, civic groups and social movements, professional groups and environmental groups were the results of strong struggles despite the closed structure of nuclear policy, and have acted as a strong deterrent to nuclear policy.

With the Yeongdeok struggle, there have been massive, militant national anti-nuclear movements in Anmyon Island in 1990, Koolup Island in 1994, Buan in 2003, Gyeongju in 2005 and in Samcheok in 2011. As soon as a proposed site of a nuclear power station or waste disposal unit is announced, anti-nuclear movement forces are organized intensively and publicize nuclear issues nationally, beginning with local and national protests, campaigns, debates, open hearings, media plays and so on. In the case of the Anmyon Island struggle, most of the formal and informal associations in Anmyon Island joined and led the struggle. More than 100 national and local associations outside Anmyon Island supported and allied, including some of the civil associations near Anmyon Island, the grassroots anti-nuclear organizations of nuclear power station sites, and national social and environmental movement organizations such as KAPMA, the National Farmers Union, the Trade Union and Teachers Union and so on (Jaejin Jun. 1993).

The new trends of the environmental movement

With the development of the anti-pollution and anti-nuclear movement led by the Korea Anti-Pollution Movement Association (KAPMA), the configuration of social movements began to increasingly diverge into people's movement sectors and civil sectors, producing new trends of the environmental movement. The life (or bio)-peace movement, which demanded a transformation of industrial civilization, the CCEJ, which demanded environmental reform within the system 1989, and Green Korea, which demanded the conservation of nature in 1991, emerged with new and different views and approaches to the environment and the society. Accidents, for example, the phenol pollution of the reservoir and tap water by the illegal discharge of an electronics company in 1991 in Daegu, roused national angst, and, consequently, stimulated the urban middle class, induced civil and consumer groups to launch an environmental movement, and contributed to the generation of about 100 environmental movement organizations nationwide (Dongho Shin. 2007).

These kinds of movements began to gain momentum during the collapse of the former socialist state and during a large scale of environmental accidents; it is to be understood in the context of a civil movement rather than a class movement in Korea. Certainly, the changes of the domestic and international political configurations and of the environmental problems contributed to the activation of civil society and to the eruption of its demands and activities. This meant that environmental problems were recognized by most citizens and by the urban middle class in particular, who kept silent during the 1980s, spreading nationwide.

One characteristic of the 1990s environmental movement may be the emergence of an ecocentric movement. In particular, the emergence and development of the life-peace movement has a special significance in the sense that it has inaugurated a new horizon of the Korean environmental movement. Its advocates also came from social movement sectors, mainly the democratization movement and the peasant movement. Certainly, the existence of social movements has contributed to the development of the environmental movement. Its starting point was the criticism of modern industrial civilization, or modernity, suggesting the creation of a new alternative civilization. Its philosophical foundation was based on the life-reverence thought which may agree to intrinsic values of all beings, networks and interdependence between them, and the significance of the land (soil) and farming in particular. Advocates argue that the modern industrial civilization collapses global ecosystems and forces all forms of life to eventually die, and that a fundamental transformation of modernity is required in order to resolve the crisis of death. They criticize the political struggle of the environmental movement based on class interests, and, instead, prefer cultural struggles to detour the state.

The life-peace movement is *sallim*[7] (below *living*) with respect to killing. It includes all activities of *mosim* (worship and service) and *dolbom* (care) which respect, serve and care for all lives. It transforms the industrial civilization, the economic order and cultural mode of living in a direction toward helping overcome environmental crises. Its environmental movement has a meaning of *living*, reviving all lives (Jiha Kim. 2003: 13–15).

Its recognition of social conditions is similar to that of other environmental movements, but its action strategy differs. It suggests that the crisis the modern industrial civilization faces appears as symptoms with which most environmental movements share: (1) a nuclear threat; (2) the destruction of the natural environment; (3) resource depletion and population bomb; (4) diseases of civilization and schizophrenic social phenomena; (5) structural contradictions of the economy and their vicious cycle; (6) the control and domination of the centralized technocratic system; and (7) the old mechanic world view (Hansallim, 1990: 9–11).

However, its action strategy is based on a person's spiritual and ecological enlightenment. Only enlightenment can change people's conventional action in structures or institutions. A great transformation of a world comes from our mind in which we serve a cosmic life (Hansallim. 1990: 3) or a holistic life. The important thing concerning its action strategy is the emphasis on a personal change of lifestyle based on nonviolence and pacificism for a good life and coexistence, rather than on a structural opposition and struggle based on material interests, that is, nonviolent and peaceful individual practices as new movement methods. The methods have led to eco-friendly production and green consumerism. It has concentrated its efforts on the organic farming movement, organizing Hansallim, a kind of cooperative, which connects the organic farmers to the urban consumers and ultimately constructs a rural–urban community. Hansallim has currently developed into a community which consists of 232,000 households of urban consumers and 2,000 households of farmers with an annual sales of $150,000,000,000 (www.hansalim.or.kr/_board/20).

The life-peace movement has developed further, cooperating with religions. Initially, it was based on Donghak (Eastern Learn) and Korean traditional thoughts. Religions like Buddhism, Catholicism, Protestantism and Won Buddhism have combined their own life-peace thought with their environmental movement in the name of the life-peace movement. The combination has contributed to the activation of the Korean environmental movement.

The basis of the 1990s environmental movement may be its connection with the urban middle class. Most environmental movement organizations have been based on the membership of the urban middle class. They have to, to some extent, deal with environmental issues related to its well-being such as clean air, fresh water, healthy food, health and amenities; hence, they become reformists. The environmental movement has strengthened its solidarity with the urban middle class. Therefore it becomes a cross-class environmental movement, currently centering on the urban middle class. The comment that it is non-political is sometimes received, however, this does not indicate a failure of the perspective of the grassroots (class) environmental movement.

The 2000s environmental movement

The 1997 financial crisis in Korea gave birth to a social polarization, intensified the survival competition between individuals and lowered economic growth, all of which Koreans had not experienced before. The consequences of these changes of economic and social structures resulted in the increase of income inequality, the flexibility of the labour market, the collapse of the middle class, the increase of unemployment and irregular works, and in a spread of social grievances.

Along with the social fragmentations, there has been the advent of the information age since the early 1990s. The use of personal computers and mobile phones has been rapidly routinized, and has created and networked a numerous amount of small new communities connecting individuals, centering on the younger generation in particular. Informationalization makes a circulation of information possible beyond social, temporal and spatial limits. The access to information influences a person's action.

Most social and civil movement groups have exploited the abilities of the cyber movement, utilizing the internet for their intervention and solidarity of global issues, for support for policies and for new areas of the civil movement. They also were increasing their political and social influences in most areas of society. However, the increase of influence may not necessarily mean the development or activation of a movement.

The information age seems to change the conditions of the movement. Generally, the encroachment of material or environmental bases and the insecurity of life in social classes tend to raise conflicts and resistance on the one hand, and individualization, political indifference and cynicism on the other hand. Traditionally, social movements are connected to and try to mobilize the former altogether. However, the information age creates new conditions for the movement.

Utilizing the internet and mobile phone creates a new pattern of the movement. The new pattern of the movement and its development have not been able to be predicted by anybody. Some citizens have become audiences, reporters or journalists and/or activists in the social movement fields, using their computers and/or mobile phones. Korea has experienced and witnessed a series of great new dramatic and novel events in the 2000s. Movement organizations traditionally organize, mobilize and lead their members, information, and demonstrations and protests, respectively. This is their usual business.

In June 2002, two middle-school girls were run over and killed by a US armored vehicle. This accident could have been solved very simply if the related US drivers took legal responsibility. However, the US Forces Korea (USFK) did not take such legal action, and, rather, tried to conceal its truth. The Countermeasure Committee was established and began to declaim against a series of USFK's actions and Korean authorities. Koreans began to increasingly think that their deaths were unjust. There had been a small scale of protests and demonstrations as usual, which involved tens or hundreds of protestors and some civic groups for five months until the two drivers were found innocent of the charges by the US military court in November 2002. After acquitting, the case raised huge anti-American protests.

With protests of the movement organizations online and offline, related information was rapidly circulated, produced and debated; and the sentiment of unfairness and public rage were rapidly spread through the internet. This can be called the online movement, which is not yet connected to the offline movement. In such a process, netizens came to realize the reality of the two girls' death, which was unjust, and the structural problem caused by the inequality of the SOFA (Status of Forces Agreement between Korea and the USA).[8]

A netizen, declaiming against the verdict, suggested a candle demonstration at Gwanghwamun Plaza via the internet. It got into a new phase quite different from its previous aspects, connecting the online movement to the offline movement. Citizens voluntarily came together, declaimed, discussed agendas and issues of the movement, and promised to meet the next day at the plaza. The events of the candle demonstration continued over a period of 100 days. The citizens' volunteerism, autonomy and initiative had an impact on the content, form and path of the anti-war and peace movement.

Its characteristics may be as follows. (1) Participants ranged from hundreds to tens of thousands a day for about 100 days. (2) The candle demonstration was a national movement which joined 64 cities (or towns) in Korea. (3) It was also held by Korean residents in 16 countries abroad. Related to (2), it was the movement beyond national and local boundaries. (4) Social characteristics of voluntary participants through the internet varied, including children, housewives, white collar workers, internet communities and the elderly, and was based on mainly the middle classes and the young generations who had been relatively indifferent to social and political issues. (5) The candle demonstration was a movement in which 700 civil movement groups or organizations joined beyond their special movement areas, such as religious groups, cultural/artist groups, lawyers, teachers, Trade Unions, social movement organizations and so on. (6) Citizens, who were on the sidelines in the past, became a positive and subjective participant if motivations for participation were provided. (7) The candle demonstration was a cross-class, cross-region, cross-generation and cross-gender solidarity movement. (8) These characteristics of the candle demonstration are possible in the information age. (9) Contemporary Korean society tends to make the middle class radical. (10) A computer and a mobile phone play a role of the amplifier of the movement

These characteristics appeared to be reiterated in subsequent candle demonstrations; in particular, the mad cow disease candle demonstration in 2008 was a much more amplified form of the candle demonstration.

Environmental movement organizations and activists keep the traditional movement methods and activities to organize and mobilize resources and to attract public participation, with utilizing the internet and the mobile phone. In the process of the movement, movement methods are developed and renovated, raising great public concerns. The methods include the Three Steps, One Bow (a Buddhist pilgrimage walk) and hunger strikes. The methods allow a few activists to amplify the effect of an environmental movement on society.

The Saemangeum Reclamation Project and the Korea Train Express Project had been launched since the early 1990s. The Saemangeum Reclamation Project was designed to convert about 40,000 ha of mudflats by building a 34 km seawall off the coast. The construction of the seawall finished in 2010. According to the Korea Train Express Project, the 13 km tunneling work through Mount Cheongseong was launched in 2002 and ended in 2008. Environmentalists have objected to the Saemangeum Project, but did not object the Korea Train Express Project, demanding an environmental impact assessment at some areas instead.

The Saemangeum Project was controversial from its initiation and environmental movements for the protection of mudflats and the fisherman's right to live have developed fiercely at the local, national and international levels. Amidst the movements, protests, legal actions, lobbies and lawsuit for future generations (at first in Korea), four activists decided to take the ascetic action of the Three Steps, One Bow for the saving of the Saemangeum mudflats for 65 days and for 305 km long, starting from Buan, via towns and cities, to Seoul in 2003.

There had been environmental movements against the tunneling works at Mount Geumjung and Mount Cheongseong. Jiyul, a Buddhist nun in Mount Cheonseong, started protests and a lawsuit concerning Salamanders (who become the plaintiff at first in Korea). She also underwent the four-times hunger strikes, risking her life, with the collaborations of environmental groups, demanding the government to suspend the tunneling works that would endanger rare animals and swamps. She demanded strongly the temporary stop of excavation and the new joint research of the EIA in particular. Her last fast continued to be over 100 days at the front of the Blue House. The government, fearing her possible death from the fast, accepted her demands for the new joint research team of the EIA and for the temporary halt of the tunnelling work (Jiyul. 2005).

Although the cases of the above failed ultimately to solve the related problems, they imply important significances in the history of the Korean environmental movement. Their performances of resistance are based on their authenticity which rouses the great public interest and sympathy. Their messages are transmitted to the public via this authenticity. Their performances create great movement scenes, which attract media attentions that engage the public interest and represent repressed civic desires, organizing citizens to join up with movement forces and occupy cyber space in particular.

Here, the most important thing for the social movement is that the citizen's initiative and the activists' (or movement's) authenticity represent, sympathize with and weave together the numerous civic grievances, repressed desires and conflicts which neoliberal society has produced, and ultimately create the powerful social solidarity. Conflicts and grievances are ubiquitous, and are ready to mobilize and be expressed voluntarily and/or negatively. The hold and stitching together of the civic grievances and desires is the imperative of all social movements and a source of solidarity for emancipation.

Notes

* This paper was supported by the National Research Foundation of Korea Grant Funded by the Korean Government (MEST) (NRF-2009-413-B00002).

1 Sources of the anti-pollution movement used in this chapter largely rely upon KRIPP's (1986) *The Korean Map of Pollution.*

2 It is located near the Ulsan Industrial Complex.

3 The epidemiological survey took a long time and needed many experts and money – for example, in the case of Minamata in Japan, hundreds of experts examined it for five to ten years.

4 The emigration was initially supposed to be finished in 1988, but came to an end in 1993. The emigration plan included 34,533 residents and 333.7 billion won (Ministry of the Environment. 1992: 342–343).

5 Even the academic study of pollution was strictly controlled (Dongho Shin. 2007: 260).

6 Korea had 70,000 victims from the explosions in Japan in 1945. About 40,000 Korean-Japanese died and about 30,000 have been survivors of the atomic air raid – they have organized the Korean Association of Victims of Atomic Bombing (Hankuk Wonpok Heesangja Hyuphoi) (www.wonpok.or.kr/).

7 The word, *sallim*, has a subtle implication in Korean, which means "save a life," "revive," "a living" or "a domestic work." It is used as a meaning of "the sacred labor to revive all lives" in the context of life-movement.

8 About 600 criminal acts a year were committed and environmental problems have been continuously generated by the USFK in Korea.

References

Beck, Ulrich. 1997. "Global Risk Politics." *Political Quarterly* 68(issue B): 18–33.

Dobson, Andrew. 1990. *Green Political Thought.* London and New York: Routledge.

Dongho Shin. 2007. *Friends of Nature 1 and 2.* Seoul: Dyosae.

Goldblatt, David. 1996. *Social Theory and the Environment.* Cambridge: Polity.

Hansallim. 1990. *The Hansallim Manifesto.* Seoul: Hansallim.

Inglehart, Ronald. 1990. *Culture Shift in Advanced Industrial Society*. Princeton, NJ: Princeton University Press.
Jaejin Jun. 1993. *Nuclear and Struggle of Anmyon Island*. Cheonan: Choongnam Journal Press.
Jiha, Kim. 1993. *A Learning of Life 1*. Seoul: Whanam.
Jiyul. 2005. *Green Resonance*. Seoul: Samin.
Jungjun Lee, 1994. *Green Economics*. Seoul: Hangilsa.
KAPMA. 1988–1993. Survival and Peace (vol. 1–22).
KRIPP. 1982–1992. Pollution Study (vol. 1–22).
KRIPP. 1986. *The Korean Map of Pollution*. Seoul: Ilwalseogak.
Ministry of the Environment. 1983. *The 1992 White Paper of the Environment*. Seoul: Ministry of the Environment.
O'Connor, James. 1998. *Natural Causes: Essays in Ecological Marxism*. London and New York: Guilford.
See-jae Lee. 2000. "Korean Environmental Movement and its Political Empowerment." *Korea Journal* (Autumn): 131–160.
Sookyoung Lee. 2001. "Onsan Disease and Onsan Residents' Collective Emigration, in the Aftermath of...." The Society for the Environment and Pollution Study, http://ecoi.tistory.com/category/자료실.
Sungtae Hong. 2007. *Criticize Developmentalism*. Seoul: Dangdae.
To-wan Ku. 1996. *Sociology of Korean Environmental Movement*. Seoul: Literature and Intelligence.
Yol Choi. 1990. Human Environment and Pollution. In *For All of Us, the Sky and the Earth* (The anniversary casebook for the 1990 Earth Day), ed. KAPMA.
Yongsun Oh. 2008. *Reflexive Environment*. Seoul: Arche.
Yun, Sungbok. 2001. "Development, Democracy and Environmental Movements in South Korea." PhD thesis, University of Essex.

13 South Korea – the "making" of a working class in a newly industrialized country

John Minns

Introduction

The title of this chapter brings to mind E.P. Thompson's pathbreaking 1963 work "The Making of the English Working Class". Recalling that immense contribution in the title means that, for the purposes of modesty, as well as clarity, it is necessary to make clear what this chapter is and is not.

It is not an attempt, even briefly, to sketch a history of the South Korean working class. Thompson's work itself is not a comprehensive history of the early English working class. It is a history of the growth of their class consciousness; an attempt to trace workers' concept of themselves as a distinct class and of other classes in relation to them. In doing so, Thompson is keenly aware that consciousness is never a simple reflection of class interest. Rather it develops in a complex process by which material interest interacts with ideas, institutions and values; in one sense of the word, with culture.

> The class experience is largely determined by the productive relations into which men [sic] are born – or enter involuntarily. Class consciousness is the way in which these experiences are handled in cultural terms: embodied in traditions, value-systems, ideas and institutional forms.[1]

The English factory operative, craftsman or miner of the late eighteenth century had few traditions, values or institutions which were distinctly the creation of the working class. No sizeable working class had existed before him or her which might have created them. So inevitably, many of the first "cultural terms" which are used to handle these new class "experiences" were derived from the pre-industrial society in which they grew up and were socialized.

The same is the case with all "new" working classes. Yet while there are many studies of working class consciousness in developed capitalist societies, much less attention has been paid to class consciousness in Newly Industrializing Countries (NICs) where the transformation of farmers into workers has been spectacularly rapid in the last three or four decades. It is easy to forget that England, in the period of the "making" of its working class, was a NIC. Indeed, it was the first.

This chapter is not an attempt to draw close parallels between the development of different working classes across different centuries and continents – the English in the late eighteenth and early nineteenth centuries and the Korean in the last few decades. On the contrary, much of the point of Thompson's work was to deny that there was a single, predictable and triumphal march of a newly formed proletariat to a "high" level of class consciousness. Unexpected ideas occupy the minds of these workers. Some are drawn from peasant struggles against oppression, some from real or imagined national history, others from religious dogma. They mingle with the emerging realization of workers that their ways of life, the foes they face and the weapons they have to hand are different from those of their forebears. The notion that they are being dealt with unfairly and the possibilities inherent in the great potential power of their position is filtered through these ideas.

Class consciousness, in Thompson's history, veers this way and that and sometimes even turns back the way it had come. Rather than a highly structured, almost inevitable process, Thompson emphasizes agency – the activity of the workers themselves – and the continuity of, often pre-capitalist, national and regional ideologies and popular traditions which precede the physical formation of the working class itself.

Such local traditions, by their nature, differ greatly from one another. Regional differences are, if anything, more important in pre-industrial societies because the regional cultures of such societies are more varied than those of industrialized societies with their ubiquitous and highly standardized systems of communications, production and consumption. That being so, comparisons, especially between working classes in the early stages of their "making", can be as misleading as they are useful.

However, Thompson's insights about the English working class may alert us to a number of matters in the development of class consciousness of which it is useful to take note in dealing with the development of other working classes. Three such are: the continuity or discontinuity of labouring traditions; pre-industrial, possibly folkloric, customs, traditions and ideas which help to shape early working class consciousness; and the role of religious institutions and ideas.

For at least one part of the 1980s, and through some of the 1990s as well, the South Korean working class was perhaps the most militant in the world. Mostly under conditions of severe repression it conducted, between 1987 and 1990, the most widespread campaign of industrial militancy anywhere in the previous quarter of a century. Furthermore, this activity and militancy had enormous political ramifications. To the extent that there has been an important democratic transformation of South Korea it was the working class and, significantly, students and intellectuals politically oriented towards the working class, who played a huge part in it.

Proletarianization and traditions

Thompson's working class was, by and large, new. But industrial capitalism in England was preceded by a long period of small-scale manufacture. Thus the growing working class of the late eighteenth century had at least some traditions of a labouring class on which to draw. It had, to an extent, absorbed the experience of the artisan, journeyman, apprentice and cottage worker (the outworker of the eighteenth century).[2] Thus one can find a woolcombers' union ticket of 1838 which recalls similar tickets produced by woolcombers as early as 1700.[3] Early English unionism owes much to this tradition of a labouring poor engaged in small-scale manufacture.

Korea also has a tradition of working class organization and activism which stretches back before the Second World War. However, these organizations, along with their legacy of ideas and even individual activists, were destroyed in the post-war period.

As in many countries which had been occupied by defeated powers, the end of the Second World War left a power vacuum in Korea. The ruling elites had mostly been compromised by the occupation and they and the police were widely regarded as collaborators. Resistance to the Japanese had been dominated by the left.

With the Japanese surrender, a People's Republic of Korea was established with the Communist Party (CPKI) as its backbone and with its capital in Seoul.[4] The situation remained complex and unstable through 1945 and much of 1946. Then in autumn 1946 there began a peasant and working class upsurge known as the Autumn Harvest Risings. Over 250,000 workers took part, calling for economic improvements and also making a revolutionary demand – the transfer of power to the People's Committees.[5] More than 200 policemen – considered to be collaborators and servants of the landlord class – were killed.[6] Workers occupied factories throughout the country, in some cases taking them over and contracting out managerial positions to those with the necessary expertise.[7] But the risings were defeated. The left was the big loser. With the unions crushed, membership fell from 553,408 to just 2,465 in a few years.[8] The smashing of the risings meant that peasants and workers effectively lost the organizations which had defended their interests.

Even such a calamity might have left behind a tradition, at least in the underground. But the Korean War of 1950–3 completed the task of the destruction of this impressive working class movement. Physically, the working class was most damaged by the devastation of the industrial and capital base of the country.[9] In Seoul over 80 per cent of industry, public utilities and transport facilities and over half the dwellings were destroyed. Nationwide 68 per cent of factories lay in ruins and industrial production dropped 52 per cent between 1949 and 1951 alone.[10]

Troops of the Republic of Korea routinely executed suspected leftists and northern sympathizers before they were forced to retreat southward and later when retaking areas occupied by the north. Tens of thousands were murdered;

one report suggests 29,000 in Seoul alone.[11] The war forced most radicals who survived to flee to the north to escape from the terror initiated by the government of Syngman Rhee.[12]

> through kidnapping, murder, and defection during North Korean occupation, the war served to destroy the final remnants of the moderate and Left-leaning leadership that had opposed Rhee before independence. It also delivered the final blow to the Left in South Korea.[13]

A student revolution against Rhee in 1960 gave workers a brief chance to assert themselves independently of the government – but this changed dramatically after the military coup of 16 May 1961 which brought General Park Chung-Hee to power. A union federation – the FKTU – was allowed to work openly. But it was effectively government controlled, its officials bought and paid for. In addition a battery of anti-union legislation introduced by Park between 1961 and his assassination in 1979 made industrial action illegal. The Korean CIA infiltrated hundreds of agents into factories to identify militants and to play a role in FKTU elections. To win office at the national level without KCIA support was practically impossible.[14]

Thus when rapid industrialization from about the mid-1960s began to create a large working class, it had few traditions or memories of the post-war militancy – even fewer than were left to the English working class of the eighteenth century.

Proletarianization was much faster in South Korea in the 1960s and 1970s. Whereas, in England, until at least the 1830s, factory workers were a minority of the workforce, even in "leading-edge" industries such as weaving, in South Korea, factories and large firms became the core of industry within half a decade. The industrial workforce alone rose from 10 per cent of the labour force in 1965 to 23 per cent in 1983. The service workforce increased from 31 to 47 per cent in the same period. Farm labour fell from 65 per cent in the early 1960s to 38 per cent in early 1980s.[15]

Moreover, it was, at first, a workforce of very young, often female, rural migrants, to whom the militant tradition of Chun Pyung was completely unknown. About 30 per cent of the employed workforce in the 1960s were young women, typically aged 14–24 and employed in textiles and related industries and other light manufacturing.[16] Even if some older activists had survived the purges of the 1940s and 1950s, the level of repression under the Park regime made impossible any dissemination of the Chun Pyung tradition to this new group of workers.

Class consciousness

Lacking the ways of thinking about society which develop in working classes over time, new working classes commonly reach back to pre-industrial traditions and ideas with which to understand their situation.[17]

In the English context, notions such as the "Freeborn Englishman" were important; the idea that at some point English people had been free and were entitled to liberty as their right of birth. It is a belief which long predates the English working class and is not necessarily even the product of subaltern classes at all. Yet it took on real importance as a way for workers to interpret the situation in which they found themselves. Thompson writes:

> In the contest between 1792 and 1836 the artisans and workers made this tradition [of the "freeborn Englishman"] peculiarly their own, adding to the claim for free speech and thought their own claim for the untrammeled propagation, in the cheapest possible form, of the products of this thought.[18]

Such traditions are not simply historical hangovers, stubbornly outliving the circumstances from which they sprang. Rather they are a result of a process of selection and reinvention. Some remnants of the pre-capitalist past are discarded, others come to greater prominence. In some cases old ideas are retained, but are given new content as a result of the lived class experience of workers. In others an "invention of tradition" takes place.

In Korea, old notions of popular democracy and nationalist egalitarianism, summed up by the word *minjung*, come to play a similar and crucial role in the workers' movement of the 1970s and 1980s – precisely at the key point in the formation of the independent labour movement.

Minjung literally means "people", but it has connotations of the popular will and of an oppressed community; much as the word "pueblo" is sometimes used in Spanish-speaking Latin America. As the term came to be used in the 1970s it suggested that the *minjung* are:

> Koreans, predominantly workers in agriculture and urban industries, who retained the values and sentiments of the Korean masses in the face of militaristic rule and cultural and economic systems imposed directly or otherwise by foreign governments or interests, along with those among intellectuals, writers, politicians or professionals who have supported their aspirations.[19]

The idea of *minjung* is especially connected to the *Tonghak*, or Eastern Learning, a "nativistic" movement which began in the early 1860s in response to the growth of Western influence in Korean politics and culture. By 1894, *Tonghak* peasant rebels in the south-west were in open revolt. They were finally defeated by the Korean government and Japanese troops.[20]

The rebellion was simultaneously nationalist and populist – linking the struggle against foreign incursion to the demand for improvements in the people's welfare.[21] Resistance to Japanese colonial control over Korea from 1910 was considered a battle by the suffering *minjung*, as is resistance to the division of Korea, and to great power (especially US and Japanese) involvement in the country.

Minjung finds an echo in Thompson's work in ideas such as the "Norman Yoke". Common amongst working people in Thompson's period was the belief that there had been a period of "English freedom before the time of the 'Norman bastard [William the Conqueror] and his armed banditti' "[22]. According to the myth, a foreign aristocracy imposed itself on ordinary English people in 1066, usurping their ancient liberties and impoverishing them materially.

This form of working class radicalism looks back to an idealized past, as well as forward to a just future. It is aimed at rallying workers but it reveres the poor, including the small proprietor (with his own field or his own loom), as a whole. It is nationalist – but not only nationalist. Moreover it casts the contemporary class struggle in cultural terms; as a struggle for "old English times, old English fare, old English holidays" as well as "abundance". It is a struggle against oppression partly expressed in cultural terms.

Thus, as Thompson points out, it is possible to have a rebellious *traditional* culture.[23] Whether that culture is truly representative of what happened in the past, or is distorted or invented for the political ends of later times is not the point. The point is that new working class movements, lacking clear traditions from their own class, made these other traditions peculiarly their own. *Minjung* ideology played a similar role in newly industrializing Korea.

Students and intellectuals were commonly considered part of the *minjung*. This reflects the fact that, especially under the increased repression after the imposition of the authoritarian Yushin constitution in 1972, many opponents of the regime, including students, writers, journalists and church leaders, sought to reach out to and mobilize workers and peasants.[24] As in eighteenth century England, the most prominent champions of the working class, such as the proprietors of the "unstamped press", were not workers themselves at all but small business people, preachers or independent craftsmen.

In the hands of intellectuals, *minjung* forms of sociology, literature, theology and art were developed.[25] On university campuses in the 1980s it was common to see students performing revived peasant music, dance and drama.[26] Shamanist rituals – considered the native "folk" religion of the Korean masses – were often performed at demonstrations.

The mask-dance drama, which had originally evolved from harvest ceremonies, has always been an important form of cultural expression in Korea. In the 1980s it was taken over by the proponents of *minjung*. *Minjung* activists felt "a sense of mission – to revive the lost art of the people and return it to them".[27] This idea of going back to the people, in the Korean context, often meant the use of cultural forms derived from peasant life, combined with a practical orientation to the industrial working class. In the 1970s and 1980s, an estimated 3,000 or more students took jobs in industry with the explicit aim of helping to organize independent unions.[28] In one year alone, 1985–6, the police claimed to have unmasked 671 such agitators.[29]

Intellectuals influenced by *minjung* ideas increasingly oriented their work towards the labour movement and risked a great deal in doing so. But the nationalist element of *minjung* could also be appropriated by the regime. And folk culture was not necessarily the preserve of opponents of the government–chaebol alliance. They could be used by the right for its own purposes. Eric Hobsbawm warns that the culture of exploited classes is never developed by them alone.

> The world of the poor, however, elaborate, self-contained, and separate, is a subaltern and therefore in some sense incomplete world, for it normally takes for granted the existence of the general framework of those who have hegemony, or at any rate its inability for most of the time to do much about it. It accepts their hegemony, even when it challenges some of its implications because largely it has to.[30]

The nationalist element in *minjung* ideas was particularly prone to incorporation by the government. The military or ex-military men, who formed the core of governments between 1961 and 1992 also styled themselves nationalists – determined to develop the country to prevent dependency. "National" culture was contested. Government funds were poured into the discovery, preservation and dissemination of popular (folk) culture throughout the worst periods of dictatorship.[31]

Similarly, at the time of the "making" of the English working class, popular notions of the Englishman's "birthright" could inspire right-wing, "Church and King" mobs to attack radicals, although the same ideas were held by the radicals themselves.

In any case, *minjung* appealed to workers with no working class tradition, with little history as workers and with strong collective memories of the countryside. By the middle 1980s, large sections of the working class had considerable experience of their own in battles against employers and the state. Cultural methods of transmitting a political message, however, continued. But they became more explicitly steeped in the experience of the working class. A working class literature had developed, often encouraged by student activists who help set up small publishing houses for the purpose.

By the mid-1980s, there were some well-known worker writers, including poets such as Pak No Hae – whose verse dwells on workers' alienation and the injustice by which great wealth is concentrated in the hands of the chaebol.

Like a snake shedding skin the Korean workers had begun to outgrow *minjung*. Eventually its influence became very much weaker. However, working class cultural activities – newspapers, magazines, evening schools, dance groups and writing contests – remained an important part of the labour movement. Many unions sponsor cultural activities: mask dances, plays, music. In 1988 a National Council of Workers' Cultural Movement Organizations was formed to coordinate their activities.[32]

Church and class

Religion and religious institutions played an important part – although a transitory one – in both Korean and English working class movements in their early stages. Methodism and various forms of Dissent provided many English workers with a belief system within which they might feel justified in objecting to their condition and which might sustain their faith in a better future. If the oppressors were ungodly then rebellion was justified by scripture. In Korea also, Christianity, or sections of it, played a similar role.[33]

That workers could find solace, and even a rallying point in religion, should be less surprising to Marxists than may be obvious. Marx's oft repeated maxim – that religion "is the opium of the people" – is usually quoted without the rest of the paragraph of which it is a part. That reads:

> Religious suffering is at one and the same time the expression of real suffering and a protest against real suffering. Religion is the sigh of the oppressed creature, the heart of a heartless world and the soul of soulless conditions. It is the opium of the people.[34]

In Korea by the 1970s, as in early industrial England, there was plenty of real suffering and soulless conditions. *Minjung* thought provided a point of intersection between political action and the beliefs of Korean Christians. Two organizations in particular, the Catholic group, Young Christian Workers (JOC) and the Protestant Urban Industrial Mission (UIM), began to involve themselves in the welfare of the factory worker during the 1960s. Lessons in labour law and union organizing were combined with classes in scripture. Some clergy even took factory jobs as part of their mission.[35]

At first they offered legal courses, with the support of the labour department of the government, in how to run a union within the FKTU official structure. But they rapidly became associated with some of the most important disputes of the 1970s. About 20 per cent of new unions formed in that decade were assisted by the UIM.[36]

Thompson's discussion of English Methodism makes it clear that the relationship between religious ideas of deliverance and the worldly success or failure of a labour movement is complex. He argues that: "it is possible that religious revivalism took over just at the point where 'political' or temporal aspirations met with defeat."[37] In other words, workers turned to religion as a replacement for the victories which eluded them in daily life. The spread of religion could be symptomatic of a movement in retreat. But in Korea, the sequence was different. There Christianity played its greatest role in the workers' movement in the early stages of its formation – especially in the late 1960s and the 1970s. But, in those stages the movement was young and small, state repression intense and therefore victories were rare. As independent unionism developed, organized nationally and, eventually exploded in the great burst of militancy between 1987 and 1990, Christianity played a less significant role. Its influence in the labour movement waned greatly.

There were several more temporal and obvious ways in which the Christian churches became attractive to worker activists in the 1960s and 1970s. One was that they provided social bonds for people who had been removed from a network of family and friends by the process of industrialization. Young rural migrants, working long hours in factories far from their homes, experienced extreme isolation. Many found themselves housed in factory dormitories, closely supervised by management. Workers were frequently shifted between dorms in order to prevent the growth of solidarity or networks of resistance. These isolated, uprooted workers were searching for companionship and solidarity and shelter from a brutal and intrusive management as much as they were looking for a religious belief system.[38]

Although the factory system did not develop in the same way in England, Thompson discovered that the dislocation of people from their old communities made an open, relatively democratic church a social, as well as political, haven.

> Methodism, with its open chapel doors, did offer to the uprooted and abandoned people of the Industrial Revolution some kind of community to replace the older community-patterns which were being displaced.... Indeed, for many people in these years the Methodist "ticket" of church-membership acquired a fetishistic importance; for the migrant worker it could be the ticket of entry into a new community when he moved from town to town.[39]

Finally, the church provided those who wanted to organize a union with some resources and with a degree of "cover" – a site to organize which, for a time at least, remained just on the safe side of the law and its enforcers. This legal "window" was vital in the early period. Under church influence, about 40,000 workers were organized into unions at about 100 enterprises during the late 1960s.[40] Many of the activists who went on to help found the large independent unions of the 1980s and unite them in the Korean Confederation of Trade Unions (KCTU) in the 1990s got their original experience here.

Yet, during the 1980s, church influence on the labour movement declined. Several explanations for this decline seem to fit the circumstances. First, just as its attraction in an early period was to a recently dislocated workforce, so when workers became more settled, they could form social bonds in their own community without the church. Second, the growth of the labour movement began to create a different sense of community – a community of activists. Finally, increasing confrontation – on broad political as well as economic questions – between the new unions and the state radicalized unionists further.[41] Activists shifting leftward, some influenced by Marxism, often found the church too mild.[42]

Conclusion

One of E.P. Thompson's important contributions to Marxist thought was to draw attention to the apparently irregular ways in which class consciousness develops or, in many cases, fails to do so. It is necessary now to remember that he was writing in circumstances where most Marxist discussion was still dominated by those who had only friendly criticism for the Soviet Union – if they had any at all. For that tradition, the working class was, as often as not, a category to be manipulated in practice as well as in theory. A stage army, it was to be brought into play at the appropriate moment, expected to think the thoughts and take the action it was supposed to in response to the objective development of industry or economic crisis. Thompson shows that the growth of working class consciousness, especially in "new" working classes cannot be predicted before the fact. The attempt to do so contains considerable political as well as theoretical dangers in which predictive certainty becomes authoritarian practice.

> There is a cultural superstructure through which this recognition [of class] dawns in inefficient ways. These cultural "lags" and distortions are a nuisance, so that it becomes easy to pass from this to some theory of substitution: the party, sect or theorist, who disclose class consciousness, not as it is, but as it ought to be.[43]

In the lives of ordinary people, proletarianization is an enormous transformation. Such a transformation is still occurring throughout the world and affecting the lives of millions. That fact alone makes the study of how workers come to understand and react to it important. In Korea, as in early England, workers did, in fact, develop something that deserves to be called "class consciousness". What's more they did so under conditions where repressive forces of various kinds sought to frustrate its development.

Repression may set the limits allowed by rulers. But try as it will, it cannot always intrude on the furtive rebellious conversation in the factory dormitory, the secret evening meeting, the church service or evening class. In those arenas, ways of thinking, speaking, joking and even praying begin to develop that is common to this new class. In ways in which they think about society, proletarians begin to resemble each other culturally more than they resemble those of their parents or siblings who remained to till the soil.

Notes

1 Thompson (1963).
2 Thompson (1963, p. 913) writes:

> The slow, piecemeal accretions of capital accumulation had meant that the preliminaries to the Industrial Revolution stretched backwards for hundreds of years. From Tudor times onwards this artisan culture had grown more complex with each phase of technical and social change. Delaney, Dekker and Nashe: Winstanley and Lilburne: Bunyan and Defoe all had at times addressed themselves to it.

3 Thompson (1991, pp. 60–61). Both tickets include the patron saint of woolcombers – Bishop Blaize. They are reproduced on Plates 1 and 3.
4 Chiu (1992, p. 130).
5 Jones and Sakong (1980, pp. 352–354).
6 Ibid., p. 379.

7 Ibid., p. 77.
8 Bello and Rosenfeld (1992, p. 30).
9 Kim *et al.* (1995, p. 183).
10 In all nearly one million civilians and over 300,000 troops from South Korea alone (whose population was only around 22 million) were killed in the war. About 25 per cent of population became refugees. For the extent of destruction due to the war see Chiu (1992, p. 113); Whelan (1990, p. 373); Cole and Lyman (1971, p. 22); MacDonald (1986, p. 258); Rees (1964, p. 441); Haggard *et al.* (1997, p. 872).
11 Cumings (1990, pp. 699–702).
12 Chiu (1992, p. 137).
13 Cole and Lyman (1971, p. 27).
14 Bello and Rosenfeld (1992, p. 33).
15 Ibid., p. 23.
16 Ogle (1990, p. 20).
17 Many theorists have argued that the key cultural aspect of Korean society which must be taken into account is Confucianism. Some have argued that the Confucian value system is the key to understanding economic success in East Asia. See for example, Pye (1985). There are many objections to this line of argument – not the least that it is an ethnocentric misunderstanding of the varied cultures of the region and that it fails to explain the often turbulent histories of working class and peasant militancy. In addition, in the case of Korea, it is possible to argue that Confucianism has been the culture of the elite, not the masses. See, for example, Wells (1995, p. 6) and Chung (1995, p. 62).
18 Thompson (1963, p. 805).
19 Wells (1995, p. 2). For critical discussion of recent *minjung* theorists see Kim (1995). Also see Dalton and Cotton (1996, p. 279); and Koo (1993, p. 143).
20 Chung (1995, p. 69).
21 Irwan (1987, p. 389).
22 Thompson (1963, p. 254).
23 Thompson (1991, p. 9).
24 Koo (1993, p. 143).
25 Ibid., p. 144.
26 Clark (1995, p. 95).
27 Choi (1995, p. 111).
28 Koo (1993, p. 150).
29 Ogle (1990, p. 99). The penalty for being discovered was severe. In 1986, Kwon In Sook, a woman student was discovered working in a factory. She was arrested, sexually assaulted and tortured with electric shock. She attempted suicide. Finally she was sentenced to a year-and-a-half in jail for lying on her employment application. Close links were built between radical students and the developing workers' movement – some of which remain today. In my own experience, some of the student and former student activists I have met spent some time in industry for the purpose of organizing. And some workers who had been victimized were using the limited cover of the university to continue organizing. So it was that I met the former (victimized) president of a local Hyundai car workers' union in a little office in a university in Seoul.
30 Hobsbawm (1978, p. 20).
31 Choi (1995, p. 111).
32 Koo (1993, p. 160).
33 It is important here to note that not all Christians in Korea were sympathetic to the workers' movement. Indeed large sections of both Protestant and Catholic hierarchies denounced those of their colleagues who looked to the workers' movement and preached resistance. Methodism in England was similarly divided – vertically between the high Toryism of its founder, John Wesley, on one side and many itinerant preachers and worker activists in its ranks.

34 Marx (1975, p. 244).
35 About 25 clergy went to factories in this way; Ogle (1990, p. 87).
36 Koo (1993, p. 140).
37 Thompson (1963, p. 428).
38 Dormitory inspectors and matrons were commonly used as overseers of workers outside production in order to break social ties. Lee (1988, p. 141).
39 Thompson (1963, pp. 416–417).
40 Lee (1988, p. 143).
41 A discussion of these conflicts and the most recent struggles of the Korean labour movement is beyond the scope of this chapter. Readable accounts in English for various periods can be found in the Asia Monitor Resource Center (1987), McNally (1988) and in Moody (1997).
42 Koo (1993, p. 150).
43 Thompson (1991, p. 9).

Bibliography

Asia Monitor Resource Center. 1987. *Min-Ju, No-Jo, South Korea's New Trade Unions*, Hong Kong: AMRC.

Bello, W. and Rosenfeld, S. 1992. *Dragons in Distress: Asia's Miracle Economies in Crisis*, London: Penguin, London.

Chiu, Stephen Wing-Kai. 1992. "The State and the Financing of Industrialisation in East Asia: Historical Origins of Comparative Divergences", PhD thesis, Princeton University.

Choi, Chungmoo. 1995. "The Minjung Culture Movement and the Construction of Popular Culture in Korea", in *South Korea's Minjung Movement: The Culture and Politics of Dissidence.* Ed. Kenneth Wells. Honolulu: University of Hawaii Press.

Chung, Chai-sik, 1995. "Confucian Tradition and Nationalist Ideology in Korea", in *South Korea's Minjung Movement: The Culture and Politics of Dissidence.* Ed. Kenneth Wells. Honolulu: University of Hawaii Press.

Clark, David. 1995. "Growth and Limitations of Minjung Christianity in South Korea", in *South Korea's Minjung Movement: The Culture and Politics of Dissidence.* Ed. Kenneth Wells. Honolulu: University of Hawaii Press.

Cole, David C. and Lyman, Princeton N. 1971. *Korean Development, the Interplay of Politics and Economics*, Cambridge, MA: Harvard University Press.

Cumings, Bruce. 1981. *The Origins of the Korean War, Vol 1, Liberation and the Emergence of Separate Regimes, 1945–1947*, Princeton, NJ: Princeton University Press.

Cumings, Bruce. 1990. *The Origins of the Korean War, Vol. 2, The Roaring of the Cataract, 1947–1950*, Princeton, NJ: Princeton University Press.

Dalton, Bronwen and Cotton, James. 1996. "New Social Movements and the Changing Nature of Political Opposition in South Korea", in *Political Oppositions in Industrialising Asia.* Ed. Garry Rodan. London: Routledge.

Haggard, Stephan, Kang, David and Moon, Chung-In. 1997. "Japanese Colonialism and Korean Development: A Critique". *World Development*, 25(6): 867–881.

Hobsbawm, Eric J. 1978. "Religion and the Rise of Socialism". *Marxist Perspectives* 1: 20.

Irwan, Alexander. 1987. "Real Wages and Class Struggle in South Korea". *Journal of Contemporary Asia*, 17(4): 385–408.

Jones, Leroy P. and Il Sakong. 1980. *Government, Business and Entrepreneurship in Economic Development: The Korean Case*, Cambridge, MA: Harvard University Press.

Kim, Hyung-A. 1995. "Minjung Socioeconomic Responses to State-led Industrialization", in *South Korea's Minjung Movement: The Culture and Politics of Dissidence.* Ed. Kenneth Wells. Honolulu: University of Hawaii Press.

Kim, Joon-Kyung, Shim, Sang Dal and Kim, Jun-Il. 1995. "The Role of the Government in Promoting Industrialisation and Human Capital Accumulation in Korea", in *Growth Theories in Light of the East Asian Experience. National Bureau of Economic Research: East Asia Seminar on Economics Series*, Vol. 4. Eds Takatoshi Ito and Anne O. Krueger. Chicago, IL, and London: University of Chicago Press.

Ko, Won. 1977. "Kim Chi-ha: Poet of Blood and Fire". *Bulletin of Concerned Asian Scholars*, 9(2): 20–25.

Koo, Hagen. 1993. "The State, *Minjung*, and the Working Class in South Korea", in *State and Society in Contemporary Korea.* Ed. Hagan Koo. Ithaca, NY, and London: Cornell University Press.

Lee, Jeong Taik. 1988. "Dynamics of Labor Control and Labor Protest in the Process of Export-Oriented Industrialisation in South Korea". *Asian Perspectives*, 12(1): 134–158.

MacDonald, C. 1986. *Korea: The War before Vietnam*, New York: The Free Press.

McNally, David. 1988. "Globalisation on Trial: Crisis and Class Struggle in East Asia". *Monthly Review*, 50(4): 1–13.

Marx, Karl. 1975. "Critique of Hegel's Philospohy of Right", in *Karl Marx: Early Writings.* Harmondsworth: Penguin.

Moody, Kim. 1997. *Workers in a Lean World*, London: Verso.

Ogle, George E. 1990. *South Korea: Dissent Within the Economic Miracle*, London: Zed Books.

Pye, Lucian, 1985. *Asian Power and Politics: The Cultural Dimensions of Authority*, Cambridge, MA, and London: Belknap Press of Harvard University Press.

Rees, D. 1964. *Korea: The Limited War*, London: Macmillan.

Song, Byung-Nak. 1994. *The Rise of the Korean Economy*, Oxford: Oxford University Press.

Sung, Yeung Kwack. 1990. "The Economic Development of the Republic of Korea, 1965–1981", in *Models of Development: A Comparative Study of Economic Growth in South Korea and Taiwan.* Ed. Lawrence J. Lau, 2nd edn. San Francisco, CA: ICS Press.

Thompson, Edward P. 1963. *The Making of the English Working Class*, London: Penguin.

Thompson, Edward P. 1991. *Customs in Common*, London: Penguin.

Wells, Kenneth. 1995. "Introduction", in *South Korea's Minjung Movement: The Culture and Politics of Dissidence.* Ed. Kenneth Wells. Honolulu: University of Hawaii Press.

Whelan, R. 1990. *Drawing the Line: The Korean War, 1950–1953*, London: Faber.

14 Neoliberal globalization and labor relations in Korea

Byoung-Hoon Lee

Introduction

"Globalization" is now a buzzword frequently used by academics and policy-makers to depict the epoch-making transformation of human life that is evolving in nearly every societal dimension: economic, political, cultural, and technological. Despite on-going debate[1] regarding the definition of globalization, its causal mechanism, and consequences, it is undeniable that globalization has, to a certain extent, reshaped the way people everywhere live, work, and do business.

Against this backdrop, globalization has been the subject matter of intense contention in Korea among organized labor, business circles, and the government. Labor unions are adamantly critical of contemporary globalization, presuming that it is stirring the "forces of evil" that victimize workers by imposing neoliberal economic restructuring and the race-to-the-bottom. The other parties – the government and business groups – view globalization not only in the given context of irresistible worldwide economic integration, but also as imperative for economic reforms to enhance national competitiveness under the growing competition of global markets. Over the last two decades, while creating ideological debates among concerned parties, globalization, combined with social democratization and economic reforms, has exerted a significant influence on the transformation of countrywide labor relations. In this light, my chapter is to examine what impact globalization had on Korean labor relations and how labor relations has, in turn, been transformed during the 1990s, by focusing on the two administrations, led by Presidents Kim Young-Sam and Kim Dae-jung.

Dual face of globalization: environmental pressure and government policy

The effect of globalization on labor relations in Korea can be conceived as being twofold – that is, the structural context of socio-economic integration and the government's policy agenda.[2] On the one hand, globalization, which becomes a key contextual factor to influence labor relations in any countries (including Korea), has been propelled by the new order of international free trade, increasing cross-national mobility of capital (and labor in the less extent) with the strengthening role of international finance institutions, the growing significance of global standards for both business and labor, and breakthroughs in information-communication technology (ICT) during the 1990s. On the other hand, globalization has manifested itself into the Korean government's policy agenda, a core part of which was to reform the existing institutional systems of labor relations and labor markets in its strategic pursuit of enhancing the competitiveness of its national economy under the environment of economic integration in the mid-1990s and coping with the economic crisis that struck in late 1997. In this light, globalization could be treated as an interwoven force of environmental pressure and the government's responding strategies, which triggered and conditioned the reshaping of Korean labor relations.

It was around 1994 that the term "globalization" came to the fore in Korea. The Uruguay Round, starting in 1986 to expand global free trade, reached a final agreement in 1994 and, as a consequence, the GATT (General Agreement on Tariffs and Trade) was replaced in January 1995 by the World Trade Organization (WTO), which has stronger regulatory power to enforce the new norms of free trade to member countries. Under the WTO system, the Korean government began to evolve its so-called globalization strategy to enhance the competitiveness of the national economy and promote economic liberalization. President Kim Young-Sam announced his "Grand Idea of Globalization" in November 1994, and the Globalization Committee, formed in January 1995, formulated a set of new national development strategies in the era of globalization, covering government administration, diplomacy and unification, economy, social dimension, education and culture, and politics (Globalization Committee 1998). Moreover, President Kim made active efforts for the country to gain membership to the OECD (Organisation for Economic Co-operation and Development) as part of his plan to elevate the country to the elite status of advanced economies. Korea's successful accession to the OECD in mid-1996 was a result of steps taken by the government to further expand economic liberalization for foreign capital in such areas as M&A, portfolio investment, real property investment, and direct investment (International Solidarity Policy Information Center 1999).

In 1996, the government initiated extensive reform of the existing labor laws by resorting to the process of tripartite consultation, by which it intended to promote labor market flexibility required for the improvement of national economic competitiveness as well as meet international labor standards as a condition for joining the OECD. In 1996, President Kim Young-Sam announced his "Grand Idea for New Industrial Relations" and formed the Presidential Commission on Industrial Relations Reform (PCIRR), in order to reshape labor relations in the new era of globalization and information society. The labor laws, which were finally revised after intense tripartite dialogue and labor–state confrontations, reflected a compromise of differing interests between employers and labor unions. For employers, the revised Labor Standards Act (LSA) introduced lay-off procedures along with the flexible and selective working hour system, thereby promoting the flexible use and adjustment of the labor force. At the same time, the new Labor Union Act expanded labor unions' rights to the level of international labor standards by doing away with existing anti-union provisions, which prohibited multiple union organizations, third party involvement, and unions' political activity.

The outbreak of the foreign exchange crisis in November 1997 was to a certain extent attributable to the globalization strategy pursued by the government and business groups.[3] The government, which was obsessed with its ambitious plan to advance the national economy in the era of globalization, adhered to the mistaken foreign exchange policy for a strong Korean won and mismanaged the external liabilities and balance of payment, as shown in Table 14.1. Business groups, which over-expanded production capacity both at home and overseas in order to advance as global competitors, also contributed in crippling the national economy with their excessive debt. As vast amounts of foreign capital fled the country under the worsening economic conditions, Korea abruptly fell into a serious crisis in late 1997.

Ironically, the economic crisis has deepened the impact of globalization on the Korean economy. In coping with the foreign exchange crisis, the government entered into a stand-by agreement with the IMF for a bailout program that provided emergency loans amounting to US$19.5 billion. The stand-by agreement included various economic restructuring programs to be carried out by the Korean government.[4]

The stand-by agreement between the IMF and the Korean government included reform of corporate governance, restructuring and liberalization of the financial market, dissolution of import regulations, enhancement of labor market flexibility, and expansion of the social safety net. Under the context of the economic crisis and in accordance with the economic reform guidelines imposed by international finance institutions (i.e., IMF and World Bank), President Kim Dae-jung, elected in December 1997, led extensive restructuring policies targeting four sectors – corporate, financial, public, and labor – since early 1998. His economic restructuring policy basically aimed to transform the existing state-dominated economy toward a market-driven system by benchmarking the neoliberal model of Anglo-Saxon countries (i.e., the US and the UK). In addition to its various reform steps in the private, finance, and public sectors,[5] the Kim Dae-jung administration made a partial change in labor laws in accordance with the IMF agreement, particularly for promoting flexibility of the labor market. Gaining labor unions' endorsement as part of the Social Pact of the Tripartite Commission, the government amended the LSA to put the lay-off provision into effect and enacted the Dispatched Workers Protection Act in February 1998. At the same time, it guaranteed that civil servants' works councils and teachers' unions could be established in 1999. As such, globalization, seen as a combined force of the newly emerging politico-economic environments and the government's strategic responses, offers the most significant contextual background to the reshaping of labor relations

Table 14.1 Indices of the Korean national economy (billion US$)

	1993	*1994*	*1995*	*1996*	*1997*	*1998*	*1999*	*2000*
GDP growth (%)	5.5	8.3	8.9	6.8	5.0	–6.7	10.9	8.8
GNP per capita	7,381	8,998	10,823	11,380	10,307	6,723	8,551	9,628
Balance of payment	0.99	–3.87	–8.51	–23.01	–8.17	40.56	24.48	11.04
External liability	43.9	97.4	127.5	163.5	159.2	148.7	137.1	136.3
Foreign currency reserve	18.3	22.4	29.4	29.4	8.8	48.5	74.1	96.2
Exchange rate (won/US$)	803	804	771	805	951	1,399	1,189	1,131

Source: Center for Economic Information, KDI (http://epic.kdi.re.kr/home/english/index.html).

Note
The figures for external liability and foreign currency reserve are as of year-end.

Transformation of labor relations

Establishment of social dialogue system

In pursuit of the globalization strategy (Kim Young-Sam administration) and neoliberal restructuring policies (Kim Dae-jung administration), the government implemented a model of social dialogue as a means of promoting concerted efforts for three parties to deal with various challenges derived from globalization (i.e., labor law reform by the PCIRR and economic restructuring via the Tripartite Commission).[6]

The establishment of the PCIRR in May 1996 is viewed as the first genuine attempt at tripartism. The PCIRR, formed as a presidential advisory body and composed of representatives from labor unions, employers' associations, academics, and public interest groups, provided a formal and open forum of social dialogue among various stakeholders with regard to the reform of labor laws. In particular, the PCIRR included representatives of the Korean Confederation of Trade Unions (KCTU), the second national center of democratic labor unions, which was formed in November 1995, but not legally recognized until 1999. After a number of public hearings and workshops of its subcommittees and following lengthy discussion in plenary sessions, the PCIRR prepared policy recommendations of labor law reforms and sent them to the government.[7] The PCIRR might be regarded as a significant experiment of tripartism to adopt policy-consultations over the labor reform, although it drew little attention from organized labor and public press after the intensified labor–state confrontations of early 1997, caused by the government's action to disregard its recommendations and revise labor laws in a unilateral manner.

The financial crisis breaking out in November 1997 created a condition for expanding the agenda of social dialogue and encouraging tripartite policy consultations. Under the unprecedented economic crisis, President Kim Dae-jung established the Tripartite Commission in January 1998 in order to promote joint efforts of three parties to cope with the crisis. The Tripartite Commission enables labor unions to directly address their demands to and discuss with government officials. It also covers a more extensive agenda, including economic reforms and social welfare policies, as well as labor issues. The historic "Social Pact," which the first Tripartite Commission made by the 25-day intensive negotiation in February 1998, embraced 90 agreed items of socio-economic policy areas. Note that most items of the social pact were basically to endorse the stand-by agreement imposed by the IMF and World Bank (i.e., corporate transparency, labor market flexibility, and social security for the unemployed) or to reflect the concerned issues over basic labor rights by international labor institutions, such as the ILO (International Labour Organization) and the trade union group (TUAC) of the OECD.

From mid-1998, the Tripartite Commission attempted to have prior policy consultations over the direction and principles of economic restructuring for the finance and public sectors, which was the core part of the IMF-guided reform programs. The Tripartite Commission has since played a role of the intermediating forum to negotiate newly raised labor issues, like the reduction of working hour, protection of non-standard workers, and unionization of civil servants. As Vogel and Lindauer (1989) suggest, social dialogue, exemplified by the PCIRR and the Tripartite Commission, has been a key instrument of new governance for national-level labor relations since the mid-1990s, even though recurrent labor–state confrontations and the withdrawal of the KCTU weakened those bodies' operation.[8]

The social dialogue system has been implemented by the government's strategic choice to handle the policy issues, generated by the globalizing context (and the economic crisis). It has also become an institutionalized vehicle for both labor unions and employers to advance and intermediate their interests in the connection with global standards (i.e., the enhancement of labor rights for the former, and the promotion of labor flexibility for the latter). In particular, labor unions have tried to gain the assistance or demand the pressure from international society for fulfilling their interests in social dialogue processes, by gaining support from the ILO and the OECD.

Changes of enterprise-level labor relations and union structure

The late 1990s have witnessed substantial changes in labor–management relations under the context of globalization. The contention between labor unions and management has shifted from economic issues such as wages and welfare benefits to employment security or flexibility. This is evident in the reasons of labor disputes, as demonstrated in Table 14.2. Labor disputes, which largely

Table 14.2 Trends of labor disputes by reasons

	Total	*Overdue wages*	*Wage increases*	*Dismissal*[1]	*Contract languages*	*Others*[2]
1990	322	10 (3.1)	167 (51.9)	18 (5.6)	49 (15.2)	78 (24.2)
1991	234	5 (2.1)	132 (56.4)	7 (3.0)	56 (23.9)	34 (14.5)
1992	235	27 (11.5)	134 (57.0)	4 (1.7)	49 (20.9)	21 (8.9)
1993	144	11 (7.6)	66 (45.8)	1 (0.7)	52 (36.1)	14 (9.7)
1994	121	6 (5.0)	51 (42.1)	3 (2.5)	42 (34.7)	19 (15.7)
1995	88	0 (0.0)	33 (37.5)	1 (1.1)	49 (55.7)	5 (5.7)
1996	85	1 (1.2)	19 (22.4)	0 (0.0)	62 (72.9)	3 (3.5)
1997	78	3 (3.8)	18 (23.1)	0 (0.0)	51 (65.4)	6 (7.7)
1998	129	23 (17.8)	28 (21.7)	3 (2.3)	57 (44.2)	10 (7.8)
1999	198	22 (11.1)	40 (20.2)	0 (0.0)	89 (44.9)	47 (23.7)
2000	250	7 (2.8)	47 (18.8)	2 (0.8)	167 (66.8)	27 (10.8)
2001	235	6 (2.6)	59 (25.1)	0 (0.0)	149 (63.4)	21 (8.9)

Source: Korea Labor Institute 2002.

Notes
1 Dismissal due to management's disciplinary action or union activities.
2 Including various reasons for lay-offs, merger and acquisition, spin-offs and outsourcing, etc.

came from wage negotiations until 1994, were mainly caused by the issue of union members' employment security. Management at many firms were concerned over a growing global market competition and attempted to expand labor flexibility by such various action as outsourcing, spin-offs, organizational restructuring, and early retirement plans, whereas labor unions tried to gain labor contracts for constraining those managerial steps from making their members' employment insecure. Labor–management relations worsened during the years of the economic crisis, largely owing to management-led downsizing and business restructuring.[9] As shown in Table 14.2, the number of labor disputes, which had fallen below 100 prior to the crisis (1995–1997), increased from 129 in 1998 to 250 in 2000. Particularly, a series of intense labor disputes at large firms took place as labor unions opposed the government's economic restructuring policies for the public and financial sectors as well as the management-led downsizing action (e.g., Hyundai Motor in 1998 and Daewoo Motor in 2001). Moreover, management initiated the reshaping of the existing personnel scheme under the context of economic crisis. According to a KLI survey, conducted in 2000, the vast majority of Korean companies have made noticeable changes in such personnel schemes as wage system, performance evaluation, job promotion, and career management from 1998 on, as illustrated in Table 14.3 (Park and Noh 2001). In particular, the same survey reported that 45.2 percent of respondent companies have implemented a merit pay plan (called "annual salary"), particularly for white-collar employees.[10]

As such, globalization and, more significantly, the economic crisis, which placed labor unions into a defensive position, laid down favorable conditions for enabling employers to introduce a performance-based personnel system, and more closely linked workers' wages and employment to market situations.

Labor unions have made remarkable efforts to enhance their interest representation and transform organizational structure under the context of globalization. The unionization of teachers and civil servants, allowed as part of the 1998 social pact, contributed in the regain of union membership, which declined mainly due to de-industrialization of the national economy and massive downsizing until 1998, as illustrated in Figure 14.1. The unionization of both teachers and civil servants has, to a certain extent, been aided by both international labor institutions and foreign unions, which pressured the governments to implement labor rights.

Table 14.3 Changes in personnel schemes

	Wage system	*Performance appraisal*	*Job promotion*	*Career management*	*Organizational structure*
Change rate	992.8%	887.7%	887.8%	773.7%	96.8%

Source: Park and Noh 2001, p. 11.

Note
Change rate denotes the percentage of companies that have changed their personnel schemes.

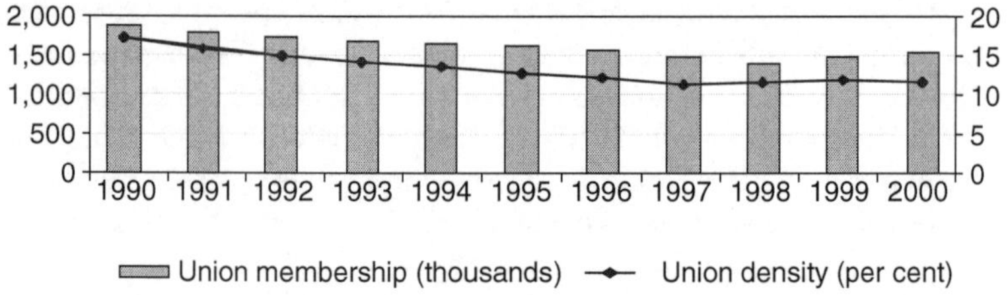

Figure 14.1 Trends in union membership and union density.

In addition, many industrial federations (mainly affiliated with the KCTU) achieved organizational amalgamation and, more significantly, some of them, including the Health and Medical Workers Union (1998), the Banking Workers Union (2000), and the Metal Workers Union (2001), transformed their organizational structures into the industrial union model. The main reason for the organizational restructuring of labor unions is that the decentralized structure of the enterprise model constrained labor unions from effectively responding to the challenges of globalization and economic restructuring, and, therefore, need to be transformed toward the bigger and concentrated one. Along with the organizational transformation toward the industry unionism, labor unions demanded an industry-wide centralized bargaining structure. However, the unions' demand has not yet been accepted by employers, who prefer the decentralized structure of the existing enterprise bargaining. Accordingly, the globalization has made an indirect, yet crucial impact on the reshaping of union structure and bargaining arrangements.

Increasing labor issues of marginal workers

The globalization has contributed in a noticeable change of labor market situation in Korea. In particular, employers' new employment strategies, which were boosted by the globalizing environment as well as the government's responding policies, has led to a proliferation of marginal workforce, such as foreign and non-standard workers, and the unemployed in the labor market. The growing presence of those marginal worker groups, in turn, has created new labor issues in the contested arena of labor relations during the 1990s.

Under the tight labor market condition that the country continued to have a very low unemployment rate of below 3 percent before the outbreak of the economic crisis in late 1997, the influx of foreign workers, which might be viewed as an indicator of the globalizing labor market mechanism, grew rapidly from the early 1990s to 1996, as illustrated in Figure 14.2. The increase of foreign workers can be explained from the dual aspects of supply and demand. On the side of demand, the severe labor shortage of small manufacturing firms, which was due to domestic workers' aversion of 3D (difficult, dangerous, and dirty) manufacturing jobs, engendered the inflow of foreign workers.[11] On the supply

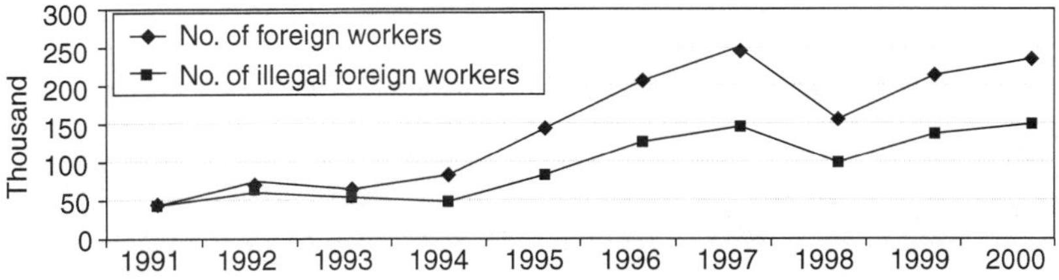

Figure 14.2 Trends in foreign workforce in Korea (source: Ministry of Justice).

Note
Data for 1991–1999 is as of year-end, and that of 2000 as of April.

side, those foreign workers from countries with much cheaper labor immigrated in search of the "Korean dream" of earning relatively higher wages.

The problem is, however, that foreign workers, particularly those with illegal visa status, were excluded from the protection of Korean labor laws and suffered from inferior working conditions of small manufacturing firms. In this context, many civil activist groups, which had big concerns over the precarious status of foreign workers, were formed and undertook various activities to draw social attention to the inhumane employment situation of those workers and demand the government's action to improve the legal protection of their working conditions. Even foreign workers organized their own collective demonstrations with the aid of those civil groups. Confronted with mounting pressure from civil activist groups and social attention given to foreign workers, the government began providing partial legal protection, such as basic labor standards and occupational safety, from the mid-1990s, and attempted to introduce the "work-permit" program for guaranteeing foreign workers' legal employment status in 2000. Yet, the government's attempt was brought to a halt, due to strong resistance from employers of small firms, who were concerned about the increasing costs of foreign labor. The work permit program went through the heated policy debate for a while and was finally implemented in 2004.

The sharp growth of the non-standard workforce, including temporary workers, part-timers, temporary agency (or dispatched) workers, and independent contractors, has been another "hot potato" of labor relations. As shown in Figure 14.3, the share of the non-standard workforce in the total working population continued to soar since the mid-1990s and, in particular, has shown a drastic increase during the period of economic crisis. The government's official reports reveal that the share of non-standard workers increased from 45.9 percent in 1997 to 52.4 percent in 2000 and, therefore, exceeded that of regular workers. According to the research of recent years, it turns out that the non-standard workers, in general, are revealed to be under very precarious working conditions, compared to regular ones. In fact, the 2000 Working Population Survey of the Labor Statistics Office demonstrates that wages of non-standard workers reach only about 54 percent that of regular workers, and that over 70 percent of

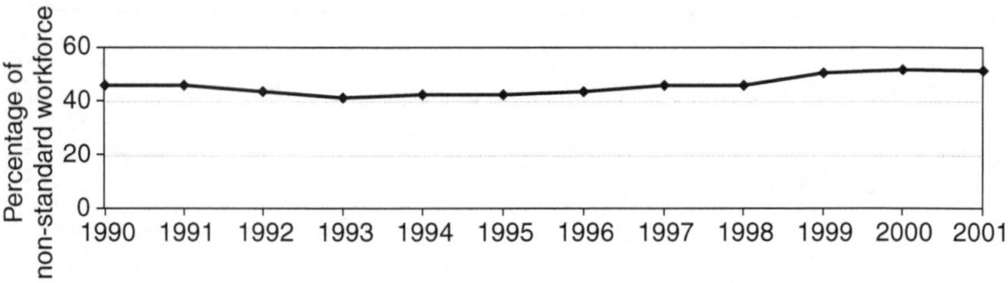

Figure 14.3 Shares of non-standard workforce (source: Korea Labor Institute 2002).

non-standard workforce is excluded from social security programs (i.e., national pension, medical insurance, and unemployment insurance) and legal labor standards (i.e., paid leave, extra working time allowances, severance pay, and bonuses) (Kim 2001). Concerned about the rapid proliferation of the non-standard workforce and their poor employment conditions, the national centers (the FKTU and the KCTU) of labor unions began pressuring the government to reform the existing labor laws for protecting those marginal workers and regulating employers' excessive use of the non-standard labor, while launching their own organizing campaigns to unionize the unprotected workers. As a consequence, the special committee to discuss labor law reforms and the government's policy to protect and regulate the employment terms of the non-standard workers was established as part of the Tripartite Commission in July 2001. Some groups of those non-standard workers were successful in organizing themselves, which invoked intense conflicts with management and, sometimes, regular workers. Moreover, labor unions and civil activist groups jointly engaged in collective demonstrations to demand the government's active efforts to improve the inferior employment status of those marginal workers. As such, the rapid proliferation of non-standard labor, prompted by management's strategic move for expanding labor flexibility under the globalizing context, has generated a core contested issue among three parties (and civil activist groups).

The economic crisis, occurring in the pathway to globalization, put the unemployed on focal attention of the society, as the unemployment rate soared to over 6 percent in 1998–1999. The sharp rise in the unemployment rate was attributed to the bankruptcy of numerous companies and massive downsizing undertaken by employers during the economic crisis.[12] Given social attention to soaring unemployment, the government and labor unions agreed upon special policy steps to protect the unemployed as part of the social pact in early 1998. The government spent a huge amount of special budget on assisting the livelihood of the unemployed and their job placement efforts in 1998, and expanded the coverage of employment insurance.[13] Although the unemployment rate declined to 3–4 percent along with the economic recovery after 2000, the unemployment of the youth (15–24 years old) remained as high as over 10 percent, becoming an hot issue of the government's labor market policy-making.

In sum, the liberation and market-driven restructuring of labor markets, pursued by the government and employers under the context of globalization, has led to the growing presence of a marginal workforce, such as foreign workers, non-standard workers, and the unemployed, which results in the growing labor market segmentation.

Conclusion: the causality of globalization and labor relations

Globalization alone cannot account for all the changes that took place in Korean labor relations during the 1990s. Yet, it is definitely one of most influential forces that have created the transformation of the country's labor relations. As summarized in Figure 14.4, the impact of globalization over labor relations can be understood as the combination of the two sets of interplaying factors: the contextual factors to condition the national economy and country-level labor relations, and the agent factor, particularly the government's policy strategies to respond to the globalizing context and enhance the national economy competitiveness. Some factors of the two categories, like growing influx of foreign capital and labor, labor reforms, and economic restructuring policy, had the

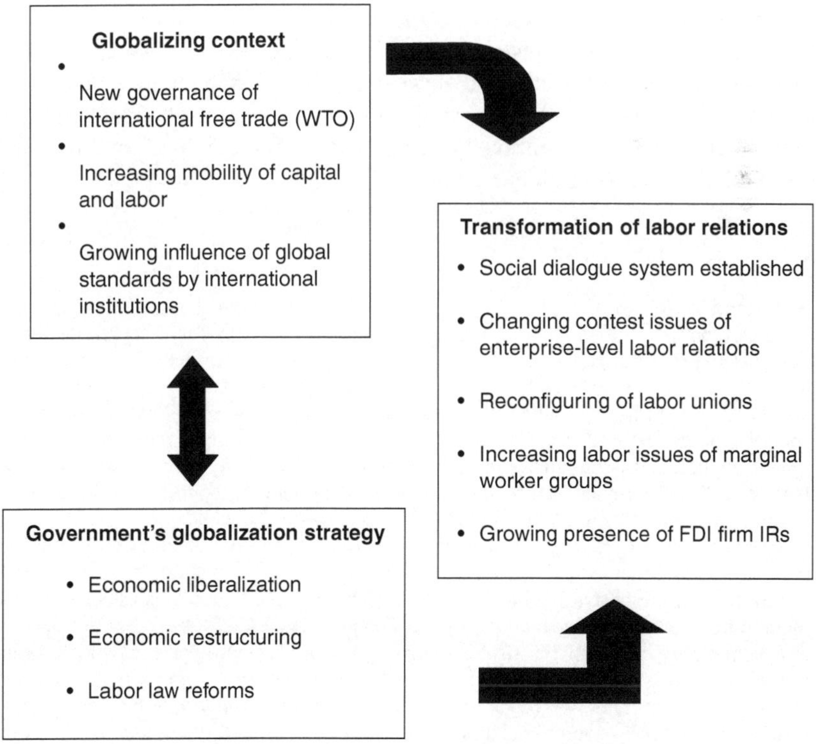

Figure 14.4 Diagram of globalization's effect on labor relations.

direct and immediate effect on the reshaping of labor relations, while other factors, such as the new order of international free trade (the establishment of the WTO system), global standards set by international institutions, and the government's economic liberalization policy, affected the game-playing of labor relations actors in an indirect and conditioning manner.

Globalization, as an interwoven pressure of the ever-integrating international environment and the government's responding policies, has led Korean labor relations to change to a certain extent. At the national level, a social dialogue system of tripartite policy consultation was implemented as a means to deal with challenges given by globalization, despite in an unstable form. The enterprise-level labor relations have shifted from the wage-focused and labor-offensive pattern to the employment-focused and labor-defensive one, along with growing labor-management confrontations and the organizational renewal of union structures and bargaining arrangements. Moreover, this period of globalization witnessed the growing presence of marginal workforce, such as foreign workers, non-standard employees, and the unemployed, which has generated a new contested terrain in Korean labor relations.

As Giles (2000) indicates, globalization has turned Korean labor relations into a more complicated game, involving domestic actors and institutions as well as overseas agency and institutional norms. The evolution of labor relations over the 1990s also shows a contradictory combination of social dialogue and neoliberal (or market-dominated) restructuring. To sum up, Korean labor relations, confronted with ever-growing challenges from the globalizing circumstance, have entered into the era of uncertainty, in that the terrain of labor relations embraces complex and contentious interplays, involving domestic and overseas actors under the context of globalization.

Notes

1 According to Held *et al.* (1999: 2–10), it is possible to distinguish three broad schools in conceptualizing globalization: hyperglobalizers, skeptics, and transformationalists. For the hyperglobalizers, contemporary globalization is interpreted as becoming increasingly subject to the disciplines of the global marketplace. By contrast, the skeptics maintain that globalization is essentially a myth that exaggerates worldwide socio-economic integration in that national governments remain powerful. For the transformationalists, globalization is conceived as historically unprecedented, such that states and societies across the globe are experiencing a process of profound change toward a more interconnected but highly uncertain world.

2 In a similar vein, Park (1999) distinguishes the contemporary evolution of globalization using two dimensions – the experiential dimension (the integration of the global economy) and the normative dimension (the developmental strategies of the government to integrate the national economy into the global economy).

3 The economic crisis can be also explained by structural problems of the Korean economy, such as the government-dominated finance system, business inefficiency of the corporate conglomerate (*chaebol*) system, and the corrupted ties between politicians and business. Moreover, labor unions and radical academics contend that the economic crisis was attributed to the conspiracy of international hedge funds.

4 The stand-by agreement between the IMF and the Korean government included

reform of corporate governance, restructuring and liberalization of the financial market, dissolution of import regulations, enhancement of labor market flexibility, and expansion of the social safety net.

5 The exemplary reform action in the three sectors is the enhancement of corporate governance transparency, business swaps, finance industry restructuring with raising the soundness of assets, and privatization.

6 For the details of historical evolution of social dialogue in Korea, see Lee (1999).

7 In the PCIRR's recommendation report, 107 out of 148 labor law issues were agreed upon, while 41 issues, including multiple labor unions, redundancy dismissal, teachers' right to organize, and replacement of striking workers, remained uncompromised among different interest groups.

8 In May 1999, the Tripartite Commission Act was legislated, so that the institutional status of the Commission was promoted to a permanent body for social dialogue.

9 A KLI survey indicates that during the economic crisis many employers carried out organizational restructuring, including spin-offs (74 percent), outsourcing (57.6 percent), and de-layering (49.2 percent), while undertaking downsizing actions and expanding the use of the non-standard workforce.

10 The survey, conducted by the Korea Employers Federation, reports that 15.3 percent of companies with more than 50 employees introduced the merit pay scheme in 1998, while another survey by the Ministry of Labor shows that 12.7 percent of companies with more than 100 employees implemented the same plan in 1999. Similarly, the government introduced performance-based pay for civil servants and employees of the public sector from 2000 on.

11 According to Kang (1996), the overall shortage rate of production labor in the manufacturing sector ranged from 5.5 to 9.6 percent between 1990 and 1996. In particular, the labor shortage of small manufacturing firms was even more severe at a rate of 8.6 to 16.4 percent.

12 The monthly average of bankrupt companies more than doubled from 430 in 1996 to around 1,000 in the fourth quarter of 1997 and the first quarter of 1998. According to a KLI survey of 400 companies listed on the stock market, 52.2 percent and 28.2 percent took downsizing actions in 1998 and 1999, respectively (Park and Noh 2001). The same survey reports that the rate of employment reduction in 1998 reached 16.2 percent.

13 The coverage of employment insurance has expanded to include small firms with more than five employees in March 1998 and later to all firms, including those with fewer than five employees, in April 1999. Moreover, the government began to apply employment insurance to temporary employees from July 1999 and plans to expand its coverage to daily workers beginning in 2003.

References

Giles, Anthony. 2000, "Globalization and Industrial Relations Theory," *Journal of Industrial Relations* 42(2): 173–194.

Globalization Committee. 1998, *White Paper on Globalization* (in Korean).

Held, David, Anthony McGrew, David Goldblatt, and Jonathan Perraton. 1999, *Global Transformations: Politics, Economics and Culture*, Stanford, Stanford University Press.

International Solidarity Policy Information Center. 1999, *From UR to IMF and New Millenium Round* (in Korean).

Kang, Soo-Dol. 1996, *Employment and Management of Foreign Workers and Policy Recommendations*, Korea Labor Institute (in Korean).

Kim, Yoo-Sun. 2001, "Size and Situation of Non-standard Workers," *Labor Society Bulletin* 54: 98–102.

Korea Labor Institute. 2002, *2002 Labor Statistics* (in Korean).
Lee, Byoung-Hoon. 1999, "Social Dialogue and Labor Union's Involvement," Paper presented to the ILO-KLI Regional Meeting on Organized Labor in the 21st Century.
Park, Jin-Do. 1999, "Neo-Liberalistic Globalization and WTO," Paper presented to the Training Camp for the National Farmers Association (in Korean).
Park, Woo-Sung and Yong-Jin Noh. 2001, *Changes of Human Resource Management and Labor Relations since the Economic Crisis*, Korea Labor Institute (in Korean).
Vogel, Ezra and David Lindauer. 1989, "Toward a Social Compact for South Korean Labor," Development Discussion Paper presented the international KLI conference in Seoul.

15 Labor movements in democratized Korea

An old or new social movement?[1]

Yoonkyung Lee

Introduction

Is a labor movement in a democratizing polity an old or new social movement? The new social movement literature developed from the rising articulation and mobilization around the issues of gender, ecology, and peace in Western democracies explicitly places labor into the "old" camp. Labor movements are considered to be old as they purport to represent the working-class interest, which has become too obsolete to reflect the diversified concerns of post-industrial society (Johnston *et al.* 1994). On the other hand, labor has gained a novel conceptualization of "social movement unionism" from the experiences of new democracies like South Africa and Brazil or those of old democracies like the United States and Canada to capture the broad coalitions of labor and other movement actors mobilized for general social justice agenda. Then, is the labor movement in the context of democratizing Korea on the old or new side of social activism? The organizing argument of this chapter is to show that Korean workers' movements developed and diversified to include both the old and new dimensions of the movement conceptualization. This chapter discusses the evolution of this duality where a part of the Korean labor movement has become institutionalized by primarily focusing on material and labor rights issues along with another part of the movement that is closely tied to civic activism for intersecting justice concerns.

Since the 1987 democratic transition, Korean unions have achieved significant gains in terms of wages and other working conditions while establishing themselves as an important collective actor to participate in the national tripartite institutions and to form their own political party with elected seats in the national legislature. At the same time, the organizationally narrow, union-centered movement was faced with two predicaments on its way of becoming an encompassing and representative political force. Established parties in democratized Korea have continuously failed to represent labor and distributional agenda in national politics and consequently placed organized labor as an institutional "outsider." Union movements themselves have revealed inadequacies in responding to new labor issues stemming from the increasing irregular employment, gendered labor practices, and the influx of migrant workers. These marginalized voices have organized outside the union structure but in close relations with civil society actors to engage in new modes of collective action.

To analytically assess the development and transformation of the Korean labor movements over the last two decades, this chapter is organized as follows. The first section discusses the organizational development of the Korean labor movement since 1987. The second section focuses on unions' gains in wages, labor policy, and political representation. The last section examines the predicaments and limitations that Korean unions have exposed and identifies the evolution of new sources for contentious activism from within the labor movements. The chapter ends with a brief conclusion that recapitulates the major discussions of this study and emphasizes the importance of understanding the progression of Korean labor movements within the context of democratic development.

The development of the Korean labor movement since 1987

The democratic breakthrough in 1987 did not only reinstitute electoral democracy in Korea but also created political space through which workers were able to claim their long-suppressed labor rights. When the massive protests in May and June of 1987 ended authoritarian rule, workers across the nation erupted to demand decent wages and basic labor rights. During this Workers' Great Struggle that lasted the months of July, August, and September of 1987, over one million workers in more than 4,000 unionized and un-unionized shop floors participated in a variety of collective actions such as sit-ins, strikes, rallies, and street demonstrations (Cho 1998: 275–276). In the ensuing years, the number of labor unions increased and workers organized into unions soared. However, the unionization rate reached its peak in 1989 at 18.6 percent of all paid employees and slid back to pre-democratization rates around 11–12 percent in the following years (Korea Labor Statistics).

This upheaval in workers' collective action and union organizing was rather a natural course of events due to accumulated frustrations under previous authoritarian governments that relied on labor repressive measures both at the national and factory levels. Korean workers had been deprived of an adequate mechanism to resolve their political and economic grievances that had snowballed along the years of compressed industrial development (Song 1991). Although the state had co-opted a segment of workers into the state-sponsored union, the Federation of Korean Trade Unions (FKTU), this union center failed to represent workers' interests and thus lacked grassroots' support from the rank-and-files.

Against the monopoly of the FKTU that had been politically and financially dependent upon the past authoritarian regimes, new and independent unions were organized outside the FKTU. Under the banner of "democratic union movement" (*minju nojo undong*), they first formed the Korean Confederation of Trade Unions (KCTU) in 1990. In 1995, the Korea Confederation of Trade Unions (KCTU) was formally organized as the second national center by amalgamating the KCTU (primarily based on small and medium enterprise unions), *chaebol* unions, and white-collar workers' unions (Lee 2003). The KCTU, which began with some 400,000 unionized workers, has now grown to represent over 630,000 members (KCTU webpage).[2] As of 2006, both the FKTU (over 60 percent of its membership) and the KCTU (over 70 percent of its membership) rely on unions in metal, chemical, automobile industries, banking, white-collar professionals, taxi, and public transportation (Korea Ministry of Labor 2007). By the late 1990s, the majority of regular the workforce employed in large firms became organized, with a notable exception of Samsung. Workers employed in firms with more than 300 employees account for 78.3 percent of total union membership in 2000 (ibid.). This indicates that almost all of the large firms are unionized while very few small firms have unions at all.

The union density stagnating at around 11–12 percent despite the favorable political environment under democratic governments is rather puzzling. This is related to the structural changes within the Korean economy such as the shrinkage of the manufacturing sector and increased fragmentation of the labor market. As of 2007, the manufacturing sector employs 17.7 percent of the total labor force in contrast to 75 percent in the service sector (Korea Statistical Information). The labor market also became fragmented with massive layoffs, rising contingent labor, and heightened precariousness in employment conditions in the aftermath of the Asian Financial Crisis.[3] These structural changes severely undermined the traditional trade union constituency. The industrial sector that had been the organizational basis of Korean unions was shrinking while the labor force's fragmentation, diversity, and precariousness made union organizing a formidable task.

Another clear observable trend in the rising contingent labor is a gendered disparity. As Table 15.1 shows, 67 percent of all female workers are employed in non-regular positions and 68 percent of all non-regular jobs are occupied by female workers. This disproportional share of female labor in contingent employment is further reflected in the unionization data. The gap between the share of unionized male workers and that of female workers dramatically increased over the last 20 years. While the gap in 1985 was 15.5 versus 11.1 percent, it diverged to 13.5 versus 5.3 percent in 2006 (Ministry of Labor 2007).

Since political democratization in 1987 the Korean union movement has experienced an organizational expansion to the extent to form a second national center and to engage in militant mobilizations for union rights, higher wages, and decent working conditions. Its growth and achievements, however, were

Table 15.1 Disparities in employment and union representation (in thousands)

Total paid employees (15,351)	*Regular workers*	*Non-regular workers*
Number and percentage	6,910 (45%)	8,450 (55%)
Male : female	4,830 (54%) : 2,080 (32%)	4,080 (46%) : 4,360 (68%)
Not represented by unions	61.8%	89.6%
Unionization rates	21.6%	2.8%
Share in total union membership	86.3%	13.7%

Source: Korea Labor Statistics.

largely confined within enterprise unions, large conglomerates, and full-time male workers. The labor movement that developed based on large individual enterprise unions failed to penetrate into the shop floors of small enterprises or into the increasing segment of non-regular workers. The following section presents what the labor movement has gained in terms of wages, labor policy reforms, and political representation over the last two decades.

The gains of the Korean labor movement: wages, labor policy, and political representation

Newly empowered labor unions vigorously engaged in wage negotiations to make up for the low wages imposed by previous authoritarian governments and as a result they were able to make significant gains in their wage levels in post-1987 period. Korean workers who were paid a monthly wage less than USD350 (KRW351,000) in 1986 pushed up their wage levels almost seven times to USD2,353 (KRW2,823,000) in 2007 (Korea Labor Statistics).[4] If inflation rates are taken into account, the real wage increased about 3.4 times (ibid.).

However, a closer look at the wage data indicates that the benefits of the labor movement were unequally distributed. Korean unions, mostly organized within large firms, have been able to exert their mobilizing strength to maximize firm-level gains. The annual spring offensive for wage negotiations have been led by unions in heavy industry and transportation, such as *Daewoo* Shipbuilding, *Hyundai* Heavy Industry, *Hyundai* Automobile, and Seoul Metro, often involving strikes, walkouts, factory occupation, and street demonstrations (Choi *et al.* 2001). Due to these powerful unions, workers employed in large manufacturing and public-service firms have experienced higher and quicker wage increases than their counterparts in small firms. The ratio of 100:111 in 1986 found between firms with less than 30 employees and firms with more than 500 employees widened to 100:171 in 2004 (Korea Labor Statistics). This means that labor unions in large corporations have pushed their wage levels disproportionately higher than the wages at the remaining smaller companies that remain mostly un-unionized.

The concentration of unions in large firms did not only widen a wage gap among workers across different firm sizes, but also created a disparity in non-wage welfare benefits. Korean employers are responsible for providing two kinds of non-wage benefits to their workers: one is social welfare contributions that are defined by legislation on health care, unemployment insurance, retirement allowance, and public pension, and the other is company welfare expenses that are determined by collective agreements with their respective unions. Social protection programs that first began to be implemented in large firms remain to have limited coverage for workers in small firms or non-regular workers. These workers are hugely disadvantaged in the coverage of unemployment insurance, retirement allowance, and public pension (Yang 2010). In addition, company welfare benefits have created further fragmentation among workers. The average monthly non-wage benefits in large firms that were 100,000 won (approximately

USD830) in 1992 increased to 180,000 won (approximately USD1,500) in 2000. In small firms, they rose from 80,000 won only to 100,000 won in the same period (Korean Labor Statistics).

Besides increased wages and social welfare benefits, Korean labor unions gained social legitimacy and legal recognition through various labor law reforms in post-1987. The new labor legislations lifted the restrictions that originated from previous authoritarian governments to infringe upon workers' freedom of association. The three vicious articles in the labor law that prohibited multiple unionism (to prevent the formation of independent unions outside the government-sponsored FKTU), a third party intervention in union affairs (to hinder the connections between industrial workers and democratic movement circles), and unions' political activities (to avert possible linkages between unions and opposition parties) were repealed in a series of labor law amendments (Lee 2009a). These achievements, however, were not without costs for labor. Labor unions had to concede to the revisions that would allow greater flexibility in the labor market (making hiring and dismissing of workers easier and expanding the employment of non-regular workers). Table 15.2 summarizes the major changes in the labor law reforms since 1987.

With the growing ascendancy of union movements, particularly the one led by the KCTU, the government had to acknowledge the presence of a second national union and to include it in tripartite consultations. The Labor Reform Committee formed in 1996 as a tripartite body under the Kim Young Sam government invited both of the FKTU and the KCTU, plus employers' organizations and labor scholars to discuss necessary changes in existing labor policies. This first round of tripartite consultation, however, failed to produce an agreement. The passage of a unilateral labor bill (with stipulations on increased labor market flexibility) by the ruling New Korea Party in the National Assembly in December 1996 provoked a general strike organized by the two national unions for the first time in post-Korean War history. In the next round of tripartite consultation that took place under the Korea Tripartite Commission in the aftermath of the Asian Financial Crisis, the KCTU gained formal and legal recognition but at the exchange of further labor market flexibility. The KCTU leadership was soon denounced by their union members for "selling out" the general labor cause and has since pulled out of the Tripartite Commission. The Kim Dae Jung government that oversaw the post-Financial Crisis economic reforms was quick to implement the agreed measures to flexibilize the labor market but incomplete to carry out corporate restructuring especially reforming the Korean *chaebols* (You 2010).

Another distinctive sign of progress for Korean labor unions was the formation of the Democratic Labor Party (DLP) in 2000. Considering the predominance of ideologically conservative, organizationally shallow, and non-programmatic parties in Korean politics, the successful entrance of the DLP into the electoral arena is a phenomenal event. This labor party is primarily based on the KCTU (about 40 percent of the party membership) as well as other sectoral and civic organizations (DLP webpage). According to the 2007 Report on

Table 15.2 Labor law reforms and major changes in post-1987 Korea

Year	*Major changes*
1987	Prohibition of political activities by labor unions (–) No multiple unionism (–) Prohibition of a third party intervention (–) Right to form unions without membership guidelines (+) Reduction of defense industries where unions are not allowed (+) Elimination of the ordinance for union dissolution (+) Shortening of the cooling period (+)
1989	No multiple unionism (–) Permission of political activities by labor unions (+) Partial permission of a third party intervention (0)
1997	Multiple unionism at the national level (+) Permission of a third party intervention (+) Prohibition of teacher and public employee unions (–) Permission of massive layoffs (–) Flexibilization of work hours (–)
1998	Political finance laws to allow political activities by unions (+) Permission of teacher union and public employee work council (+) Permission of massive layoffs and dispatch workers (–)
2003	Weekly 40 hour workweek (+) Permission of public employee union (+) Protection of non-regular workers (+) Protection of foreign workers (+)

Source: compiled by the author with information from Choi *et al.* 2001.

Note
The + and – signs in parentheses indicate the positive and negative effect of each labor reform on organized labor.

Political Parties' Activities and Finance, the DLP has the highest percentage of due-paying members at 62.8 percent compared to the Grand National Party's 12.2 percent and the United Democratic Party's 7.1 percent (National Election Commission 2008).

The change in the electoral system in 2002 that introduced a proportional representation element critically contributed to the DLP's electoral success.[5] In the legislative election of 2004, the DLP earned two seats from single-member districts (SMDs), Changwon and Ulsan, and eight seats from the proportional system by earning 13.1 percent of nationwide support.[6] While the party's performance in the 2008 election was reduced to five seats (two from SMDs and three from the proportional list) due to the factional split to the Progressive New Party, the presence of the DLP has raised the importance of distributional issues and social protection programs in the national legislature.

Since political democratization in 1987, the Korean labor movement has been able to develop its organizational and mobilizational capacities to the extent to establish itself as a legitimate social actor and institution. Based on their organizational strength, unions engaged in various actions to improve their wage levels, social protection policies, legal provisions on collective industrial relations, and formal political representation. With the formation of the Tripartite Commission and the Democratic Labor Party, in particular, the union movement seems to have gained institutionalized access to formal political processes to be able to influence labor policy making. However, unions' participation in such political arenas produced either dubious outcomes or outcomes that were restricted to the constituency represented by the narrowly organized labor unions.

New labor movements from within

For the past 20 years, Korean society underwent a concomitant process of political democratization and economic liberalization. Political democratization has obviously created a nurturing environment for the empowerment of the labor movement. However, the processes of economic liberalization and changing labor market conditions created novel challenges to the Korean labor movement. The size of the industrial manufacturing sector declined and undermined the traditional bases of union membership. Public and private firms underwent restructuring that often accompanied massive layoffs. Full-time jobs went through reductions only to be replaced by contingent workforce. Women have been disproportionally employed in the service sector particularly under precarious employment conditions. The number of migrant workers also soared to fill the dangerous and difficult work in small firms that Korean workers were hesitant to take.

Yet, these diverse subgroups of working population lacked an adequate organizational voice to be able to affect the direction of macro-economic changes. Narrowly organized Korean unions have been inadequate in responding to and representing these labor issues stemming from the fragmented and stratified labor population. As such, a large sway of labor issues had to be pursued outside union structures. Beginning from the late 1990s, women workers, non-regular workers, and migrant workers emerged as the new sources of labor activism often articulating intersecting social justice concerns in conjunction with other social movement forces.

The activism of these marginalized workers manifested resemblances with the labor protests of the 1970s and 1980s. National union centers often fell short of offering effective representation to these labor grievances; the strikes tended to turn prolonged, isolated, and radicalized with the "hit and run" tactics by the employers and the government;[7] and although the mobilizations were first precipitated by unlawful layoffs or unfair labor practices, workers' demands evolved to be framed beyond labor issues but in intersections with notions of gender equality, anti-racism, and human rights. Most critically, these protests were closely linked with and supported by social movement organizations that have developed as important mechanisms of interest articulation and representation in democratized Korea (Lee 2009b).

The recent strikes by non-regular women workers in E-Land, Giryung Electronics, and the KTX (Korean bullet train) have all shown these characterizations. It has been the social movement organizations, such as the Korean Womenlink and the Council of Korean Women Workers, that have aided these prolonged mobilizations by non-regular women workers. These women who were involved in strikes have expressed serious discontent with the insufficient levels of support they received from national unions such as the KCTU and FKTU (Moon 2007).

Labor activists, in reaction to the inadequacies of existing union structures to represent the labor grievances faced by women workers, chose to form separate organizations of their own that were often cross-sectional and community-based (Oh 2003). The Council of Korean Women Workers (CKWW) was set up in 1992 to organize and represent women workers in the manufacturing sectors, while the Korean Women's Labor Union (KWLU) was organized with 2,000 members in 1999 to support women workers in part-time tutoring, insurance consulting, substitute teaching, housekeeping services, and hospice services (ibid.). Many of their activities were more closely linked to other civil society actors, most notably the women's movement circles, than existing union organizations. The Korean Womenlink in particular has been intensively involved in these labor issues. Through these connections, the labor questions faced by women and/or non-regular workers have been framed not just as job and pay issues but more as general social justice agenda for human rights and gender equality.

Another source for a new labor movement came from migrant workers who made inflows into the Korean labor market in recent years. While their numbers have increased in dramatic phases since the early 1990s, their workplace experiences and daily discriminations have been in depressing conditions. The number of migrant workers, both legal and illegal, is around 400,000 as of 2007, accounting for 2.5 percent of Korea's total labor force (Ministry of Justice). They were first admitted under the Industrial Trainee System (1991–2004) and not recognized as "workers" even though they worked the same as regular Korean workers. They were paid less, usually less than 50 percent of a regular worker's wage, and were often subjected to inhumane discrimination and violations of their labor rights (Seol 2006).

Migrant workers began to challenge this trainee system and the prevailing discriminatory practices against foreign workers in Korean society. Their actions have been supported, again, not by existing labor unions but by social movement groups. As evidenced in the protests by migrant workers in 1994, 1995, and 1996, their mobilization developed with the direct and substantial linkages with domestic civic organizations such as the Citizens Coalition for Economic Justice and the Joint Committee with Migrants in Korea (Lim 2003; Lee 2009b). While labor unions were largely absent or hesitant in this involvement, new civic organizations were formed with an aim to support the rights and interests of migrant workers in Korea. The number of migrant-supporting groups is known to have grown to reach around 200 (Seol 2006).

The linkages between migrant workers and these domestic civic organizations increased the significance of migrants' issues and the effectiveness of their actions. The demands raised in the coordinated protests and campaigns by migrants and domestic civic actors were not merely about securing unpaid wages and extended stay in Korea but cast hard questions about Korean society beyond labor issues. They questioned issues of racial discrimination and exclusive ethno-nationalism, while promoting universal human rights and democratic inclusiveness that were beyond the scope of traditional labor unions' articulation. Their sustained activism resulted in the replacement of the Industrial Trainee Program with the Employment Permit System in 2004, which recognizes migrant workers' equal eligibility for labor protection programs (Lee 2009b).

Overall, institutional "outsiders" in democratized Korea were not limited to women workers, non-regular workers, and migrant workers. Working people in general, both unionized and un-unionized, have lacked an effective political organization to represent the distributional issues in the formal political arena where established political parties have been organizationally unstable, policy-wise undifferentiated, and resiliently reliant on regionalistic appeals to mobilize votes. Although the DLP is organizationally based on labor unions and purports to represent the interests of the working people, it is a minor party in the National Assembly. The DLP lawmakers find it extremely frustrating to work in the National Assembly where the basic procedural rules are often violated by the majority party politicians (Park 2006). Under these circumstances, Korean workers do not have meaningful political representation in the formal political process that would give them access and influence in policy-making processes. Due to these political predicaments, labor unions themselves have often drawn into contentious politics and militant mobilizations.

Organized at the enterprise level, the Korean union movement was able to raise wages and other material benefits for its members but was incapacitated in gaining substantive political representation to affect the formation of socio-economic policies that were beyond the realm of firm-level remunerations. Therefore, Korea's diversified working populations, whether unionized or un-unionized, remain to brew new labor activisms that are hard to be contained within union-oriented wage negotiations.

Conclusion

Since the democratic transition in 1987, Korean workers and unions have significantly gained in terms of wages, social welfare, labor law reforms, organizational strength, and social influence. Although every step of labor ascendance involved intense conflict with employers and the government, Korean unions are now entitled to greater freedom and political legitimacy. The union monopoly under the conservative FKTU was broken and the KCTU emerged as a powerful alternative national center for Korean workers. Company-level unions have vigorously engaged in wage bargaining and collective agreements to improve the wage levels and other material benefits. Two national unions gained political legitimacy to the extent to participate in the national tripartite consultations. The formation of the DLP and its modest electoral success, in particular, signaled the beginning of political representation of labor interest in national politics. Union-based labor movements, at least, seem to have acquired the signs of an "old" movement with their organizational stability and institutionalized sectoral claims.

Yet the processes of economic liberalization that paralleled political democratization in Korean society produced fundamental changes in the labor market conditions and created novel challenges to the Korean labor movement. Korean workers have become highly diversified and stratified and came to raise broad social justice issues that are beyond the scope of "traditional" labor unions. In recent years, it has been the women workers, non-regular workers, and migrant workers who got mobilized and articulated intersecting socioeconomic issues that fundamentally question the depth and inclusiveness of Korean democracy.

In this sense, Koran labor movements since democratic transition in 1987 have evolved to breed both the old and new dimensions of social movements. In one direction, the union-oriented movement focused on articulating material issues and gaining legal recognition. However, the organizational structure of enterprise unionism has limited the equitable distribution of such economic and political gains. Therefore, the labor movement itself diversified into another direction to spin-off various social justice claims and mobilization flexibilities. Yet, what these two directions commonly point to is the predicaments of Korean democracy. Democratization is not just about instituting the mechanism of electoral contestation and granting basic civil rights. Democracy is fundamentally about possibilities and imaginations of representation and inclusiveness, particularly of those who raise the most aching questions to its political system. As long as Korean democracy remains aloof from this social discontent, it will constantly face new waves of labor activism. From this perspective, Korea's labor movements remain to be ripe with possibilities for novel claims and contentious activism.

Notes

1 An earlier version of this chapter ("Labor Movements and Democratic Consolidation in Korea: Gains and Losses") was presented at the Conference on "Social Movements and Democratic Consolidation: Korea and Taiwan Compared" (Academia Sinica, July 23, 2003, Taipei, Taiwan) and published in *Asia-Pacific Forum* (No. 21, September 2003). This chapter makes two important revisions. First, the diversification of Korean labor movements is closely analyzed by examining the evolution of new activism by non-regular, women, and migrant workers. Second, new labor-related data have been added to reflect changes in recent years.

2 The membership size of the FKTU and the KCTU has gradually changed over the last 20 years with the KCTU increasingly challenging the FKTU's organizational dominance.

3 According to the Korean Labor Standard Law, non-regular workers are those who have terminal labor contract, those who are dispatched to different work locations, or those who provide part-time labor.

4 For employees in non-agricultural sectors and manufacturing industries. Exchange rates for 1986: USD1 = KRW950, for 2004: USD1 = KRW1,200.
5 Under the new electoral system, voters cast one vote for a candidate in the given district (242 out 299 seats) and a second vote for a party (for the remaining 57 seats).
6 These two cities are huge industrial towns where heavy industry and export manufacturing facilities are concentrated. Such concentration of large conglomerates and factories transformed these towns into the capital of labor union movements in democratized Korea.
7 Employers would lay off workers, ignore the existence of unions, or close down factories (most of the time violating legal procedures) and completely shut down negotiations with the affected workers.

References

Cho, Hee-Yeon. 1998. *Democracy and Social Movements in Korea*. Seoul: Dangdae Publication [in Korean].

Choi, Young-gi, Jun Kim, Hyo-rae Cho, and Beom-sang Yu. 2001. *Korean Labor Movements since 1987*. Seoul: KLI [in Korean].

Johnston, Hank, Enrique Larana, and Joseph R. Gusfield. 1994. "Identities, Grievances, and New Social Movements." In *New Social Movements: From Ideology to Identity*, edited by Hank Johnston, Enrique Larana, and Joseph R. Gusfield, 3–35. Philadelphia, PA: Temple University Press.

Korea Ministry of Labor. 1997. *Annual Report on Trade Unions*. Seoul: MOL.

Lee, Yoonkyung. 2003. "Labor Movements and Democratic Consolidation in Korea: Gains and Losses," *Asia Pacific Forum* No. 21.

Lee, Yoonkyung. 2009a. "Divergent Outcomes of Labor Reform Politics in Democratized Korea and Taiwan," *Studies in Comparative International Development* 44 (1): 47–70.

Lee, Yoonkyung. 2009b. "Migration, Migrants, and Contested Ethno-nationalism in Korea," *Critical Asian Studies* 41 (3): 363–380.

Lim, Timothy. 2003. "Racing from the Bottom in South Korea: The Nexus between Civil Society and Transnational Migrants," *Asian Survey* 43 (3): 423–442.

Moon, Ji-sun. 2007. "Solidarity between Non-regular Women Workers and Citizen Movements," *Journal of Korean Sociology Conference* 6: 79–98 [in Korean].

National Election Commission. 2008. *Annual Report on Political Parties' Activity and Finance*. Seoul: National Election Commission.

Oh, Mi-kyung. 2003. *Women's Labor Movements and the Politics of Civil Rights*. Seoul: Arche [in Korean].

Park, Kyung-mi. 2006. "The Competition Structure of Party Politics since Korea's Democratization," *Social Research* 11: 113–141 [in Korean].

Seol, Dong-hoon. 2006. "Migrant Workers and Poverty." In *The New Poor in Korean Society*, edited by Korea Urban Research Institute, 375–412. Seoul: Hanwool [in Korean].

Song, Ho-geun. 1991. *Labor Politics and the Market in Korea*. Seoul: Nanam [in Korean].

Yang, Jay-jin. 2010. "The Political Economy of the Korean Welfare State," unpublished manuscript.

You, Jong-Il. 2010. "The Political Economy of Reforms in South Korea," unpublished manuscript.

Internet sources

Democratic Labor Party: www.dlp.org
KCTU: http://nodong.org/
Korea Ministry of Justice: www.moj.go.kr
Korea Labor Statistics: http://laborstat.molab.go.kr
Korea Statistical Information Service: www.kosis.go.kr

16 Mobilizing public opinion for/against foreign labor policies in Korea, 1995–2005

NGOs, trade unions, and employers' associations in contested terrain[1]

Dong-Hoon Seol

Introduction

The year of 1987 is a turning point not only in the history of Korea's democratization but also in its international labor migration history. Around this year, outflow of indigenous workers has significantly decreased, while migrant workers from abroad started flowing into Korea to work. Since then, the number of foreign migrant workers rapidly increased with more diversity in their country of origin. Furthermore, Roh Tae-woo government's *Nordpolitik* (North-bound Policy) opened up economic and cultural exchanges with China and the USSR and, in the process, the government actively hosted ethnic Koreans' visit to Korea. Since then, the number ethnic Koreans from China (*Joseonjok*) and the former Soviet Union including Russia, Uzbekistan and Kazakhstan (*Goryeoin*) increased in Korea. Whether they were ethnic Korean visitors from China and the former Soviet Union or tourists from the less developed countries in East, South and Southeast Asia, the visitors and tourists settled in Korea as migrant workers. As their numbers increased, Korea became one of the labor-importing countries.

The inflow of migrant workers was proof of success of the Korean government's industrialization policy propelled since the 1960s. The labor market of Korea was suffering from labor shortage in manufacturing sectors. Citizens, having achieved a fast economic development, were no longer willing to take difficult, dirty and dangerous (so called "3-D") jobs. Thus, small and medium size manufacturing firms and construction companies were experiencing chronic shortage of labor. Furthermore, when the Korean government eased restriction on Koreans traveling abroad, it equally allowed easy entrance to foreigners. As a result, Korea became a "country of opportunity," where migrant workers could easily enter and find a job.

The government, however, did not take any significant action to manage this new phenomenon until 1990. There was no identification card for the foreign migrant workers to legally work in Korea. No single foreign manual worker could find an appropriate document under the Departures and Arrivals Control Act (DACA), thus becoming an undocumented worker. In the pretext of coping with the labor shortage, the government left the employment of undocumented migrant workers undisturbed until 1991 when it finally adopted the *Industrial Technical Training Program* (ITTP) for foreigners, which, however, imported "trainees" but not "workers." ITTP was an expedient policy aimed at providing foreign labor to small and medium size business, while easing criticisms of the trade unions who opposed importation of a foreign labor force. ITTP was put into effect on November 1, 1991 and still exists today as the ITTP of Korean companies with foreign investments.

The government designated the period of June 10 to July 31, 1992 as "voluntary self-report period for overstayers" and accepted applications to find out the situation of undocumented migrant workers in Korea. The number of undocumented migrant workers self-reported during that period was 61,126 and the number of employers was 10,796. The government extended the permitted overstay period until the end of that year. In addition, in September 1992, the government imported trainees and placed them in companies with no foreign investment records. Ten 3-D small and medium size manufacturing businesses which included dyeing, gliding, heat-treat, metal works, machinery, shoe manufacturing, glass-work, leather, electronics and electric work were permitted to employ a maximum of 10,000 industrial technical trainees with the recommendation from the Minister of Commerce and Industry. But this policy was suspended within a year since its start in April 1993 (Seol 1999: 118–119).

The government tried to replace every undocumented migrant worker with industrial technical trainees by establishing the "1992 Voluntary Self-Report Period." The government (Ministry of Industry and Commerce) on January 4, 1994 appointed the Korea Federation of Small and Medium Business (KFSB, *Junggihyeop*) as the implementing body of ITTP to import industrial technical trainees. Afterwards, the Construction Association of Korea (CAK, *Geonhyeop*), the National Federation of Fisheries Cooperatives (NFFC, *Suhyeop*) and the National Agricultural Cooperative Federation (NACF, *Nonghyup*) were added as implementing agencies of ITTP to recruit and manage the industrial technical trainees designated to construction, fisheries, and corporate farming sectors and pasture industries.

Before the launch of the *Employment Permit Program* (EPP) for foreigners on August 17, 2004, ITTP was the key foreign labor policy of Korea. In most cases, "trainees" under the ITTP are not being trained for any specific jobs, but rather filling menial jobs that Koreans refuse to take. Since they are not classified as workers, they are denied the rights of regular workers in Korea, which includes unionizing, collective bargaining and collective action. Therefore, they are regarded as "disguised workers."

Although the formal foreign labor policy of Korea was ITTP, the Korean employers utilized undocumented workers much more than trainees (Seol and Skrentny 2004). Before the regularization of undocumented workers in September 2003, only 16 percent of foreign workers residing in Korea were industrial technical trainees and post-training workers, while 78 percent were undocumented migrant workers. The remaining 6 percent are professionals or high-skilled workers. Undocumented migrant workers alleviated Korea's labor shortage and contributed to its economic development, but suffered from unpaid or delayed wages, industrial accidents, occupational illnesses and unreasonable lay-off or dismissal because of their illegal status (JCMK 2001; HRSWM 2002).

The government's foreign labor policy resulted in uncontrolled illegal overstays of migrant workers, human rights abuses and corruption in recruiting trainees (Seol *et al.* 2002). Migrant workers who worked in Korea during the late 1980s and early 1990s suffered from extreme wage delays or nonpayment, industrial accidents, physical assaults and sexual violence (see Yoo 1997; Hahm 1997; Seol and Han 2004).

Nevertheless, there also were individuals who took care of the migrant workers when they became victims of such human rights violations, by organizing social groups to assist migrant workers. They have also asked the government to abolish ITTP. The government has modified its foreign labor policy when faced with the criticisms by NGOs. The Act on Employment of Foreign Workers, Etc. was passed in the Korean Assembly on July 31, 2003, which was officially announced on August 16 after a one year preparation period, and was put into effect on August 17, 2004.

At the turning point of foreign labor policy, the objective of this chapter is to look into Korean citizens' attitudes toward foreign migrant workers for the previous ten years. Koreans have formed their attitude toward migrant workers through direct encounters with them and have found solutions to the problems. The major actors of Korean society in this issue are small and medium size business owners or managers who employ migrant workers, fellow workers who interact with them in everyday life, trade union activists and human rights campaigners. I examine the responses of the different social groups to the influx of migrant workers in order to understand attitudes of accommodating migrant workers.

Employers and their associations

Small and medium size businesses, suffering from labor shortage, began hiring migrant workers around late 1980s. ITTP was one of the solutions to the manufacturing sector's labor shortage since 1991. Abella *et al.* (1994: 75) conducted a survey which asked managers of small and medium size business to cite two solutions to labor shortage in the manufacturing sector. According to their survey, "improving wage level and working conditions" (59 percent), "extending extra-work hours of the existing workers" (44 percent), "adopting labor-saving manufacturing technology" (36 percent) were followed by the "employment of foreign labor" (20 percent) as the fourth solution. They also showed preference in employing migrant workers over "hiring housewives or elderly" (8 percent), or "temporary or expeditionary workers" (5 percent).

An important fact found in this survey is that companies do not sorely rely on employing migrant workers to resolve labor shortage; they at the same time look for alternative solutions. Nonetheless, the labor shortage in the manufacturing sector cannot simply be resolved by the efforts listed above. Structural improvement of small and medium size companies and employment of migrant workers have to take place at the same time. As the labor market grows tighter, employers continue to seek workers from abroad. Employment of the elderly, increased labor force participation by women, and the application of technology to the service sector are expected to reduce the need for migrant workers.

It is important to notice that businesses cannot find a domestic labor force, and the wage level of migrant workers is low. The factors can be explained in two ways. First, the fundamental reason of being unable to find indigenous workers is not on the quantity of workers but on the quality of working life (Kang 1996). Three-D jobs became undesirable to indigenous workers, and thus became works for migrant workers (Abella *et al.* 1994). This means that even if the wage level slightly increases, 3-D jobs will not be attractive to indigenous workers. In other words, migrant workers do not compete with indigenous workers for the same jobs, but rather take undesirable jobs, forming a mutually beneficial relationship between the migrant workers and indigenous workers.

Second, businesses hire migrant workers because of their low wages. Migrant workers are hired with concentration in "marginal companies" or "sunset industries" (Lee *et al.* 1995). "Sunset industries" are suffering from chronic labor shortage; hence, it is rather correct to interpret low wages as an additional cause of hiring migrant workers. They hire migrant workers primarily because they cannot find indigenous workers, and are additionally beneficial because labor price of migrant workers is cheap. In particular, wage level of industrial technical trainees is much lower than unskilled indigenous workers and even undocumented migrant workers. Therefore, ITTP benefits marginal companies (Yoo *et al.* 2005).

Employers generally view migrant workers as "cheap and docile laborers who perform tasks not taken by Koreans" (Seol 1999: 389–390). Employers regard migrant workers as "servants," "farmhands," or "maids" of traditional Korean culture who can be hired with much lower wages (Seol and Han 2004: 49). Small and medium size businesses minimize the cost of employing migrant workers and strictly control their everyday life in order to secure cheap labor. Companies who hire industrial technical trainees often confine them and prohibit them from making outside contacts to prevent escape. Many companies hiring undocumented migrant workers delay wage payment and seize their passports for the same reason. Employers of migrant workers consider such discrimination as natural. The greater problem is that such discriminatory treatment is backed by the Korean government's foreign labor policy – ITTP.

Although companies employing migrant workers show positive position on using foreign labor force, they do not show a unified opinion on the abolition of ITTP and adoption of the EPP. The position of the Korea Employers Federation (KEF), the Korea Chamber of Commerce and Industry (KCCI) and the Federation of Korean Industries (FKI) is that as far as companies suffering from labor shortage can secure supply of labor force, the kind of foreign labor programs does not matter: they are willing to accept the abolition of ITTP. However,

KFSB, CAK, NACF and NFFC, all of which work as agencies recruiting industrial technical trainees, strongly oppose the abolition of ITTP.

ITTP not only provides benefits to each of these employers' associations but also reflects the interests of each government body overseeing them, such as the Small and Medium Business Administration (SMBA) – KFSB, the Ministry of Construction and Transportation (MOCT) – CAK, the Ministry of Maritime Affairs and Fisheries (MMAF) – NFFC, and the Ministry of Agriculture and Forestry (MAF) – NACF.

Fellow workers

Indigenous workers' attitudes toward migrant workers are closely related to their work experience with them. Those who have closely worked with migrant workers, their views have been influenced by their experience, while those who have not had much contact are maybe more accepting of the general attitudes of the society. The overall concept of general Koran workers toward migrant workers is close to the latter case. Most Korean workers have not had any meaningful interaction with migrant workers because of the small number of migrant workers, and are indifferent to the flow of migrant workers.

Migrant workers have been placed into jobs avoided by indigenous workers; therefore, conflict between the two groups on job opportunity and wages has not yet been an issue. However, because problems migrant workers face today is increasingly becoming a labor rights issue, and policy resolutions are being sought, it is necessary to understand indigenous workers' understanding of the situation with migrant workers.

First, indigenous workers' attitude toward employment of migrant workers in Korea is examined. When asked the question, "To what degree do you think employment of migrant workers can threaten indigenous workers' job?" 29 percent answered "encroach seriously" and 54 percent answered "encroach a little" (Seol 1999: 393). In other words, 83 percent of indigenous workers saw migrant workers as a threat to their job security.

However, indigenous workers' fear that migrant workers would take away their jobs comes from misunderstanding. As explained previously, the jobs migrant workers take are ones avoided by the Koreans, the sectors experiencing chronic labor shortage. Migrant workers are not "thieves" who snatched indigenous workers' jobs, but rather should be seen as "rescue forces" who fill up vacancies in the labor market.

Another issue the employment of migrant workforce can produce is the level of wages. To find answer, I conducted a survey of indigenous workers to determine the influence of migrant workers on level of wages (Seol 1999: 394–395). In order to find the wage level of migrant workers they think is appropriate, they were asked to write down "the reasonable percentage" compared to novice indigenous workers, given that the real wage includes housing and meals. The reasonable average wage level indigenous workers thought appropriate according to migrant workers' legal status and ethnic background was the following: ethnic

Korean industrial technical trainees 69 percent of indigenous workers' wage level, ethnic non-Korean industrial technical trainees 65 percent, ethnic Korean undocumented migrant workers 63 percent and ethnic non-Korean undocumented migrant workers 60 percent.

The responses imply several important facts. First, indigenous workers desire reform of the situation where industrial technical trainees receive lower income than undocumented migrant workers. Second, indigenous workers think that migrant workers with ethnic Korean background should receive higher wages than ethnic non-Korean migrant workers; nonetheless, ethnic Korean background cannot supersede legal status. Third, indigenous workers regard wage discrimination as natural and reasonable. It is clearly shown that wage level of even ethnic Korean industrial technical trainees, those with same ethnicity and a regular legal status has to be paid only 69 percent of indigenous workers' wages. Hence, indigenous workers also clearly discriminate against ethnic Koreans.

Indigenous workers first consider the legal status of foreigners as the first priority, and then consider ethnic background. Undocumented migrant workers with Korean backgrounds do not have any better image than non-Korean industrial technical trainees. In other words, Koreans have similar stereotypes about ethnic Koreans from China and former Soviet Union countries with other foreign migrant workers.

Some migrant workers complain that Korean fellow workers discriminate against themselves more than supervisors (Seol and Han 2004: 48). According to the survey by the National Human Rights Commission of Korea (Seol *et al.* 2002: 105), 51 percent of the migrant workers had experienced "verbal abuse and ridicule" at the workplace; 68 percent of the migrant workers answered that they had been abused by Korean fellow workers and 49 percent had experienced abuse by supervisors.

It is apparent that indigenous workers' prejudice and discrimination of migrant workers reflects the general citizens' attitude, and lack of experience of either interacting or working with foreigners. Because of their inexperience with foreigners, Koreans are largely unaware of a number of migrant worker issues (Seol and Skrentny 2004: 501).

But with globalization, a formation of global civil society became a reality, but Korean citizens still have attitudes formed in the isolationist past. In this sense, Koreans' attitude toward migrant workers may be regarded as an indicator to measure Korean society's level of globalization.

On the other hand, when indigenous workers come in contact with migrant workers at work, such stereotypes can either be destroyed or firmly settled. In the actual case studies, when indigenous workers and migrant workers work in a same place, conflict of interests develops and misunderstandings cumulate. Thus, without building informal personal relationships, relationships between the two groups with the flow of time can get worse. With the absence of better communication negative stereotypes tend to solidify.

Trade unions

Responses of trade unions should be examined in two different levels – company trade unions and their federations at the national level. Most company trade unions are affiliated with the Federation of Korean Trade Unions (FKTU) and the Korean Confederation of Trade Unions (KCTU). Looking at FKTU and KCTU separately, FKTU does not have an office solely responsible for migrant worker matters. They do provide individual counseling in regional headquarters or in each federation by industries; however, the actual matters are consigned to human rights organizations supporting migrant workers. On the other hand, KCTU prior to its establishment on November 11, 1995 showed deep interest in migrant workers and has participated in establishing measures. KCTU has a separate section dealing with issues of migrant workers. The two trade union federations have put efforts to establish policy directions of trade unions and to educate their member unions at company level. The two federations' policies toward migrant workers are not that different. They are both adding voices to the abolition of ITTP and the implementation of EPP. Although they are against unlimited importation of a foreign labor force, the federations support equal treatment for migrant workers if the company has to import foreign labor due to labor shortage. By prohibiting discrimination against migrant workers, they also aim to block off additional benefits of the employers, and, thus, protect indigenous workers. And the two federations are strongly recommending their affiliated trade unions at company level to proactively accept migrant workers as members of unions. However, neither union group makes the migrant worker issue a priority.

Company trade unions in Korea are not largely against their companies' employment of migrant workers. It is because the presence of migrant workers does not directly violate union members' employment (Uh and Kwon 1995).

The majority of trade union officers, however, agree that rights of migrant workers also have to be protected by trade unions since migrant workers are also subjects of the unions (Seol 1999: 404–405). However, it is very difficult to organize migrant workers. Not only is it hard to unify opinions of union members, but also migrant workers consider the disadvantages they may receive from companies in case of participating in union activities. Industrial technical trainees do not have the right to join trade unions since they are "trainees" not "workers." Undocumented migrant workers have worries of losing their job. Furthermore, companies put pressure to restrict migrant workers' activities; in many cases, this is the major reason for such a small number of migrant workers wanting to join the unions. Nevertheless, domestic trade unions at company level were generally indifferent to the tasks of organizing migrant workers

Therefore, there have been very few significant efforts to improve the discriminatory situation of migrant workers from the trade union at each company level. The largest reason was on concentration of migrant workers in small and medium scale businesses. In particular, the majority of companies hiring undocumented migrant workers did not have trade unions. Normally, companies designated for industrial technical trainees have a trade union, but the managers tried to shut contacts among migrant workers. In particular, businesses in 3-D sectors have oppressed labor movement since they have had continuous difficulties with trade unions while the companies were facing labor shortage. In sum, each trade union of the companies has left migrant workers ignored.

The federations under their auspices established trade unions covering migrant workers. Under KCTU, the Equality Trade Union Migrants' Branch in Seoul, Gyeonggi, and Incheon Areas (ETU: *Pryeongdeung nojo yiju jibu*), covering undocumented migrant workers, was established in May 2001. ETU however has its focus on political activities rather than economic activities reflecting individual members' interests. It began anew as the Migrants' Trade Union on May 3, 2005.

Since the Supreme Court's decision allowed the unemployed to organize unions, an official union centered on the unemployed and undocumented workers was established with the help of the federations at national level; its activities, however, are not yet significant.

NGOs supporting foreign migrant workers

Unlike the situation in many nations in Europe, where socialist parties have worked for migrant rights (see Jacobson 1996), Korean political parties generally have not taken the lead in immigration. Only some nongovernmental organizations (NGOs) have served as supporters of migrant workers' human rights.

With increasing cases of human rights abuses, the new social movement to protect migrant workers was initiated by the civil society rather than the trade unions. A Filipino priest at Jayangdong Catholic Church in Seoul celebrated Mass in Tagalog in May 1992. Hundreds of Filipino workers started to gather on Sunday afternoons, and it received the media's attention. At the same time, human rights abuses of migrant workers were revealed in the media. To many human rights campaigners interested in migrant workers, this became a starting point. They have established NGOs for supporting foreign migrant workers since 1992.

The growth of NGOs supporting foreign migrant workers associates with the influx of migrant workers. Before the financial crisis in 1997, the number of NGOs steadily increased. Since 1992, counseling centers for migrant workers were established starting from Seoul Metropolitan area spreading throughout the nation. Most of the organizations initially established were faith based – Catholic, Protestant, Buddhist and Muslim – with strong religious characteristic/background. Although the number was relatively small, NGOs with little religious color were also established, and some existing labor counseling centers started counseling services for migrant workers.

However, in 1997–1998 with the Korean economy suffering from the financial crisis, the situation changed. With the return of migrant workers to their home countries, the rate of increase in the number of NGOs supporting migrant workers also decreased. In 1999 with the improvement of the economy, the number of foreign migrant workers started to rise again.

These NGOs provide shelter for migrant workers, provide counseling services and try to resolve difficult situations such as industrial accidents and wage delay or nonpayment, and provide legal and medical services. They also conduct surveys on migrant workers with scholars, publicize the results to raise public awareness and suggest specific policy alternatives. Domestic NGOs supporting migrant workers have a strong character in advocating human rights protection. The major activities can be summarized as six categories: (1) Counseling Services, (2) Provision of Shelters and Medical Services, (3) Educational Services, (4) Research and Advocacy, (5) Religious Services and (6) Supporting the Associations of Migrant Workers (Seol 2003).

Apart from these ordinary everyday activities, the NGO groups have staged demonstrations for improving foreign labor policy (Seol 2003; Lim 2002, 2003). The Joint Committee of Migrant Workers in Korea (JCMK, *Oinohyeop*) was organized after the protest of Nepalese industrial technical trainees at Myeong-dong Catholic Cathedral in January 1995, has continuously requested abolition of ITTP and to put EPP into force. JCMK and the Solidarity for Migrant Workers' Human Rights in Korea (SMHR, *Yijuingwon yeondae*) was established in January 2004, have enlightened the public to improve human rights conditions of migrant workers through protests, sit-ins and bringing in lawsuits. The NGOs' way of struggle is the legacy of the democratization age in 1980–1990s. Rather than independently supporting migrant workers, they expanded activities to form broader solidarity with FKTU and KCTU as well as general civil society groups including the People's Solidarity for Participatory Democracy (PSPD), and Citizens' Coalition for Economic Justice (CCEJ). They also have cooperated with NGOs supporting migrant workers in labor-sending countries including the Philippines and Indonesia as well as labor-importing countries including Japan, Hong Kong, Taiwan, Malaysia and Germany. The enactment of EPP in 2003 may not have been possible without these NGOs' activities.

Conclusion

It is generally understood in the public that discrimination against foreign migrant workers is the worst of all kinds of discrimination that exist in today's Korean society. Migrant workers' pitiful image in Korean citizens' minds is raised by mass media (see Seol and Han 2004). The print media give the plight of foreign workers front-page treatment, and television coverage frequently includes disturbing videos on their abuse. The public is not friendly to rounding up and deporting "pitiful" undocumented workers.

In reality in Korea, discrimination against migrant workers still prevails. The main reason causing human rights problem is pointed out as uncontrolled number of undocumented migrant workers. The discrimination is based on some Korean citizens' exclusive attitude toward migrant workers.

However, the matter should be carefully approached. Chung (2004: 4) shows that Koreans' exclusionist sentiment against foreigners (including migrant workers) is not so serious in comparison with that of other countries. Analyzing the Korean General Social Survey (KGSS) data on "national identity" conducted in 2003, she argues that Koreans have a strong nationalistic sentiment; however, this is not directly related to their exclusionist attitudes toward migrant workers. In the assessment of the positive attitude level toward migrant workers, Korea was placed on the fifth out of 24 countries.

Korean people's general attitude toward migrant workers should be seen as "immature hospitality" shaped in a country with a relatively small number of foreign migrants concentrated in particular areas. While the attitude of citizens in traditional immigration countries is formed through direct contact with immigrants, Koreans' attitude still remains imaginative, unproven by experience. The general attitude of the public is formed simply by accepting images shown in media. Therefore, whether the hospitality will be maintained in the future, when more real life experiences are made and shared, is still questionable.

In the meantime, new social movements to reform the human rights situation of migrant workers and improve their labor rights started to rise since 1992, and led to the establishment of various NGOs. These NGOs have provided shelters, counsel services on industrial accidents and nonpayment or delay of wage, provided medical and legal assistance, along with other services needed. Furthermore, they have disseminated the results to raise social awareness, provided alternative policies and cooperated with NGOs abroad supporting migrant workers. Such NGOs aim to remove discriminatory policies and ultimately root out discriminatory elements in Koreans' socially accepted views.

Recently, far right groups with racially discriminatory characters have been organized in Korea. In addition, there are increasingly more people making anti-foreigner comments on the internet. However, Korean society in general still remains on the side of civil movement making efforts to meet international norms of human rights (Jacobson 1996; Seol and Skrentny 2009). Human rights norms are already internalized by NGOs supporting migrant workers and apparently the wider Korean society, and their legitimacy and rectitude are self-evident. The NGOs, in solidarity with trade unions and other civic NGOs, continue to make efforts to improve the Korean government's foreign labor policy, and further to awaken conscience of the citizens by actively taking a role of public education.

The Korean government established the National Human Rights Commission of Korea as an independent status body in 2001. The Commission checks the human rights of migrant workers, and made recommendations to the government to abolish ITTP and adopt EPP in 2003. NGO activists usually resort to the Commission to solve human rights violations. International norms serve as standards for Korean citizens to strive for as part of the nation's development.

Note

1 Paper presented at the 46th annual meeting of the International Studies Association. Hilton Hawaiian Village, Honolulu, HI, USA, March 2, 2005. The original title is "Korean Citizens' Responses to the Inflow of Foreign Workers: Their Impacts on the Government's Foreign Labor Policy."

References

Abella, Manolo I., Young bum Park and W. Roger Böhning. 1994. *Adjustments to Labor Shortages and Foreign Workers in the Republic of Korea*. Geneva: International Labor Organization.

Chung, Kiseon. 2004. "Analysis of Korean Citizens' Attitude toward Foreign Immigrants: A Comparison with the Cases of the United States, Canada, Australia and Japan." Paper presented at the Summer Meeting of the Korean Sociological Association. Kyungpook National University, Daegu, Korea, June 18, 2004 (in Korean).

Hahm, Hanhee. 1997. "Foreign Workers' Conflict and Adaptation: Challenges and Responses seen in a Culture facing Another Culture." *Journal of Labor Studies* 13: 99–130 (in Korean).

HRSWM (Human Rights Solidarity for Women and Migrants in Korea). 2002. *White Paper on the Human Rights of the Industrial Trainees in Korean Companies with Foreign Investments: A Field Report of Human Rights Violations*. Anyang: HRSWM (in Korean).

Jacobson, David. 1996. *Rights across Borders*. Baltimore, MD: Johns Hopkins University Press.

JCMK (Joint Committee of Migrant Workers in Korea). 2001. *White Paper on the Human Rights of the Foreign Migrant Workers in Korea*. Seoul: JCMK (in Korean).

Kang, Su Dol. 1996. *Employment, Management, and Policy Alternatives for Foreign Workers in Korea: From the Standpoint of Comparison with Corporate and Social Rationality*. Seoul: Korea Labor Institute (in Korean).

Lee, Bun Song, Moon Kyung Choi, Joo An Kwon, Joonmo Cho and Kyung Hee Shin. 1995. *A Study of Foreign Workers in Seoul*. Seoul: Seoul Development Institute (in Korean).

Lim, Timothy C. 2002. "The Changing Face of South Korea: The Emergence of Korea as a 'Land of Immigration.'" *Korea Society Quarterly* 3(2/3): 16–21.

Lim, Timothy C. 2003. "Racing from the Bottom in South Korea: The Nexus between Civil Society and Transnational Migrants." *Asian Survey* 43(3): 423–442.

Seol, Dong-Hoon. 1992. "International Labor Migration and Foreign Workers in Korea." *Society and History* 37: 231–325 (in Korean).

Seol, Dong-Hoon. 1999. *Foreign Workers in Korean Society, 1987–1998*. Seoul: Seoul National University Press (in Korean).

Seol, Dong-Hoon. 2003. "New Social Movement for Foreign Migrant Workers in Korea, 1992–2002." Pp. 76–99 in *Politics of Struggle, Solidarity and Memory*, Volume 2, edited by Jin-Kyoon Kim. Seoul: Munhwagwahaksa (in Korean).

Seol, Dong-Hoon, Hong-Yop Choi and Geon-Soo Han. 2002. *Foreign Workers' Human Rights in Korea*. Seoul: National Human Rights Commission of Korea (in Korean).

Seol, Dong-Hoon and Geon-Soo Han. 2004. "Foreign Migrant Workers and Social Discrimination in Korea." *Harvard Asia Quarterly* 8(1): 45–50.

Seol, Dong-Hoon and John D. Skrentny. 2004. "South Korea: Importing Undocumented Workers." Pp. 475–513 in *Controlling Immigration: A Global Perspective*, 2nd Edition, edited by Wayne A. Cornelius, Takeyuki Tsuda, Philip L. Martin and James F. Hollifield. Stanford, CA: Stanford University Press.

Seol, Dong-Hoon and John D. Skrentny. 2009. "Why Is There So Little Migrant Settlement in East Asia?" *International Migration Review* 43(3): 578–620.

Uh, Su Bong and Hye-Ja Kwon. 1995. *Foreign Workers and Labor Policy*. Seoul: Central Institute of the Federation of Korean Trade Unions (in Korean).

Yoo, Kil-Sang, Kyu-Yong Lee, Young bum Park and Seong-Jae Park. 2005. *Analysis of the Labor Market of Industrial Technical Trainees in Korean Companies with Foreign Investments*. Seoul: Korea Labor Institute (in Korean).

Yoo, Myung-Ki. 1997. "Foreign Workers and Korean Culture." *Journal of Labor Studies* 13: 69–98 (in Korean).

Index

Page numbers in *italics* denote tables, those in **bold** denote figures.